Target Score

A preparation course for the TOEIC® test

Charles Talcott   Graham Tullis

Teacher's Book

TOEIC® is a [registered] trademark of Educational Testing Service (ETS).
This publication is not endorsed or approved by ETS.

CAMBRIDGE UNIVERSITY PRESS
Cambridge, New York, Melbourne, Madrid, Cape Town, Singapore, São Paulo

Cambridge University Press
The Edinburgh Building, Cambridge CB2 2RU, UK

www.cambridge.org
Information on this title: www.cambridge.org/targetscore

© Cambridge University Press 2006

This book is in copyright. Subject to statutory exception and to the provisions of relevant collective licensing agreements, no reproduction of any part may take place without the written permission of Cambridge University Press.

First Published 2006

Printed in the United Kingdom at the University Press, Cambridge

A catalogue record for this book is available from the British Library

ISBN-13   978-0-521-543736 Student's Book
ISBN-10   0-521-543738 Student's Book

ISBN-13   978-0-521-602631 Teacher's Book
ISBN-10   0-521-602637 Teacher's Book

Contents

Introduction		4
Overview of the TOEIC®		6
Unit 1	Careers	9
Unit 2	Workplaces	16
Unit 3	Communications	22
	Review Test 1 Answer Key	30
Unit 4	Retailing	34
Unit 5	Industry	42
Unit 6	Trade	49
	Review Test 2 Answer Key	56
Unit 7	Leisure	61
Unit 8	Money	69
Unit 9	Travel	78
	Review Test 3 Answer Key	85
Unit 10	Environment	89
Unit 11	Health	95
Unit 12	Society	102
	Review Test 4 Answer Key	109
Classroom Activities for the TOEIC®		114

Introduction

This Teacher's Book has been designed to help both you and your students to make the best of *Target Score,* and to give you guidelines and suggestions for using the Student's Book material as effectively as possible with your class. *Target Score* is a dual-purpose course, built around the framework of the Test of English for International Communication (TOEIC®); it offers students an opportunity to acquire professional communication skills while preparing them for a benchmark assessment of their language competence, using the model of the TOEIC® test. The authors have combined their experience of teaching general business English and TOEIC® preparation classes to create *Target Score.* Most general business English coursebooks do not provide an outcomes assessment of students' performance, and most TOEIC® preparation courses do not offer students an opportunity to develop active communication skills. *Target Score,* however, does both.

In addition to comprehensive explanations of how best to approach the twelve units of the Student's Book, in the Teacher's Book you will find ideas and suggestions for developing your own activities and exercises, photocopiable exercises and full explanations of all review test questions.

Contents

In each unit of the Teacher's Book, you will find the following sections:
- **An overview** of the contents of each unit in the form of a table. This shows the order in which the different components are presented, and includes a short description of each section, with an estimate of the time necessary to complete it. The times are presented with a range from minimum to maximum. How much time you spend on each section will depend on the level of the class you are teaching, and also on whether you choose to take full advantage of the suggested activities for discussion, debate and speaking practice.
- **A detailed description** of each section of the corresponding Student's Book units. Each of the sections in a unit is introduced by a short summary which indicates the part of the TOEIC® test that it prepares for, together with the specific aims in terms of language and test-taking skills. Each section contains full explanations of all the different types of activities, and gives suggestions for how best to exploit these with your class. Potentially troublesome vocabulary is highlighted, and extension activities are provided. The principal difficulties that face test-takers in each section are also explained.
- **A full set of answer key** explanations for all four review tests. The reviews are an important component of the Student's Book and have two functions. Each review test recycles the language, vocabulary and structures that have been presented in the previous three units, allowing teachers to evaluate students' language acquisition as they complete the course. In addition, the review tests follow the TOEIC® question format and include questions for each section of the actual test. This enables students to familiarize themselves with the test format as they progress through the Student's Book. The answers explain each of the questions in detail and give a full analysis of both correct and incorrect answers.
- **Writing activities**. Although the test does not evaluate students' writing competence, a selection of proposed writing activities has been included which can be used with classes where writing is a component.

Troubleshooting the TOEIC®

The principal difficulties that students face on each section of the test are outlined below and will help you to focus on specific test-taking strategies as you use the Student's Book.

Timing

The TOEIC® is a two-hour test, allowing 45 minutes for the Listening section, and 1 hour and 15 minutes for the Reading section. The rapid pace of the test is one of the built-in challenges that measures students' ability to work quickly in English. It is very important for students to understand that on the Listening section of the test, they will have to adapt to the speed of the audio recording. None of the questions in Parts I–IV are repeated, so it is crucial for students to remain focused and to concentrate fully on the audio recordings as they are played. For the Reading section, students are able to decide how to manage their time, and can choose the order in which they answer Parts V–VII but they must work quickly and pace themselves accordingly.

Listening
Part I

Part I audio recordings are relatively short, as they consist of only four short statements about each picture. However, this section requires focused listening, as very often the statements contain words that are similar in sound. Make sure that students anticipate by looking at the photos before they hear the questions.

Part II

In Part II, the main difficulty is that there is no written or visual material in the test book. Everything students need to answer the questions is on the audio recording. If they miss the beginning of the question, they will not be able to select the correct answer. It is therefore essential that students listen to each question as it is played. If they do not understand a question, they should mark an answer at random and prepare to listen to the following question.

Part III

In this part, students listen to the audio recording of a dialogue in order to answer the question printed out in the test booklet. They therefore have to switch from listening to reading. Students should always try to read the first line of the question in the test book before they focus on the audio recording. They will not have time to read the complete question, and should stop reading to focus their complete attention on the recording as only highly proficient language learners can listen and read simultaneously.

Part IV

This part presents other difficulties as the recordings of the short talks are between 1 minute and 2 minutes in length. Students not only have to memorize the information that they hear, but they also have to switch between listening and reading. If at all possible, students should try to read the first lines of the questions for each recording before the recording begins. The audio recording always indicates which questions refer to a particular short talk before it is played, using the following words: "Questions 97 and 98 refer to the following announcement/news bulletin 11", etc. However, if students wait for that information, they will not have time to read the first lines of the questions. Even if it is not always easy to identify precisely which questions refer to the next short talk, students will have read a selection of questions and be better prepared to listen for and memorize the relevant information. It is also important to tell students that they should not attempt to read and listen simultaneously.

Reading

Students should set themselves time limits for answering the questions on the different parts of the Reading section. Remember, there are only 75 minutes available and 100 questions to answer; in other words, students have no more than 45 seconds to spend on each question. They should allow more time for Parts VI and VII, and try to answer the questions on Part V as quickly as possible. Some students may prefer to answer the sections that present them with the least difficulty first. As a general rule, students find the Part VI error recognition questions the most challenging, whereas the Part VII reading comprehension questions are often more straightforward. Sometimes, students will be faced with questions that are beyond their ability. They need to understand that spending time on these questions may mean they have less time to do questions that are within their ability range.

Part V

Part V consists of incomplete sentences which are quick to read. Students should allow 20 seconds to choose the correct answer for each. They should read the question and mark the first answer choice, then move to the next question. Hesitating and changing the answer will slow them down and often results in choosing the wrong answer.

Part VI

Part VI is also simple to read. However, as four parts of each sentence are underlined, it takes longer to analyze the sentences and identify the errors. Students should allow 30 seconds per question on this part. Once again, they should not spend too much time thinking about any question because it will not necessarily help them to correctly answer the most difficult items.

Part VII

Part VII involves texts and documents of differing lengths. If students have been able to answer the questions in Parts V and VI in less than 45 seconds, they will be able to devote extra time to reading the texts and questions on this part. In some cases, the documents may be quite long and in others quite short. Since students can usually handle this type of question well, it is important that they budget enough time to read all the texts and answer the questions.

Overview of the TOEIC®
Test of English for International Communication

What is the TOEIC®?

The TOEIC® is a test of international English that is taken every year by three million students and business professionals in different countries around the world.* The two-hour test includes 200 multiple-choice questions and is divided into two sections: Listening and Reading. There are 100 questions on each section.

Listening (45 minutes)
- Part I Picture identification
- Part II Question/Response
- Part III Short conversations
- Part IV Short talks

Reading (1 hour 15 minutes)
- Part V Incomplete sentences
- Part VI Error recognition
- Part VII Reading comprehension

Students will find a description of each part of the test below, followed by a box with specific strategies that will help them to maximize their score.

*For more information, consult the TOEIC® web page at www.TOEIC.com

The Listening section

This section of the test has four separate parts and lasts 45 minutes.

Part I Picture identification (20 questions)

In Part I, students will see a selection of 20 black and white photographs and will hear a series of 20 recordings. For each photo, they will hear four descriptive statements. They must identify the one statement that best describes what they can see in the picture.

Students should:
- always look closely at each photo and ask themselves:
  Who is in the photo?
  What objects are visible?
  Where was the photo taken?
  What are the professions of the people?
  What actions are being performed?
  What are the positions of the people and the objects?
- make sure they listen to the complete statement. Some statements may only be partially true.
- watch out for homonyms and similar-sounding words that have different meanings.

Part II Question/Response (30 questions)

Part II features 30 recordings of questions and responses. Each question is followed by three responses. You must select the appropriate response.

As the questions that students will hear will be of different types, they should:
- try to determine what type of question is being asked, and what the purpose of the question is. Some questions ask for information, but others may be invitations, suggestions or comments.
- listen carefully to the beginning of the question, especially for question words such as *who*, *what*, *where*, etc.
- not expect the answer to a question to contain the same verb and tense time as the question.

Part III Short conversations (30 questions)

Part III includes 30 recordings of three-part conversations between two people. After listening to each conversation, students have to answer one written comprehension question. Each question has four multiple-choice answers, only one of which is correct.

Students should:
- always read the question before they hear the recording. This will help them to focus on what is said, and they may even be able to guess the meaning of words that they do not understand.
- try to identify who the speakers are, where the conversation takes place and what the speakers are talking about, while they are listening to the conversation.
- listen for keywords that will help them to identify the context.

Part IV Short talks (20 questions)

Part IV presents several recorded short talks that may include announcements, weather reports, travel advisories, etc. Students must answer two or more written comprehension questions about each talk. Each question has four multiple-choice answers, only one of which is correct.

Students should:
- read as many questions as they can before they hear the short talk – but they must not read the answers. They will not have time and the answers will distract them.
- focus on the introduction and the first part of the talk to determine the context.
- memorize key information as they listen and not try to answer any questions before they have listened to the whole talk.

The Reading section

This section of the test has three parts and lasts one hour and 15 minutes.

Part V Incomplete sentences (40 questions)

The questions in Part V consist of sentences that contain a blank. Students are given four possible answers to complete the sentence. They must choose the correct one.

Students should:
- ask themselves if the question is about vocabulary or grammar.
- analyze the sentence and try to identify the parts of speech, i.e. noun, adjective, etc. This will help them to choose the correct answer, especially on vocabulary questions.
- figure out the meaning and/or the type of word by looking at prefixes and suffixes.
- look for grammatical relationships in the sentence, i.e. cause/effect, conditionals, verb tense agreement, etc.

Part VI Error recognition (20 questions)

Part VI includes 20 sentences that each have four underlined and lettered segments. One of these segments contains an error. Students must identify which underlined segment contains the error.

Students should:
- check the underlined parts of the sentence for errors that relate to the entire sentence structure.
- look carefully at the relationship between parts of the sentence, i.e. subject/verb agreement, especially with count/non-count or irregular nouns, verb tense/time expressions, etc.
- watch out for prepositions and gerund/infinitive errors.

Part VII Reading comprehension (40 questions)

In this section of the test, students must read several documents and answer comprehension questions about them. The documents may include announcements, notices, letters, advertisements, news articles, etc. Each document is followed by a set of questions.

Students should:
- skim the questions before reading in order to establish a focus for reading.
- be familiar with the layout of common types of texts such as emails, memos or formal letters in order to facilitate their reading.
- read the title and the first line of the text to determine what kind of text it is and identify the main idea.
- remember that an answer may require that they understand information in different parts of the text.

General test-taking strategies

The following simple strategies can help students to perform better on the test:
- Bring a good quality pencil and eraser.
- Make sure that they are familiar with the instructions for each section of the test before they take it. That will help them to concentrate on the questions and they will be able to use their time more effectively.
- Not to panic if they hear or read words that they do not understand. Focusing on the general context will usually help them to answer correctly.
- Remember that they are not penalized for incorrect answers, so to always give an answer to each question.
- If they cannot find the right answer to a question in the Listening section or they have not understood part of the recording – they must not panic! They should choose an answer that they think is possible and move on to focus on the next question.
- Not let themselves be distracted by a difficult question in the Listening section. They only have several seconds between each question, so they must answer quickly and be ready to listen to the next one.
- Make sure that they do not run out of time when doing the Reading section. They must remember that their time is limited.
- Even if they do not have enough time to finish all the questions in the Reading section, they should still complete the answer grid by guessing.

1 Careers

Unit Focus • Professions • Recruitment • Training

Unit overview

Unit components	Focus	TOEIC practice	Duration
Snapshot	Employment	Part I	15–25 mins
Listening 1	Temp agency	Part III	15 mins
Grammar Check 1	Present simple and present continuous	Part VI	20–30 mins
Vocabulary Builder	Suffixes: people and professions	Part V	20 mins
Viewpoint	Business etiquette: Indian companies	Part VII	20–30 mins
Grammar Check 2	Wh- questions	Parts II/III/IV/VII	20 mins
Listening 2	Job interview	Part II	20 mins
Listening 3	Job Fair talks	Part IV	20 mins
Communication	Temporary work agency interviews		40 mins
		Total	3 hrs 10–3 hrs 40

Snapshot

Aims
- TOEIC Part I practice: identifying the context of a photo
- Vocabulary development: employment
- Discussion

The activities in this section introduce the themes of careers and employment which are developed throughout the unit. The pictures provide students with practice in identifying the context of images that they will encounter in Part I. Explain to students that they should always look for visual clues that give information about the situation that is shown in the picture. The exercise provides a list of possible situations that could correspond to those shown in the pictures. Students should use their dictionaries to find the meanings of these terms, then decide which ones are the most likely. The discussion questions that follow are designed to encourage students to exchange their knowledge and experience of the professional environment in their countries in order to enhance their speaking skills.

Picture descriptions
Picture 1
This picture shows two people *shaking hands* in a room where the *representatives* of two sides in a *negotiation* are *meeting*. The man on the left, who is wearing a *business suit*, is most probably a manager and he is shaking the hand of one of the men on the other side of the *conference table*. These men are more casually dressed and are wearing *short-sleeved shirts*. Some documents are laid out on the table. The situation is not a *board meeting* because the participants would all be dressed in the same way, but the setting for the photo could be a *boardroom*. It is unlikely that the situation is a *general assembly* as the representatives are shaking hands after reaching an agreement about something.

Picture 2
This picture shows a *demonstration* in a city street. In the foreground, a *police officer* is positioned in front of some metal *barriers*. On the other side of the barriers, a crowd of people is *gathered*. They are all wearing the same color clothes which suggests that they may all be *employees* of the same company. They are holding *banners* and *signs* with slogans on them. We can read the words '… with justice' on one banner. The situation is not a *company picnic* since the employees are protesting about something. It cannot be a *fire drill* because they would not be carrying banners.

Picture 3
This picture shows two people in an *interview* situation. The women are seated across from each other at a table in a room. One woman is *writing notes* on a *sheet of paper* on a *clipboard*. The other woman is sitting with

(9)

her legs *crossed* and her hands *clasped*. She is speaking to the other woman. There are a number of empty chairs *lined up* against the wall. The picture does not show a *sales presentation* since neither person is presenting a product. It does not show a *conference call* because neither person is using a telephone.

Picture 4
This picture shows three middle-aged men in *business suits* in a *meeting room*. The man on the right is presenting an *award* to the man on the left, and a third man is *clapping*, or *applauding*. The situation is most probably a ceremony for a *member of staff* who is about to take *retirement*. Behind them on the table we can see some *wine glasses* and an *ice bucket*. The situation is not a *press conference* as only three people are present. Neither is it a *product demonstration* as there are no products visible.

Answers			
1 c	2 b	3 b	4 a

Listening 1

Aims:
- TOEIC Part III practice: short conversations
- Listening for specific information in telephone calls

The recorded telephone conversations present three situations that a temporary agency manager has to deal with. These are in the form of short conversations and although they do not follow the exact format for Part III of the test, they allow students to develop strategies for this section. Students are asked to listen for the specific information to help them to identify the context of each conversation. In the first two conversations, the callers are enquiring about the availability of temporary personnel, and in the third, the caller is informing one of her clients that an employee has interrupted his contract. Although telephoning is dealt with in detail in Unit 3, you may want to focus students' attention on the following language:

This is …
Speaking.
I'm calling to …
What can I do for you?
Can you get back to me …?
Can I help you?

You may want to pre-teach the following vocabulary:

1	schedule	department store	to sort out
2	HR (human resources)	staff	truck driver
		to involve	deliver merchandise
3	to give notice	full time	short-staffed

Answers
A
- a replacement   3
- availability   1, 2
- a previous assignment 1
- contracts   1, 2, 3
- an assignment abroad   2
- meeting arrangements   2

B
1 if she can do the assignment
2 to discuss the conditions of the contract
3 call Mr. Liebe asap

AUDIOSCRIPT
A and B
1
Man Hi Laura. This is Jason Jackman from ShowKase stores.
Woman Hi Jason. What can I do for you?
Man Well, I'm calling to ask you if there's any chance of getting Sabrina Marquez to do another contract with us. You know, she worked at our Lexington store last year during the holiday period. Is there any way we can get her back again this year?
Woman Just let me have a look at her schedule. OK, here it is. Well, right now she's working on a two-month contract for a department store. But that finishes on the fifteenth – when do you need her to start?
Man It would be great if she could start right after that and work through the end of January.
Woman She's down for another contract in January, but that hasn't been finalized yet. Let me check with her on this.
Man I really need to get this sorted out pretty quickly. Can you get back to me before the end of the week?
Woman No problem. I'll let you know tomorrow.
2
Woman PeoplePower. Can I help you?
Man Yes. My name is Howard Mason. I'm the HR manager of Dextro Logistics and we need to hire some temporary staff.
Woman Fine, Mr. Mason. What exactly are you looking for?

Unit 1 | Careers

Man Well I need to hire two truck drivers for a service contract that we've just taken on. Do you have any drivers available?
Woman Yes, we do have a number of drivers available. What does the job involve?
Man It's for an international assignment. We have to deliver some merchandise to a client in Mexico. And they gave us your name. The job would be for two drivers and would take about a week, I reckon.
Woman I'll need to know the exact dates and we'll also have to discuss the conditions and go over the contract together. I think it might be better to meet.
Man Sure. Could you come over to my office tomorrow mid-morning? We're at 19 West 57th, third floor.
Woman Just let me check. OK. That's fine. Shall we say at 11?
Man Fine. See you then.
3
Woman This is Laura Alvarado of PeoplePower. Manfred Liebe please?
Man Speaking. What can I do for you?
Woman Well, actually it's about Hamish Douglas, you know, the chef who's been working under contract with you for the last two weeks. I'm sorry to have to tell you this but he's just informed me that he's accepted a full time position elsewhere without giving me any notice.
Man That's really a shame because he was working out so well. But I assume you'll be able to supply us with a replacement as soon as possible.
Woman Yes. I have a young French chef, Madeleine Legrand, who can replace him. She's just waiting for me to confirm the assignment.
Man This is a busy period and I can't afford to be short-staffed. Could you please have her call me first thing tomorrow?

Grammar Check 1

Aims
- TOEIC Part VI practice: error recognition
- Review and practice of present tenses

Depending on the level of your students, you may want to review the formation of these tenses and draw attention to the time markers that are used with them. Point out that adverbs of frequency (*occasionally*, *usually*, etc.), are normally associated with the present simple form while time markers such as *at the moment*, *right now*, *at present* are used with the present continuous.

Although the focus of this section is not on vocabulary, you may want to point out the following words:

to hire   candidate   findings
survey   release   annual
job market   job prospects   lack

Answers
A
1 c   2 a   3 b   4 d
B
1 b   2 d   3 a   4 c
C
1 ✓   2 is changing   3 ✓
4 are entering 5 compares   6 show
7 ✓   8 ✓   9 say
10 expect   11 ✓   12 possesses
13 suggest 14 ✓

Vocabulary Builder

Aims
- TOEIC Part V practice: incomplete sentences
- Suffixes: people and professions
- Vocabulary development: suffixes

The quiz at the start of this section focuses students' attention on the professions of celebrities. Ask students if they know the professions that made these people famous. Do they also know what professions they did before becoming famous? You can add your own examples of famous people who have changed profession, or ask students to think of examples of people from their country who have done this.

Answers
A
Professions Quiz

Celebrity	Profession	Previous profession
1 Paul Gauguin	painter	stockbroker
2 Charles Lindbergh	aviator	farmer
3 Alfred Hitchcock	film director	clerk
4 Marilyn Monroe	actress	factory worker
5 Ralph Lauren	fashion designer	salesman
6 J K Rowling	author	secretary
7 Hillary Clinton	senator	lawyer

Exercise B presents the principal noun-forming suffixes that are used to form words that refer to people who are active in a particular profession or participate in a given

11

activity. You can also have students think of other professions that they could add for each of the suffixes:

1	-ist	geologist	physicist*
2	-ian	politician	physician*
3	-er/-or	painter	advisor
4	-ee	retiree	
5	-ant/-ent	contestant	superintendent
6	-man**	fisherman	

* These two words refer to different professions. In U.S. English, a *physician* is a medical doctor. A *physicist* is an expert in physics.

** In modern usage, the suffix *-man* is often interchangeable with the suffixes *-woman* or *-person*, depending on the gender of the person referred to, i.e. *salesman*, *saleswoman*, *salesperson*.

Answers
B
1 (*-ist*): publicist, biologist, pharmacist, receptionist, economist
2 (*-ian*): optician, electrician, statistician, historian, librarian
3 (*-er*): laborer, designer, engineer
 (*-or*): supervisor, surveyor
4 (*-ee*): trainee, referee, trustee, addressee, interviewee
5 (*-ant*): consultant, accountant, attendant, assistant
 (*-ent*): correspondent
6 (*-man*)/
 (*-woman*): fireman*, salesman, repairman, craftsman, chairman

* A more common form of this word in U.S. English is *firefighter*.

C
1 consultants/accountants
2 chairman
3 electrician
4 economists

Extension Activity
Guess the profession. Students choose a profession from the list and other students have to ask closed questions to find out what it is:

Do you work outside? *Do you work in an office?*, etc.

Viewpoint

Aims
- TOEIC Part VII practice: reading comprehension
- Answering Wh- questions
- Discussion: business etiquette – Indian companies

The topic of the text is on one type of training that is given to staff in some Indian companies in order to prepare them to work with clients from other English-speaking cultures: cultural awareness and business etiquette training. Although the article is descriptive in tone, it raises the sensitive issue of Western cultural imperialism. Some readers, for example, may be offended to learn that employees are forced to adopt a style of dress and to change their behavior in order to conform to the Western culture of a multinational or international company's clients.

Before doing the reading activity, you may want to pre-teach the following vocabulary:

necktie	to raise a toast	interactions
conference call	to interact with	to flourish
peers	adept	compensation
alien	foreigner	project leader
to crack a joke	punctuality	a fit
competitive	benefits	garment
a bid	protocol	

Answers
1 To learn global-employee skills.
2 To learn how to interact with people from other cultures.
3 You should not slap him on the back or call him by his first name.
4 They have improved the image of Indian companies and allowed them to work on bigger projects at better rates.

DISCUSSION
The discussion questions are designed to get students to give a personal reaction to the issues raised in the article. Would they feel motivated by the kind of training offered by Indian companies? Would they find it acceptable to have to change their normal behavior and dress to suit their employer?

Unit 1 | Careers

> ⚠ *TOEIC Tip*
> This tip explains the most common forms of address. It is important to point out that *Mr., Miss., Mrs., Ms.* are never used in formal situations unless followed by a last name. It may be useful to inform students that the TOEIC® uses a selection of first names and last names from a variety of countries. You can ask the class to give some examples of common names and family names from their country.

Grammar Check 2

Aims
- TOEIC Parts II/III/IV/VII practice
- Review of Wh- questions: question forms
- Discussion

Recognizing and understanding question forms is essential in Parts II, III, IV and VII of the test. In addition, in Part II, students must be able to identify appropriate responses to different types of question. In this grammar section, the questions that are presented are information questions. These require responses which provide information about a job candidate's experience and background.

Answers
A
1 c   2 a   3 b
4 e   5 d   6 f
B
1 Where   2 When
3 How many   4 What/How many
5 Who   6 How much/What
7 Which/What/   8 How
How many

Wh- word		Legal status
1 Where	were you born?	illegal
2 When	did you graduate from High School?	illegal
3 How many	children do you have?	illegal
4 *What/How many	languages are you fluent in?	legal
5 Who	do you live with?	illegal
6 How much/What	do you weigh?	illegal
7 Which/What/How many	social organizations do you belong to?	illegal
8 How	old are you?	illegal

* In the U.S., question 4 is the only legal question. This is because employment laws make it illegal for an employer to obtain certain information from an interviewee. This ensures that minority groups are given equal employment opportunities. Question 4 is therefore only legal if the candidate's ability to speak a foreign language is part of the requirement for the position offered. In the U.S., it is illegal for any recruiter to ask about the applicant's ancestry, national origin, parentage or nationality, or to ask *how* the applicant learned to read, write or speak a foreign language. For the interviewee, he or she can choose to answer any question asked by the interviewer, even if the question is illegal. Nevertheless, if an interviewer has asked an illegal question, he or she may be subject to legal action.

> **DISCUSSION**
> You can initiate a short discussion about how interviews are conducted in the students' countries. Ask students to give examples of their own personal experience of interviews by using the questions in exercise A of the Grammer Check.

> ⚠ *TOEIC Tip*
> This tip draws attention to potentially confusing questions and gives examples of the different types of questions that begin with *How*. Ask students to think of other examples of questions that use *How* plus an adjective or adverb, i.e. *How big?, How far?* You should also point out that *How* is also often associated with *about*, and used in questions which make suggestions and invitations:
>
> *How about taking a break?*
>
> The correct response to a question with *How about?* is to either accept or refuse the invitation or suggestion.
>
> *No. Let's finish what we're doing first./*
> *Good idea. I think we all need one.*

13

Listening 2

Aims
- TOEIC Part II practice: question/response
- Listening to interview questions

Before listening, have students read the answers and check their understanding of potentially difficult vocabulary such as:

leadership skills   to strive for   to oversee
to conduct   to achieve

You may wish to ask students to prepare appropriate questions for each of the answers. After completing the listening, you can ask students to compare their questions with the ones that the speaker used in the recording.

Answers
1. A
2. F
3. E
4. G
5. C

There are no responses for questions B and D.

AUDIOSCRIPT
A What qualities make an ideal manager?
B What is most important to you in a job?
C How would you describe yourself?
D What are your long-term career plans?
E What are your present job responsibilities?
F How do you spend your free time?
G What skills have you developed recently?

Listening 3

Aims
- TOEIC Part IV practice: short talks
- Listening to an informal talk

Remind students that in Part IV, it is important to identify the context of the short talk. They can do this by listening for key phrases that indicate whether the talk is formal or informal. Tell them to look out for the use of the personal pronoun *you* which indicates a talk in the presence of an audience. Although students need to be able to filter and cope with difficult vocabulary in Part IV listenings, you may want to pre-teach the following words:

seminar   applicant   to compliment
strengths   job-seeker   job performance
advancement

Answers

A
1. recruiters, headhunters
2. job-seekers, job-hunters
3. interviewing, e-recruiting

B
1. 15-minute interview, not 50-minute interview
2. shorter, not longer
3. recruitment managers, not interviewees
4. job interviews, not advertisements
5. job-seekers, not recruiters
6. candidates, not interviewers

AUDIOSCRIPT
B

Don Stanley
Good morning. My name's Don Stanley and I'd like to welcome you to my seminar "Getting the most out of the 15-minute interview." As recruitment managers, you may find that you have less time to spend interviewing. With more applicants due to Internet job postings and tougher competition for top prospects, recruiters have to be more efficient in the hiring process. Well, today I'm going to teach you some tips on how to do that. By following a few simple steps, you can save time without giving candidates the impression that you are rushing them through a quick and impersonal interview.
First, open with small talk, but don't let it exceed two or three minutes.
Second, focus on a few essential questions.
Then, give the applicant a few minutes to ask questions about the job.
And finally, conclude by complimenting the candidate on their strengths.
So let me elaborate on my first point, small talk…

Kimberly Armstrong
At the end of most interviews, job-seekers have the opportunity to ask questions. But very few take advantage of this moment to learn more about the job. Remember, you also want to find out whether the company and the job are right for you. It's a good idea to ask what results are expected from the position. You may want to know how job performance is evaluated. You may also want to ask one or more of these questions: "What are the challenges of this job?" "What advancement opportunities can the company offer?" and "What are the long-term goals of this department?"
Questions like these can help you decide whether the job fits your career plans.

Unit 1 | Careers

Communication

Aim
- Speaking practice: asking and answering interview questions

This section gives students an opportunity to practice asking and answering interview questions. There are various ways that the activity can be organized in the classroom, depending on the number of students.

It can be done as a pairwork activity where students can take turns playing each role. Or it can be done in groups with the interviewers preparing their questions while the interviewees anticipate the questions that they think they may be asked, and prepare responses.

It also works well in groups of three with two co-directors and an applicant. One interviews the candidate and the other observes the interview and takes notes on the interviewee's performance.

Applicants can rotate several times so that interviewers have a chance to conduct several interviews before deciding on the best candidate. Interviewees can also meet after the interviews to decide which interviewers were most effective, and why.

To prepare the jobs that the candidates will apply for, you can either use the following short summaries of the main requirements for different positions, or you can clip suitable job advertisements from the newspaper, or copy them from the Internet.

Position	Requirements
Water sports instructor	- instructor level in one of the following: diving, water-skiing, sailing - 6-month contract - foreign location - excellent physical condition - previous experience required
Mystery shopper*	- able to travel - irregular working hours - good written and oral communication skills
Television sports commentator	- good speaking voice - excellent speaking skills - extensive knowledge of football, basketball and rugby - frequent travel - weekend work
Hotel receptionist	- good physical presentation - excellent interpersonal skills - knowledge of office software - foreign languages an advantage - willing to work at the weekends and late at night

* Mystery shoppers conduct quality control inspections of retail stores and service outlets. The inspectors are called mystery shoppers because they act as if they are normal clients and evaluate the store and its personnel as they are being served.

Writing Practice
Although the TOEIC® does not test writing, you may want to give your students practice with letter-writing.

Write a follow-up letter to your interview. If you were a co-director of PeoplePower, write an acceptance letter to the top candidate.

OR

If you were an interviewee, write a letter thanking the co-director of PeoplePower for the interview.

2 Workplaces

Unit Focus • Offices • Technology • Facilities

Unit overview

Unit components	Focus	TOEIC practice	Duration
Snapshot	Work environments	Part I	15–25 mins
Grammar Check 1	Count and non-count nouns	Part V	10–20 mins
Listening 1	Office complaints	Part II	15–25 mins
Grammar Check 2	Prepositions of place	Part V	20–30 mins
Listening 2	Describing a workplace	Part IV	15–20 mins
Vocabulary Builder	Word families: prefixes and suffixes	Part V	20–30 mins
Viewpoint	Workplace surveillance	Part VII	20–30 mins
Listening 3	Communication at work	Part III	10–15 mins
Communication	Safety screening		40 mins
		Total	2 hrs 45–5 hrs 55

Snapshot

Aims
- TOEIC Part I practice: identifying objects in pictures
- Vocabulary development: work environments
- Discussion

The pictures in this section introduce the theme of the workplace which is a central focus of all parts of the TOEIC® test. Students should first focus on the general settings for each picture and identify the type of workplace that is featured. Once they have done this, they should then identify the professions of the people who work there, then the tools and equipment that are used in each workplace. Explain that specific vocabulary related to the workplace is often featured in the questions in Part I of the test. You may need to help students to identify the appropriate words to describe the objects that they can see. A complete list is given on page 17.

Picture descriptions
Picture 1
This picture presents the interior of a *laboratory* where three people are working. They are all wearing *lab coats*. The man in the foreground is working with a *pippet* and is *filling* some *containers* that are *laid out* on the *work surface* in front of him. We can see various *apparatus* and *equipment* beside the containers. The two other people are working at the *counter space* in the center of the room. The walls are lined with glass-fronted *wall cabinets* and there are *drawers* under the work surfaces.

Picture 2
This picture shows an *architect* or *designer* at work at a table in her office. She is using a *triangle* to *draw a line* on the *drawing* or *plan* that she is working on. There is a *scale model* of a house on the table. Behind the woman we can see a table and chair and a *shelf unit*. There is a *picture* on the wall between the two windows which have their *blinds drawn*.

Picture 3
The setting for this picture is a *garage workshop*. A *vehicle* is parked in the *foreground* with its *hood* open. A *mechanic* is leaning over the side of the vehicle and is *adjusting* or *working* on a component in the *engine compartment*. In the background, we can see a selection of *mechanic's* tools.

Picture 4
This picture shows the inside of a *warehouse*. A man is *driving* a *forklift* and *moving* three *coils* of pipe or metal which are *stacked* on top of each other. We can see other coils which are *lined up* in *rows* to the right of the driver.

Answers
A
Suggested vocabulary

	Objects	Workplace	Jobs
Picture 1	lab equipment bottles containers pippet test tubes jars solutions	laboratory	laboratory technician
Picture 2	drawing ruler model drawing board	architect's office	architect
Picture 3	car tools battery engine hood fender wheel tire	workshop	mechanic
Picture 4	forklift stock coils pallets	warehouse	forklift driver warehouse worker

Although there is no writing component on the test, exercise B will help students to become more familiar with the types of statements that are featured in Part I of the test. You should point out that the questions in Part I are not always straightforward descriptions like *The people are working*, but more often complicated sentences which contain prepositions and adverbs. Look at the following suggestions for descriptive statements of the four pictures:

Answers
B
Possible statements
Picture 1
The man is filling some containers.
The work surface is covered with equipment.
The wall cabinets are used for storage.
He's carrying out a test.
The staff are wearing lab coats.

Picture 2
The woman is working on a plan.
There is a model on the table.
She's drawing a line on a plan.
The blinds are drawn.
There is a table behind the woman.

Picture 3
He's repairing the engine of a car.
The hood of the car is open.
The man is fixing the car.
The battery is on the floor.

Picture 4
The workman is moving some goods with a forklift.
The warehouse is stocked with goods.
The coils are stacked on top of each other.
He's moving the goods from one place to another.

DISCUSSION
The discussion questions allow students to share their personal experiences in different types of workplaces. Even if students have not had much professional experience, many will have worked part time or completed short training periods in businesses or organizations. Ask them to describe the places where they worked, the types of work that they were asked to do, and the tools and equipment that they used in their jobs.

Grammar Check 1

Aims
- TOEIC Part V practice: incomplete sentences
- Familiarizing students with the difference between count and non-count nouns

This section gives a brief introduction to the two main categories of nouns in English. Students will probably already be familiar with this distinction, but you may want to remind them that count nouns have either plural forms with *s*, or irregular plural forms (*men*, *women*, *children*, etc.), whereas non-count nouns have no plural forms. You should point out that the determiners *many* and *few* are used with count nouns, while *much* and *little* are used with non-count nouns.

You can also give students examples of other specific noun forms:

- nouns which are only used in the plural:
  premises, clothes, glasses
- nouns which are only used in the singular:
  the sun, the past, the weather
- nouns which refer to a group:
  the public, the audience, the company

It may be necessary to review some of the vocabulary that is used in the practice exercise and, in particular, the following words:

embedded   venture   microprocessor information technologies   airflow

Answers					
A					
1 a		2 b		3 b	
4 a		5 b			
B					
1 result		2 architecture		3 furniture	
4 Researchers		5 work		6 impact	
7 privacy		8 teams		9 transition	
10 people					

Listening 1

Aims
- TOEIC Part II practice: question/response
- Listening to question forms
- Discussion

Before playing the audio recording of the questions in exercise A, students have the opportunity to discuss their experience of "annoying" working conditions. It may be necessary to explain the meaning of *janitor* and *storage space*. You can then compare the students' conclusions with the official results of the survey of U.S. office facility managers (IFMA), which ranked the complaints in the following order:

1. temperatures too low
2. temperatures too high
3. poor janitor service
4. lack of meeting rooms
5. inadequate storage space
6. poor air quality
7. lack of privacy
8. inadequate parking facilities
9. unreliable computers
10. noise levels

Exercise B gives practice in listening to different kinds of questions. If you have time, ask students to select some of the questions and to prepare (in pairs or small groups) examples of possible responses. You can then ask them to role play the conversations, taking it in turns to ask and answer each of the questions.

Answers		
B		
1 J	2 A	3 H
4 F	5 D	6 B
7 G	8 I	9 E
10 C		

AUDIOSCRIPT
B
A Isn't there any way we can get the air-conditioning to work?
B Where am I going to put all these files?
C How can you concentrate with all that construction work going on outside?
D Don't you think they could provide more reserved spaces in the parking garage?
E Why can't they figure out what's wrong with my email account?
F Didn't the janitor say that he would get someone to clean the windows over the weekend?
G When are they going to turn the heat on?
H How come the conference rooms are always booked when you need them?
I Why don't you ask them to give you your own office?
J Can we close that window and keep the dust from coming in?

Grammar Check 2

Aims
- TOEIC Part V practice: incomplete sentences
- Review of prepositions of place

This grammar review section is designed to give students general practice with a wide range of prepositions that are used to describe the positions of objects and people in space. On the TOEIC®, prepositions of place are often included in statements in Part I, but are also often featured in Part V and VI questions. Exercise C is presented as a Part V blank-fill. Students will have an opportunity to practice making a description using prepositions of place in the activity that follows Listening 2.

Unit 2 | Workplaces

> **Answers**
> **A**
> 1 around 2 opposite 3 along
> 4 alongside 5 under 6 through
> 7 toward(s) 8 within 9 above
> 10 against
> **B**
> inside 8 beneath 5 with 6
> beside 4 down 3 to 7
> round 1 across from 2 over 9
> **C**
> 1 opposite 2 inside 3 down
> 4 to 5 below 6 beside

> ⚠ **TOEIC Tip**
> This tip draws attention to the other main use of prepositions which is to situate events in relation to time.

Listening 2

> **Aims**
> - TOEIC Part IV practice: short talks
> - Listening for specific information
> - Vocabulary development/acquisition
> - Speaking practice: using prepositions to describe the positions of objects in a photo

This section starts with a review of some common office vocabulary which frequently appears on the test. You may need to help students with the words to describe the objects in the picture (see the vocabulary list below). Before playing the audio recording, you may wish to ask students to practice what they have just done in Grammar Check 2 and to say where the objects are located in the picture.

> **Answers**
> **A**
> 1 paperwork:
>   faxes, envelopes, <u>documents</u>, letters
> 2 publications:
>   directories, magazines, <u>books</u>, <u>manuals</u>
> 3 office supplies:
>   stapler, scissors, <u>pens</u>, paperclips
> 4 electrical equipment:
>   <u>computer</u>, lamp, <u>fan</u>, <u>mouse</u>, <u>keyboard</u>, <u>headphones</u>
> 5 personal effects:
>   photos, <u>poster</u>, bag, <u>certificate</u>, <u>knick-knacks</u>, <u>mug</u>

> **B**
> See objects underlined in A.
> **C**
> 1 invoices: in-box tray
> 2 price lists: shelf on the left
> 3 personal items: shelf on the right
> 4 customer files: filing cabinet
> 5 printer cartridges: filing cabinet drawer

AUDIOSCRIPT
C
Welcome to my office. Yes, this is where I work. It may look a mess to you, I know, but don't worry, I know where everything is or at least I'm pretty sure I do. As you can see I have a nice big desk where I can lay everything out, so it's usually covered with an assortment of things – reports that I'm working on, documents that I have to consult. There's an in-box tray too and you can just see it under that pile of papers. That's where I keep all the important correspondence that have to deal with like invoices, bills and important emails I've printed out. Then there's the electronic heart of my working life, my computer, and I use it all the time. It's connected to a network and to the Internet and that's where I get most of the information I need. I have headphones too, so I can listen to music while I work.

On the wall behind it there are two shelves. The one on the left is where I put all the books that I need, you know, reference material, manuals, price lists, software guides and that sort of thing. And then on the one on the right, there's all my personal stuff like photos of the family and friends, and my collection of puppets. Oh, and also my two good luck charms – a silver key and a little miniature elephant. Under the desk you can just see a black filing cabinet. That's where I keep all the print documents that I need to refer to – reports and customer files. There's not that much in there because most of it's on the computer. It's also got a drawer where I keep all the office supplies that I need like staplers, tape, printer cartridges and so on.

> **ACTIVE PRACTICE**
> In this speaking activity, students are asked to work in pairs to describe a photo of an office environment by indicating where specific items are located. Each pair will be working with photos that are slightly different. It is not necessary to tell them this before starting the activity as they will discover this by listening and questioning their partner's description.

Target Score

● Extension Activity

Ask students to bring in a photo of their work area (at home or at the office) and to describe it to a partner.

Vocabulary Builder

Aims
- TOEIC Part V practice: incomplete sentences
- Review of the principles of prefixation and suffixation
- Vocabulary development: word families

This exercise focuses on how words can be generated from a base form by adding prefixes and suffixes. The more familiar students are with suffixed and prefixed forms, the easier it will be for them to identify the parts of speech that are associated with specific affixes. Questions on Part V often test this.

Answers

A
1. formerly
2. former
3. formal
4. formality
5. formation
6. conform, uniform, transform, perform

B
deformation, reformation, information
transformation, performer, informer, reformer
transformer, performance, informant

C
1. former
2. formal
3. uniforms
4. forms
5. performance

D
A complete list of the prefixed and suffixed forms of *draw, present, quest, sign, move* and *employ* is provided in the table opposite.

Base form	Prefixed form	Suffixed form	Prefixed and suffixed form
draw (v)	overdraw (v) withdraw (v)	drawer (n) drawing (n)	withdrawal (n)
present (v)	represent (v)	presentation (n) presenter (n) presentable (adj)	representative (adj/n)
quest (n)	request (v) inquest (n)	question (n/v)	
sign (v)	assign (v) resign (v) countersign (v)	signature (n)	assignment (n) resignation (n)
move (v)	remove (v)	movement (n) moveable (adj)	removal (n)
employ (v)		employment (n) employee (n) employer (n)	unemployment (n)

Viewpoint

Aims
- TOEIC Part VII practice: reading comprehension
- Vocabulary development/acquisition
- Discussion

The article deals with working conditions in some companies in the United States. It is intended to provide input for discussion and debate about the extent to which employees' behavior at work should be monitored. You may want to do the discussion in two separate parts asking students to contribute their views on the specific case that is dealt with in the text before they read the article. You can ask them to respond to the following questions:

- *What do you think an employer should do if he/she discovers that an employee is using or has used the office phone to make a personal call?*
- *What would you do if you were the boss?*

Before completing the reading, ask students to focus on the first paragraph of the text. This is a useful strategy that they can apply to Part VII, where key information is often contained at the start of a reading document. Students can list the verbs in the first paragraph that relate to surveillance, i.e.

*document   analyze   measure   monitor
count   clock   track*

Unit 2 | Workplaces

In addition to the words that students are asked to identify in the first paragraph, it may be useful to point out the following vocabulary:

to gather data	auction	instant messages
outgoing	plaintiff	attorney
polled	to fire	big business
tardiness	to outweigh	overtime pay
unemployment benefits		to sue

⚠ TOEIC Tip
This tip emphasizes the importance of scanning Part VII reading comprehension texts by focusing on key sections of the document.

Answers
B
1 a   2 a   3 c

DISCUSSION
After reading the complete text and answering the comprehension questions, start a follow-up discussion by asking students to react to the case mentioned in the article and to say whether they think that there should be limits on the degree of surveillance that employers can carry out.

Listening 3

Aims
- TOEIC Part III practice: short conversations
- Listening for gist

In this exercise, students are asked to focus on the general context of the conversations and to answer the question *What is happening in each conversation?* You can also ask them to guess the relationship between the speakers (boss/subordinate/colleagues) and to say what clues helped them to decide (i.e. forms of address, tone of voice).

Answers
A
1 request   2 issue   3 assign
4 review   5 suggest   6 express
7 discuss
B
A issue instructions   B discuss problems
C express opinions

AUDIOSCRIPT
B
A
Man Could you ask Mr. Walters. to step into my office for a few minutes?
Woman I'm afraid he's in a meeting right now. But he should be finished in an hour or so.
Man Oh well, don't disturb him right now. But please tell him I do need to see him urgently.
B
Woman Why don't we call the Brussels office? They may be able to help us out.
Man I've already done just that. They're out of stock too.
Woman So there's no way we'll be able to complete the order on time.
C
Woman Do you think I should apply for the management position in the customer service department?
Man Well, you certainly have the experience. But it will mean working much longer hours and the salary's not that great.
Woman I know. Maybe I'd be better off staying right where I am.

Communication

Aim
- Speaking practice: presenting persuasive arguments; asking questions

This activity can be organized as an informal presentation where the representatives of each group take it in turns presenting their arguments for or against the plan to introduce video surveillance. Students should take notes of what the speakers say. These can be used as the basis of a short question and answer session following each presentation.

● Writing Practice
Although the TOEIC® does not test writing, you may want to give your students practice with writing short articles. Since the article will refer to the arguments presented by the different participants at the forum, students may find it helpful to refer to the Grammar Reference on pages 135 and 136 of the Student's Book which explain reported speech and reporting words. The articles should be limited to approximately 150 words.

3 Communications

Unit **Focus**   • News • Internet • Broadcasting

Unit overview

Unit components	Focus	TOEIC practice	Duration
Snapshot	Means of communication	Part I	15–25 mins
Vocabulary Builder	Compound nouns (noun + noun)	Part V	20–30 mins
Listening 1	Conversations: information	Part III	20 mins
Grammar Check 1	Articles: *a*, *an*, *the*	Part V	20–30 mins
Viewpoint	Oral and written cultures	Part VII	25–35 mins
Listening 2	Telephoning	Part II	25–35 mins
Grammar Check 2	Present perfect and past simple	Part VI	25–35 mins
Listening 3	Radio news bulletin	Part IV	20–30 mins
Communication	Press conference: corporate layoffs		40 mins
		Total	3 hrs 30–4 hrs 40

Snapshot

Aims
- TOEIC Part I practice: picture analysis – actions and objects
- Vocabulary development: means of communication

The pictures present four contemporary means of communication: newspapers and print media, telephoning, mail and postal services, computers and Internet.

Picture descriptions
Picture 1
A woman is standing in front of a *rack* of *newspapers* at a *kiosk* or *newsstand*. The *daily papers* are *on display*. She is holding a *tabloid* newspaper and is reading the *front page headlines*.

Picture 2
A woman is using a *public phone* that is outside on the sidewalk. This phone appears to be *coin-operated*, which means that a call can be made by *inserting coins* or *change* into the *slot*. Callers can also use *pre-paid calling cards*. (Some English speakers still call this type of public phone a *phone booth* even though it is not enclosed.) She is holding the *receiver* in her right hand.

Picture 3
A woman is standing in front of a public *mailbox* that is located on the *sidewalk*. She is dropping *letters* into the *slot*.

Picture 4
A woman is sitting in front of a *computer screen* in an office. She could be *consulting* the *Internet* or reading her *email*. Her left hand is on the *keyboard* and her right hand is using a *mouse*.

Students need to practice actively looking at and describing TOEIC® Part I photographs. This opening section focuses students' attention on the particular actions and objects in the pictures. Encourage your students to practice describing photographs in newspapers and magazines in preparation for the test.

Unit 3 | Communications

Suggested vocabulary

	Actions	Objects
Picture 1	reading a newspaper looking standing	newspapers newsstand racks
Picture 2	calling phoning using a payphone listening speaking	telephone payphone street
Picture 3	mailing posting dropping her mail	mailbox letters package
Picture 4	sitting looking checking her email reading typing	computer keyboard screen mouse Internet email

In exercise A, students should choose one photo and write a statement for it. They can then read the statement out loud to a partner or to the class, who then have to identify which photo the statement refers to.

Answers
A
Possible statements
Picture 1
She's reading a newspaper.
She's at a newsstand.
There are many newspapers displayed on the rack.

Picture 2
She's on the phone.
She's calling from a public phone.
She's using a payphone.

Picture 3
She's mailing a letter/package.
She's dropping the mail into the box.
The mailbox is on the sidewalk.

Picture 4
She's working on a computer.
She's looking at the screen.
She's reading/checking her email.
B
1 D, G   2 E, H   3 A, C   4 B, F

AUDIOSCRIPT
A The woman is mailing several letters.
B The keyboard is in front of the computer screen.
C The mailbox is located on the sidewalk.
D She's reading a daily paper.
E There's a public phone next to the curb.
F The woman is checking her email.
G The newspapers are displayed in racks.
H The woman is calling from a payphone.

You may want to ask students to list other means of communication: *television*, *radio*, *telegrams*, *flyers*, *banners*, *public postings*, *bulletin boards*, *fax machines*.

Vocabulary Builder

Aims
- TOEIC Part V practice: incomplete sentences
- Vocabulary development: compound nouns; collocations

This exercise focuses on compound nouns or noun + noun combinations used in different fields of communications: broadcasting, press, information technology, telecommunications, postal services. Noun + noun combinations are commonly used in English and can be confusing for learners. The second noun is the object and the first noun describes or modifies this object. For example, in the compound noun *telephone bill*, the object is a *bill*. *Telephone* describes what kind of bill it is.

Answers
A and B

Broadcasting	news bulletin cable television
Press	feature article front page
Information technology	web browser computer screen
Telecommunications	phone booth voice mail
Postal Services	mailbox post office

C
1 voice mail
2 feature article, front page
3 mailbox, post office

23

D
Suggested answers
press
press agency
press agent
press book
press bureau
press campaign
press pass
press photographer
press release
phone
phone book
phone bill
phone booth
phone call
phone message
phone number
cell phone
portable phone
news
news agent
news agency
news rack
newsstand*
newscaster
newsletter*
newspaper*
newsprint*
newsroom*

* Note that some compound nouns become combined into single words.

● Extension Activity
Ask students to think of other common compound nouns in English not necessarily related to communication.

Listening 1

Aims
- TOEIC Part III practice: short conversations
- Listening for keywords

Begin this section by having students read the TOEIC Tip. While listening to the conversations, students should focus on keywords to identify: *who* is speaking, *where* the speakers are, and *what* they are speaking about. This is a strategy they should adopt for the TOEIC®.

The five conversations involve: buying newspapers at a newsstand; a traveler who has lost his suitcase, being paged at an airport and looking for the courtesy phone; office colleagues discussing whether they should fax or mail a contract; two people talking about watching television news coverage of an election; a person talking to a computer technician about logging into his email account.

Answers
A

	Who?	Where?	What?
1	customer and news agent	at a newsstand	buying Italian newspapers
2	traveler and airport employee	at an airport	finding a courtesy phone; a lost suitcase
3	co-workers	in an office	sending a contract by fax or by mail
4	colleagues or friends	in front of a TV	watching the news
5	computer user and computer technician	in front of a computer	typing in the email log-in and password

B
Keywords
1 newspapers, to sell out, magazines
2 name being paged, courtesy phone, baggage claim, found, suitcase
3 mail, contract, fax, to send, mail pick-up
4 to watch, evening news, station, channel, coverage
5 type in, log-in, password, check email, computer

AUDIOSCRIPT
1
Woman Would you happen to have any Italian newspapers?
Man I'm sorry. We usually sell out by noon.
Woman In that case, I'll take one of these magazines instead.
2
Man Excuse me. I just heard my name being paged. Could you tell me where the nearest courtesy phone is?

Woman There's one in the baggage claim area over to your left.
Man Thank you. I hope they've found my suitcase.

3
Woman Should I mail the contract to Ms. Kim or can I fax it?
Man Well, she'll need to sign the original so you'll have to send it. And you'd better hurry. The mail pick-up is in fifteen minutes.
Woman No problem, it's all ready to go.

4
Woman It's almost seven o'clock. Are you going to watch the evening news?
Man I don't want to miss the overseas elections results. Which station do you prefer?
Woman Channel Five has the best international coverage.

5
Man Do I have to type my log-in and password every time I want to check my email?
Woman Here, I can show you how to set your computer to do it automatically.
Man Fantastic! That'll be a real timesaver.

Extension Activity
Students can practice the dialogues from the audioscripts at the back of the book. You can also have them improvise conversations based on the first sentence of each dialogue.

More advanced students can develop their own dialogues based on one of the situations given in the exercise. Other situations might include:
- mailing a package at the post office
- asking someone to fax a document for you
- buying stamps and envelopes
- talking to an operator about making a long-distance call
- using a cell phone

Grammar Check 1

Aims
- TOEIC Part V practice: incomplete sentences
- Review of articles: *a*, *an*, *the*
- Topic: special interest group television networks and channels

The correct use of articles in English is challenging for many students. It is important that they practice determining whether a noun refers to a specific, definite object or whether the noun refers to a non-specified, indefinite object.

For example:
The television *in the room belongs to the school.* (specific, definite object)
A television *can cost a lot of money.* (non-specified, indefinite object)
Television *is an effective means of communication.* (non-specified, general)

Exercise B features the Aboriginal Peoples Television Network. The proliferation of satellite and cable television has made broadcasting much less expensive and, thus, more accessible to many special interest groups. Some groups have been able to launch their own networks and channels, creating programs that feature culturally-specific topics and issues and that can be presented in the native language.

Possible discussion questions
- *Do you know of any television channels or networks that are devoted to a particular culture or language group?*
- *How does media help to preserve and promote a particular culture?*
- *How does media influence and change culture?*

Answers
A
1   a, an, the   2   the
3   a/an   4   the
5   television (because it is a general noun)
B
1   The   2   the/no article
3   a   4   the
5   an/the   6   the
7   the   8   a
9   no article   10 no article
11 a   12 the
13 no article   14 the

Viewpoint

Aims
- TOEIC Part VII practice: reading comprehension
- Topic: changes in the way people in different cultures communicate; oral versus written modes of communication
- Discussion: culturally-specific modes of communication; how technology is affecting communication

The article encourages students to reflect on how cultures – regional, ethnic, and even professional – prefer certain modes of communication. Begin with the lead-in question in the book: *Which do you prefer – exchanging emails or talking on the phone? Why?*

Have students study the three comprehension questions before reading the article. After they have answered the questions, have students go back and identify the words that relate to communication:

signature	someone's word
handshake	a "mode" of communication
oral	written
written contract	oral agreement
written record	spoken account
cell phones	text messages
textos	Internet
email	bulletin board postings
real-time chat lines	corporate communications
information	transmit
codes	information channels
information exchange	

Answers
1 talking on a cell phone, sending text messages, email, chat lines, bulletin board postings
2 They are considered to be more reliable.
3 A company sent text messages to employees to lay them off.

DISCUSSION
Encourage students to focus on their "culture of communication". Is it primarily oral or written? Are the "communication cultures" different in public and private, at work, at school, between younger and older generations, between men and women? In terms of technology, ask students whether they think that improvements in technology have improved the *quality* of communication over the last several years. Because of cell phones, Internet, etc., people seem to be communicating more. But are they communicating with the same intensity and quality as before?

Possible responses
1
faxes, office memos, mail ("snail mail" = surface mail), telegrams, flyers, billboards, posters

Listening 2

Aims
- TOEIC Part II practice: question/response
- Vocabulary development: telephoning

In this section, students learn and review useful telephoning expressions while developing strategies to tackle the question/response format. In exercise A, students should read the ten questions and determine who would ask each question: the person calling or the person receiving the call. They can then brainstorm responses to each question.

Answers and suggested responses
A
1 Receiver. Yes, that would be fine./No, thank you. I'll call back later.
2 Receiver. I would like to speak to Mr. …/I would like extension number 523, please.
3 Caller. Yes. Just one moment./I'm sorry. All our lines are busy at the moment./Please hold.
4 Receiver. Yes, please. Tell him that I called. I can be reached at this phone number./No, I'll give him a call later in the day.
5 Caller. She's not available. She's in a meeting./She can be reached on her cell phone.
6 Receiver. May I have the number for …?
7 Caller. You need to dial/press 0./You need to call the switchboard.
8 Receiver. No, I don't mind. I think everyone should hear what we're discussing./Yes, I would. I think we need to discuss this privately before talking to the others.
9 Caller. Yes, it is. Who would you like to speak to?/No, I'm sorry, you've reached the wrong number./You've dialed the wrong number.
10 Caller. Yes, she'll be back after lunch./No, but I can leave her a message that you called.

Exercise B gives Part II practice in listening to a series of responses. Since there are ten responses, students must match the recorded responses quickly to the questions in the Student's Book. You may need to pause the audio recording for weaker students.

Unit 3 | Communications

● Extension Activity

Students can practice TOEIC® Part II with this activity. Single students or pairs can choose three questions from A and write two good responses and one incorrect response for each. Then in pairs or small groups, each reads the question and responses to the other who must choose the best response to each question.

Answers		
B		
1 A	2 H	3 B
4 I	5 E	6 J
7 C	8 G	9 D
10 F		

AUDIOSCRIPT

B
A That'd be great. I think he already has my number here at the office.
B Hold just one moment and I'll connect you.
C First dial 9 and then the number.
D Yes, it is. How may I help you?
E I can give you her cell phone number.
F She won't be in till Monday. Would you like to leave a message for her?
G Please do. That way everyone can hear the good news.
H I'd like to speak to the department manager, please.
I Please tell him Mark Hunter called.
J I'd like the phone number for radio station KZRK, please.

C

In exercise C, students refer to the models in exercise A. They should write out several telephone questions using the question phrases. Telephone questions are idiomatic. You may also want to remind students of the Wh- question forms that they studied in Unit 1, Grammar Check 2. Students can then use these questions for the Active Practice activity "Quick caller".

ACTIVE PRACTICE

This activity gives students the opportunity to further consolidate their knowledge of telephoning language and to appropriate some of the telephoning phrases presented in exercises A, B and C.

Students can pair up and exchange roles several times. You can also set up two rows of chairs opposite each other – the students on one side would make the calls.

After a few minutes, ask students to stop and to move over to the chair next to them.

Have students go through an entire rotation of callers, depending on the number of students in the class. This method of rotating students from one caller to the next makes the practice period livelier.

Grammar Check 2

Aims
- TOEIC Part VI practice: error recognition
- Present perfect and past simple
- Vocabulary development: Internet services and accounts; problem-solving

Students commonly confuse the present perfect and past simple verb tenses and thus can have difficulty with TOEIC® Parts V and VI where these items appear.
In exercise A, students begin by deducing the grammar rules from the three examples. Students should be directed to identify the verb forms and the time expressions in the examples (*for three years*, *this year*, *last month*). Ask students which time expressions indicate on-going periods of time and which ones indicate finished time periods. This is a good moment to review time expressions. The TOEIC Tip gives some examples of these.

Answers	
A	
1 past simple	2 past simple
present perfect	present perfect
	present perfect

Exercise B is an extended question-response conversation over the telephone, where an Internet hotline technician is helping a customer solve a problem. It gives students practice for TOEIC Part VI error identification. Students need to be able to determine whether the underlined verbs are correct or not, then make the corrections. This exercise can be done individually, then performed in pairs for students to check their answers.

Answers	
B	
1 C	2 I, opened
3 I, has moved	4 C
5 I, updated	6 I, have slowed
7 C	8 I, did you switch
9 I, have always used	10 C

DISCUSSION

Students interview each other about problems they may have encountered when using computers. They should focus less on the actual technical problem and more on what channels of communication helped them to solve the problem.

- Did they talk to someone? A friend? A technician?
- Did they read a manual?
- Did they go on-line to find technical help?

As students are conducting their interviews with each other, you can circulate and note down how students are using the present perfect and past tenses in their conversations.

At the end, you might also want to lead a class discussion on how certain modes of communication are more helpful than others when it comes to problem-solving.

Writing Practice

Write an email to the technical help at an Internet Service Provider (an IPS) describing a problem that you might have had with your email (lost messages, unstable Internet connections, inaccessible servers, etc.).
Be sure to practice using both the past and present perfect tenses!

ACTIVE PRACTICE

The Media Survey can be done individually or in pairs. It is designed to review media vocabulary and time expressions. After students conduct the survey, have them look for words that relate to media and then to identify time expressions.

Here are some of the important time expressions in the Media Survey:

X number of *days a week*	*every other day*
several times a week	*occasionally*
never	*every day*
once a week	*rarely*
daily	*on the weekend*

Listening 3

Aims
- TOEIC Part IV practice: short talks; radio news bulletin
- Topic: company relocations and job lay-offs

Students should read through the questions before listening to the radio news bulletin. The bulletin states that GloTelCom is holding a press conference today and that the company could be announcing lay-offs due to low profits. Encourage students to listen for the specific information that will help them answer the comprehension questions. Note that this provides background information and vocabulary for the Communication activity.

TOEIC Part IV sections often contain advanced vocabulary items that act as distracters. On the TOEIC®, students do not need to know the meaning of all the words in order to answer the questionscorrectly. They do need to practice "filtering" out the distracters in order to concentrate on the important information in the message. As a teacher, you can approach this challenge in several ways. Have students focus on the questions, then listen to the short talk. For weaker students, you may decide to pre-teach vocabulary items. However, this can result in having them focus on the difficult vocabulary rather than on the information needed to answer the questions.

Difficult vocabulary items might include: *to shut down local operations, quarterly profits, drastic measures, to be adversely affected, to be laid-off = to be let go, to undergo change, to remain an exception, to tune in.*

Possible discussion questions

Open markets and economic globalization have allowed companies to relocate and to move their manufacturing and servicing sectors to other countries in order to take advantage of less expensive labor markets.

- *Do you know of any companies that have done this?*
- *Who benefits from such relocations?*
- *Who doesn't benefit from this?*

Answers
1 hold a press conference
2 laid off 1,000 workers
3 prospects are not good
4 move operations to cheaper labor markets

AUDIOSCRIPT

GloTelCom, the communications giant, announced it would be holding a press conference today at their local headquarters. Is the industry leader preparing to shut down local operations and move overseas? With quarterly profits down again, GloTelCom has union representatives and local government officials concerned that they may take more drastic measures after 1,000 skilled workers were let go two months ago in an effort to lower costs.

This comes only two weeks after the Mayor said in a speech that the local economy was quote "strong and stable." If GloTelCom decides to reduce its workforce, the local economy and hundreds of families will be adversely affected. Moreover, the community has already seen many manufacturing jobs leave the area and according to union leaders, the future for local workers remains uncertain. It's unlikely laid-off workers would be able to find jobs in another factory.

Over the past fifteen years, the telecommunications industry has undergone enormous change. While most of the larger companies have already closed their domestic operations in order to move into cheaper labor markets, GloTelCom has remained until now, the exception.

Tune in at 3:00 p.m. for the GloTelCom press conference live.

Communication

Aim
- Speaking practice: preparing statements, questions, arguments

In this activity, students are preparing a press conference. Depending on the role they choose, students must prepare statements, questions and arguments about GloTelCom's plans to reduce its workforce and its impact on the local community.

Refer Students to the audioscript in Listening 3 in order to prepare the context of the press conference. Break students into small groups according to their roles. Give them enough time to prepare their statements.

Arrange the classroom so that GloTelCom's president, the spokesperson, and the Mayor are seated in front of the journalists and the union representatives. You may want to ask each person to stand when addressing the public. Give the journalists and union representatives full opportunity to question and challenge the statements made by GloTelCom.

Writing Practice

As a concerned member of the community, you wish to express your views on the GloTelCom issues and write a letter to send to the local newspaper and the Mayor.

Extension Activities

A

You are an expert photo editor who has been commissioned to select the best photos for a series of advertising campaigns.
- Look through the portfolio of photos. You must choose the photo that best represents the business. Remember you can only choose one!
- Write five sentences about this photo.
- Write five sentences about the location.
- Write five sentences about the actions in the photo.
- Write five sentences about the people in the photo.

B

In this activity, students develop their own radio program. The aim is to have students write and practice Part IV short talks.
- Gather sample material from newspapers and the Internet for the following suggested topics:
  Weather forecast
  Movie review
  Economic report
  Traffic advisory
  School closures due to snow
  A public announcement
  A top story from the local news
- Now, in small press teams, have students rewrite the material as a radio announcement. Tell them that they will have to adapt the written text using shorter sentences, contractions, and generally more colloquial language.
- Once they have written and practiced the radio program, they have to write four TOEIC®-type Part IV questions based on their radio news broadcast.
- Now, have them perform the program in front of the class.
- Have the rest of the class answer the TOEIC® questions.

Review Test 1 Answer Key

Units 1–3

Listening Comprehension

Part I
Photographs

1 **D** Both men are sitting (*seated*) at their desks in their cubicles. (A) Although they are using *computers*, they are not *moving* them. (B) They are not *walking through*, but are working in *the office*. (C) The employees are not *lined up outside*, but are inside *the office*.

2 **A** The two men are *working* at a table on a large document or *plan*. (B) There is paper, but there are no *pages* and, although one man (C) is drawing, they are not *painting*. (D) The paper is laid out flat, not *folded*.

3 **C** The man is *standing beside* the surveying instrument and near the truck. (A) He is *looking* through the lens on the instrument, but he is not looking for his glasses. (B) There is a *tire*, but he is not *changing it*. (D) He is *leaning over* the instrument, but not *against* the truck.

4 **D** The man is about to put some letters into a mailbox. (A) He is not *mailing* a letter, he is delivering several letters. (B) He is not *behind the post*, but in front of it. (C) He is not *opening* anything.

5 **C** The woman *is speaking into a microphone*. (A) She is not *at home* and she is not *studying*. (B) She is *talking*, but not *on the phone*. (D) She could be singing, but she is not *signing*.

6 **D** The two chefs are preparing or *cooking* food on a *stove*. (A) There are no documents, so they cannot be *reading*. (B) The food is stored *on the shelves*, but the chefs are not *stocking* them. (C) They could be chopping food, but they are not *shopping for* it.

Part II
Questions and responses

7 **C** The question *Why* asks for the reason he left his job, not for a (A) period of time. (B) The verb *to leave* refers to a job position, not to a physical object.

8 **A** *As soon as* introduces the answer to *when* they can move into the building. (B) answers a question about *how* to gain access to a *building*. (C) answers a question about *what kind* of *building* is under construction.

9 **B** This response answers the speaker's request for a *newspaper*. The other choices are replies to requests for (A) coffee and (C) photocopying facilities.

10 **B** This answer is an appropriate response to the speaker's negative opinion about television advertising. The word *station* in choice (A) refers to a train arrival, not a TV station, and (C) refers to two men who work in *advertising*.

11 **A** This choice answers the question about the location of the nearest post office. In (B), *close to* refers to the progress that has been made on a report, not to proximity. (C) refers to where information was given or *posted*, not to the location of a *post office*.

12 **B** This answer gives the information about *when* the restaurant manager started his job. Choice (A) contains the word *higher*, which has the same pronunciation as *hire*. (C) refers to a future time, whereas the question asks for information about the past.

13 **C** Only (C) gives information about frequency in response to the question *How often …?* (A) refers to *picking up* a person, not the *mail*. Choice (B) includes the word *often*, but refers to a *pick-up* or truck, not to the verb *to pick up*.

14 **A** The caller asks to speak to *Mr. Takata* and choice (A) states that he is busy. In (B), the verb *take* sounds similar to the proper name *Takata*. (C) contains the verb *to put*, but not the phrasal verb *to put through*, which means *to transfer the call to*.

Part III
Short conversations

15 **C** They both have meetings with clients on that day, so they cannot (D) attend the *training* session which (B) has been organized by the *personnel department*. (A) Although they will be away from the office, they will not be *at home*.

Review Test 1 | Answer Key

16 **C** They are discussing whether or not to buy new computers, not (A) *new software*. Answers (B) and (D) refer to the maintenance of existing computers.

17 **D** The woman is complaining about the high temperature in the office, which is the result of the *air conditioning* not working. (A) mentions cold, not hot, temperatures. (B) is about an open *window* and (C) refers to the heating system, not the hot weather.

18 **C** *Anita* has taken over from (A) *Steve*, who is no longer in charge of collecting the *money*. (B) *Dr. Camara* will receive the gift. (D) The other members of *the research team* are making contributions, not collecting them.

19 **B** Nine people will be attending the meeting.

20 **B** The man is looking for a *pay phone*, which is a synonym for *phone booth*. (A) He wants to place a call, not *buy a phone*. (C) There is no mention of a *phone book* or directory. (D) Although the phone is located next to the *bus stop*, the man does not mention taking the *bus*.

21 **A** The woman is calling to set up a new *Internet account*, not (B) to speak to an *accountant*, or (C) to make a payment on an account. (D) Although the expression *direct your call* is used, no mention is made of the *director*.

Part IV
Short talks

22 **A** The reason for the call from the *subscriptions department* is to confirm a customer's (subscriber's) full *home address*. The call is not about (B) *excess charges*, (C) *new subscriptions*, or (D) *special offers*.

23 **B** The customer has not received *Business News* because the *magazine subscription address* is *incomplete*. Consequently, (A/C/D) are true.

24 **C** The speech *welcomes* guests to the *opening ceremony* for a *business park*, (B) not a *parking lot* or (D) a *park*. (A) The *real estate development* includes *offices*, not *homes*, so the people attending are not *new homeowners*.

25 **D** The ceremony takes place at *Somerset Business Park*, which is an *office complex*, not (B) an *arts center* or (C) a *state (natural) park*. (A) It is located 15 minutes away from *downtown*.

26 **C** Only *telecommunications services* are provided to tenants. There is no mention of (A) *storage*, (B) *housing* or (D) *insurance*.

Reading Comprehension

Part V
Incomplete sentences

27 **D** The call was made *yesterday*, so the verb has to be in the *past simple* and not (A) the present continuous, (B) present perfect or (C) present simple.

28 **A** Although all four words can be used after the word *press*, a *company* can only *hold* a *press conference*, not (B/C/D).

29 **B** Only the preposition *beside* refers to a static position. (A/C/D) refer to movement.

30 **B** *Inform* is the only verb that can be followed by a direct object and the preposition *of*. (A/C/D) do not make sense in the context, which requires a verb that means *to tell*.

31 **A** Only the preposition *on* can be used with the *floor* of a building; (B) *over*, (C) *in* and (D) *at* can describe location, but not with the meaning of *floor* (*level*).

32 **B** The adverb *currently* refers to an event taking place now, so only the present continuous tense is appropriate, not (A) the present simple, (C) the present perfect or (D) the past simple.

33 **D** *Furniture* is a non-count noun and therefore cannot be qualified by (A) the indefinite article *a* or by the adjectives (B) *many* and (C) *several*.

34 **C** The indefinite article *an* must be followed by a noun. (A) The noun *account* refers to a financial item and not to a person. (B) is an adjective and (D) is a participle/gerund.

35 **B** (A) The singular indefinite article *an* is required before a word beginning with a vowel; in this case, it is the adjective *exciting* that precedes *career position*. (C) *Each* refers to the separate elements of a group, (D) *other* qualifies plural noun forms when it is not preceded by a definite article.

36 **C** *Letters* can only be collected from a *post office*. Therefore, (A/B/D) are inappropriate collocations.

Part VI
Error correction

37 **A** As it appears in the sentence, the adjective *former* is incorrect and should be changed to either the adverb *formerly* or placed in front of *president*.

38 **A** *An* is incorrect because no article is needed to qualify the plural count noun *features*.

39 **C** The preposition *above* refers to a vertical position and is incorrect. *At* is the correct preposition to use with the phrase *the end of every corridor*, which is where the *phones* are located.

40 **C** The time expression *since last month* expresses a period of time that begins in the past and continues until the present. The past simple form *went* is incorrect and should be in the present perfect form *has gone*.

41 **C** The word *train* can be a noun (a means of transport), but does not make sense in the context. The gerund *training* is the correct form of the verb *train*, which refers to teaching or learning skills.

42 **A** The verb form *are prepare* is incorrect and should be in the present continuous – *are preparing*. The adverb *currently* means "at this time" and is used with the present continuous, not the present simple.

43 **A** The present perfect tense is incorrect with the past time expression *two years ago*. The simple past (*overhauled*) should be used instead.

44 **B** The preposition *against* is incorrect because it expresses close proximity, whereas the context of the sentence requires the preposition *away from*, which refers to distance.

Part VII
Reading

45 **D** Top Assets provides full-time *expertly trained* banking personnel to its clients who are (A) banks. (B) It is an agency, but not one that provides credit or *loans*. (C) It provides a *service* by supplying staff who may be able to use the Internet (*e-banking reps*), but it does not offer *Internet connections*.

46 **C** The personnel provided by Top Assets are *trained* and have *experience*. (A) They do not have to have *insurance* or *references*. (B) There is no reference to *schedules* although we can assume that personnel are *flexible*. (D) Top Assets personnel are *right* for clients' *work environments*.

47 **A** The company offers its clients a *complimentary assessment* which is a free evaluation. (B) *18* refers to the number of steps in a process, not to a duration. (C) It offers staff for the finance industry, but not financial products such as *insurance*. (D) The noun *compliment* means "praise", not something that is free.

48 **C** Feng shui is a *practice* or method of organizing a space in a harmonious way. (A) It can be used in architecture, but it is not a place or *site*. (B) It might be included as one component of a *building project*, but cannot be defined as such. (D) It is used by *new design firms* like East/West Design Group.

49 **B** Clients use the East/West Design Group to create work environments that *enable people to work at their best*, which therefore increases *productivity*. (A) There is no mention of the effect of feng shui on *cash flow* although feng shui does generate a *flow of energy*. It is used to *design buildings*, but not to (C) *produce building materials*. Feng shui uses *natural energies*, but does not (D) r*educe the cost of energy*.

50 **B** The company first conducts *an on-site assessment* and therefore visits the client's workplace. (A) It *conducts a survey*, but not *on-line*. (C) It assesses *energy*, not *financial records*. (D) It *recommends water features*, but this is not the *first* thing it does.

AUDIOSCRIPT
Review Test I Units 1–3
Part I
1. A The men are moving the computers.
   B They're walking through the office.
   C The employees are lined up outside the office.
   D They're seated at their desks.
2. A They're working on a plan.
   B They're tearing out the pages.
   C They're painting a picture.
   D The paper's folded in half.
3. A The man's looking for his glasses.
   B He's changing the tire.
   C The man's standing beside the equipment.
   D He's leaning against the truck.
4. A He's mailing a letter.
   B The man's behind the post.
   C He's opening the package.
   D He's delivering the mail.
5. A The woman's studying at home.
   B She's talking on the phone.
   C She's speaking into the microphone.
   D She's signing a contract.
6. A The chefs are reading the menu.
   B They're stocking the shelves.
   C The chefs are shopping for vegetables.
   D They're cooking on the stove.

Part II
7. Why did you leave your last position?
   A It lasted a little more than five years.
   B I may have left it on the job site.
   C Well, I went back to school to get an advanced degree.
8. When will we be able to move into the new building?
   A Just as soon as the lease has been signed.
   B I have a badge that allows me to enter the building at any time.
   C I think they're building a new movie theater.

9 I'd like a copy of today's paper, please.
   A Certainly. Would you like cream and sugar with that?
   B I'm afraid we've sold out.
   C I'm sorry. The photocopier is out of toner.
10 Don't you think there are too many commercials on TV?
   A I think she's coming in at the other station.
   B Definitely. I'm always changing channels.
   C Yes. Both men work in television advertising.
11 Excuse me, how far is the nearest post office?
   A Just around the corner.
   B They're close to completing the report.
   C It was posted on the bulletin board.
12 When did you hire the new restaurant manager?
   A It's much higher than we thought.
   B He started two weeks ago.
   C We're eating there next week.
13 How often is the outgoing mail picked up?
   A She picked him up on the way to work.
   B He often goes out in his pick-up.
   C It's collected twice daily, at noon and at six p.m.
14 Could you put me through to Mr. Takata, please?
   A He's on another line. May I take a message?
   B Please, take as many as you'd like.
   C Sure. You can put them here in the corner.

Part III

15 **Woman 1** The personnel manager has organized a training workshop this Friday.
   Woman 2 Yes, I heard. I'd really like to go, but that's the day I visit my clients.
   Woman 1 So do I. I wish they'd let us know about these events sooner.
16 **Man** These machines are getting old. Do you think that we should replace them?
   Woman Well, the processors are very slow and we've had complaints about the small screens.
   Man Why don't we go ahead and order some new ones?
17 **Woman** Do you have any idea what the temperature is outside?
   Man I don't know exactly, but it must be up in the eighties.
   Woman Isn't that just typical? The hottest day of the summer and the air-conditioning isn't working.
18 **Man** Who should we give the money to for Dr. Camara's retirement gift?
   Woman Steve had volunteered to handle it. But since he's been transferred, Anita in the personnel department is taking care of it.
   Man OK, I'll let everyone on the research team know.
19 **Woman** Have you received confirmation for the recruitment interviews on the 15th of March?
   Man Yes. We've contacted all ten candidates. But one of them has already accepted another position and won't be attending.
   Woman No problem. Let's arrange the nine interviews at twenty-five-minute intervals starting at eight. That way we'll be finished before lunch.
20 **Man** Do you know where I might find a pay phone?
   Woman I'm pretty sure there's one right around the corner next to the bus stop.
   Man Great. Thank you. That's convenient.
21 **Man** Good morning. How may I direct your call?
   Woman I'm interested in setting up a new Internet account.
   Man One moment, I'll put you through to a service representative.

Part IV

Questions 22 and 23:
Hello. This is Tonya Jackson in the subscriptions department of Business News publications. You recently subscribed to our magazine but the postal service has returned your first three issues of Business News. They've indicated that they are unable to deliver because the address listed is incomplete. Could you please call me back to confirm your home mailing address? The toll-free number is: 1-800-825-9838. Please accept our apologies.

Questions 24–26:
Thank you for attending today's opening ceremony for Somerset Business Park. The renovation of this historic industrial complex has created over 50,000 square feet of prime office space. Swanson Development remodeled four existing structures and added two office buildings to create a mixed-use complex, which also features a conference center and an indoor sports facility. Located only 15 minutes from downtown and the airport, the 150-acre business park is also fully equipped with the latest wireless technology, ensuring high-speed telecommunications and the most reliable voice, data, and video services. Tenants already include a major insurance firm and a leading information technology company. Congratulations to everyone involved. And welcome to Somerset Business Park!

4 Retailing

Unit Focus • Stores • Products • Services

Unit overview

Unit components	Focus	TOEIC practice	Duration
Snapshot	Shopping and retailing	Part I	15–25 mins
Listening 1	Department store: shopping	Part III	20–30 mins
Grammar Check 1	Comparatives and superlatives	Part VI	15–25 mins
Listening 2	Store opening	Part IV	10 mins
Viewpoint	Camper info-shops	Part VII	25–35 mins
Vocabulary Builder	Separable prefixes	Part V	15 mins
Grammar Check 2	Tag questions	Part II	20 mins
Listening 3	Product information	Part II	20 mins
Communication	Presenting a product		40 mins
		Total	3 hrs–3 hrs 40

Snapshot

Aims
- TOEIC Part I practice: awareness of distracters
- Vocabulary development: shopping

The pictures present a selection of retail environments which can be used to generate general discussion about students' experience of shopping. This can be done either before or after the listening activities by asking questions such as:

- *How often do you go shopping?*
- *What sorts of items do you buy?*
- *Have you ever bought anything on the Internet?*

Picture descriptions
Picture 1
This picture shows a *market stall* where *fresh produce* (fruit and vegetables) is on *display*. The woman behind the stall is *serving* a customer and she is holding a *bag* for the customer to place the products in. There is a *set of scales* on the left of the picture for *weighing* produce and there are *labels* showing the prices of the produce that is for sale.

Picture 2
In the picture we can see the interior of a local *grocery store*. The walls of the store are lined with *shelves* and *display cabinets* where different types of products are arranged (tinned and packaged goods). In the center, there is a *glass-fronted counter*/display with a selection of bread and pastries for sale. The woman on the left is *stretching* her hand over the counter, probably to give change to the customer on the other side.

Picture 3
This picture shows the interior of a *television store*. *Television sets* are on display in different parts of the store and we can see the same *picture* of a woman on several *screens*. In the foreground, a *saleswoman* is assisting a couple. She is wearing a *vest* which identifies her as a member of the *sales staff*.

Picture 4
This picture is taken inside a *department store*. There are a number of different *displays* or *stands* where luxury goods and *jewelry* are on sale. A *shopper* is walking between the stands with her bag *slung over her shoulder*. She is holding two *shopping bags*, one in each hand. To her right, a *saleswoman* or *sales clerk* is leaning over the *counter* and *rearranging* the items that are on display.

Unit 4 | Retailing

Suggested vocabulary

	Items	People	Actions
Picture 1	fresh fruit vegetables fresh produce market stall	customer	buying purchasing putting in filling holding out shopping serving
Picture 2	counter shelves groceries corner store grocery store local store	shop assistant	paying counting giving change
Picture 3	Televisions (TVs) screens appliances	salesperson/ man/ assistant sales clerk	demonstrating explaining
Picture 4	department store display counter	saleswoman	arranging preparing

In exercise A, students should be able to come up with several suggested statements to describe what is happening in each picture.

Answers
A
Possible statements
Picture 1
The woman is doing her shopping at the market.
They're putting the fruit into a bag.

Picture 2
The customer is paying for the goods.
The saleswoman is handing the woman her change.

Picture 3
The saleswoman is explaining how to operate the television.
They're buying a television.

Picture 4
The sales clerk is arranging the items on display.
She's cleaning the counter.

In exercise B, after completing the listening exercise, you should draw students' attention to some of the words that are used in the statements. Explain that each statement contains one word that can be used either as a noun or as a verb. Ask them to listen again and to identify these words.

Noun	verb
1 purchase	produce
2 refund	
3 hand	change
4 produce	
5 set up	market
6 display	
7 return	damage
8 set	works

Answers
B
1 A   2 C   3 H   4 F

In exercise C, remind students that many of the questions on the test contain synonyms of words that are used in the audio recordings or in the reading texts. Learning to recognize synonyms will help them to improve their score on these sections.

Answers
C
Suggested synonyms
purchase   – buy
give a refund – reimburse
hand   – give
produce   – grow
set up   – install
arrange   – place
return   – bring back
explain   – demonstrate

AUDIOSCRIPT
B
A She's purchasing some produce.
B He's giving her a refund.
C She's handing the woman her change.
D They produce organic rice.
E They're setting up the market.
F She's arranging some items in the display case.
G They're returning the damaged goods.
H She's explaining how the TV set works.

⚠ **TOEIC Tip**
This tip draws attention to the pronunciation differences that exist between the noun and verb forms of some two-syllable words. You should point out that the majority of two-syllable words which have both a noun and a verb form are not pronounced differently i.e. *contact, practice, purchase, refund, review, service*. However, for the words which do have different pronunciations, you may want to read out the

35

> following sentences and ask students to identify which forms of the words were used.
>
> Stress is on the second syllable of the verb forms, but on the first syllable of the noun forms.
>
> 1 We **subject** all our frozen foods to rigorous hygiene controls.
> 2 The local planning officials **object** to the further expansion of the shopping center.
> 3 The company intends to **transfer** all customer service enquiries to an outside supplier.
> 4 I'm sorry, we have no **record** of that transaction on our files.
> 5 We are currently conducting a market **survey** of mobile telephone users.
> 6 The **prospects** for the retail industry are very encouraging.

Listening 1

Aims
- TOEIC Part III practice: short conversations
- Vocabulary development

The lead-in activity introduces additional retail vocabulary by focusing on a selection of goods that are sold in department stores. After students have matched the items with the categories in exercise B, you can ask them to work in pairs and to prepare a short list of other examples of items that could be bought in each of the departments. Pairs can then take turns reading out an item from their list while the other pair identify the department where it would be found.

The listening activity in exercise C gives three examples of exchanges between a sales clerk (salesperson/sales assistant) and a customer. Ask students to focus on the roles of the people in the dialogues (Who is the customer and who is the salesperson?). Students should then focus on the questions that the speakers ask and on the exact context of each dialogue. Although students may find some words in the dialogues quite difficult, you can reassure them that it is not always necessary to understand all the vocabulary in a dialogue in order to give a correct answer. Remind them to focus on what they know, not on the words they do not know.

You may want to point out the meanings of the following words after they have done the listening:

| embroidered | charge | on order |
| put aside | on display | |

● Extension Activity

If you have time, ask students to imagine a scene between a customer and a salesperson. They can then write up their own dialogues and play the scene in front of the group.

> **Answers**
> **A and B**
>
> | 1 briefcase | Leather goods |
> | 2 MP3 player | TV/Hi-Fi |
> | 3 gold bracelet | Jewelry |
> | 4 tablecloth | Household linens |
> | 5 notecards | Stationery |
> | 6 jigsaw puzzles | Toys and games |
> | 7 cashmere shawl | Women's fashion |
> | 8 perfume | Cosmetics |
> | 9 chest of drawers | Home furnishings |
> | 10 espresso machine | Electrical appliances |
>
> **C**
>
> | Location | Request |
> | 1 Teenage fashion | help with choice of gift |
> | 2 Welcome desk/ Customer services | information about a special delivery |
> | 3 Toys and games | information about a product |

AUDIOSCRIPT
C
1
Man I'm looking for a birthday gift for my sixteen-year-old daughter. What would you recommend?
Woman Well, the embroidered designer jeans have been a big success with young people so far this season.
Man Yes I know, but she already has two pairs.
2
Woman I'd like to know if it's possible to have all my purchases delivered directly to my hotel?
Man Yes ma'am, we do offer a special delivery service. I'll just need your hotel address and room number.
Woman Oh, that's great. Is there any extra charge?
3
Woman When will you be receiving the new version of the game?
Man They're on order right now. So we should have them early next week. Would you like us to put one aside for you?
Woman No, thank you. I think I'll wait to see them once they're on display.

Unit 4 | Retailing

> **ACTIVE PRACTICE**
> This section provides students with an opportunity to talk at length about their shopping experiences. It can be done as either a pairwork speaking activity or in small groups. Focus their attention on the shopping experience rather than on the specific object that they bought.
> Some suggestions for questions to ask:
> - *What sorts of things do you buy regularly/more rarely?*
> - *How do you decide where you will make the purchase?*
> - *How do you pay for the goods you buy?*
> - *How important is the price?*
> - *Are you ever influenced by special promotions?*
> - *Do you ever buy things by mail order/hire purchase?*
> - *Have you ever had to return an item that you had purchased?*

Grammar Check 1

> **Aims**
> - TOEIC Part VI practice: error recognition
> - Comparatives and superlatives

The grammar section in A provides a brief overview of the rules for comparative and superlative forms. Most students will probably be familiar with the basic rules for forming comparative and superlative sentences. If they have difficulty answering the three questions about the way these forms are used, you will need to review this aspect of grammar in more detail. (Refer to the Grammar Reference on pages 131 and 132 of the Student's Book.)

It is important to point out that it is acceptable to use the definite article with a comparative when only two items are being compared:

Of the two models I tried, this is the <u>better</u> (one).

You may also want to point out that comparative and superlative forms are also used with adverbs:

The saleswoman repeated the question <u>more slowly</u>.

Before going on to the slogans activity in B, draw students' attention to some of the most common errors for comparative and superlative forms that are included in questions on Part VI. Tell them to look out for:

- *as* instead of *than*
  The new mall will be twice as big <u>than</u> the world's largest shopping center.

- adverbial forms instead of comparative adjectives
  This is the most <u>expensively</u> item that we have on sale.
- mistakes with articles – using *a* with a superlative
  Retailers are saying that the season has been one of <u>a</u> quietest they can remember.

After completing the slogans exercise, ask students if they have other examples of slogans that contain superlative or comparative forms. They can either choose existing slogans that they are aware of, or they can invent slogans of their own and the class can guess which products the slogans are/could be used for.

You may wish to give students the names of the companies associated with the slogans and indicate the type of goods/services that they sell/used to sell.

1 Our repairmen are the loneliest guys in town.
   Maytag – domestic appliances
2 It's better than anything.
   Haagan Daz – ice cream
3 The most refreshing drink in the world.
   Coca-Cola – Coca-Cola
4 If only everything in life was as reliable as a Volkswagen.
   Volkswagen – cars
5 No battery is stronger for longer.
   Duracell – batteries
6 The world's most trusted anti-virus solution.
   Norton Symantec – software
7 The best a man can get.
   Gillette – razors
8 If you find it cheaper, we pay you the difference.
   Retail Bargains – consumer goods
9 Always the lowest price. Always.
   Wal-Mart – supermarkets

> **Answers**
> **A**
> 1
> a Comparatives: add *-er*; superlatives: add *-est*
> b Change the final *y* to *i*, then add the same endings as for one- or two-syllable adjectives.
> c Comparatives: *more/less* before the adjective
>   Superlatives: *the most/the least* before the adjective
> 2
> a *as* + adjective + *as*
> b comparative adjective + *than*

37

3
a No
b Yes

B
1 the ... *loneliest*
2 C
3 *The* most refreshing ...
4 ... as reliable *as*
5 *stronger* for longer
6 The world's *most* trusted ...
7 *The* best ...
8 If you find it ... *cheaper*, ...
9 C

Listening 2

Aims
- TOEIC Part IV practice: short talks
- Listening for specific information

Ask students to focus only on the information that they are required to fill in on the invitation. After completing this exercise, you can ask students some general questions about new stores that have opened in their countries and about what makes them unique. Ask them if they have ever been to a Camper store, or if they have heard anything about the company. Students can volunteer any information they may have about the company's products and stores. Explain that the Viewpoint reading will provide an insight into how this retailer operates.

Answers
1 opening
2 concept store
3 Sydney
4 March 26th
5 Building

AUDIOSCRIPT
The Spanish footwear chain Camper will be opening its first Australian concept store on March 26th. After setting up operations in 30 countries around the world, Camper is now turning its attention to markets further from home in its drive to internationalize the brand. The new store, located on the ground floor of Sydney's newly renovated Queen Victoria Building, will be inaugurated during a gala evening event which will be attended by well-known Australian television and show business personalities.

For many Australian shoppers visiting the new store, this will not be their first contact with the Camper brand. Their fashionable footwear has already been selling for several years in independent outlets around the country. But according to Camper management, the time has come for customers to experience for themselves the unique feel of the Camper store concept.

Viewpoint

Aims
- TOEIC Part VII practice: reading comprehension
- Scanning a text
- Vocabulary development
- Discussion: Camper info-shops

The lead-in question focuses on the graphic component of Camper's identity and invites students to react to the images that they can see on the page. You may want to point to other retail businesses that have a strong graphic identity (Benetton, Nike).

The reading material is laid out as four separate texts and students have to scan the texts in order to identify which ones contain the relevant information.

Part B focuses on specific information from each of the texts. The following vocabulary may require further explanation:

footwear   shoemaking
points of sale   non-contaminating
renewable energy boxing glove
manufacturing process padded leathers
lining   cushion
bioconstruction

The Camper company is famous for its innovative approach to store design and merchandising. It produces very original publicity materials and cultivates the image of a business that offers customers more than just a product, but a complete shopping experience. You may want to ask your students to say how they react to the type of shopping experience that Camper offers its customers. Do they find this appealing?

Answers
A
1 Text A
2 Texts B/C
3 Text B
4 Text B
5 Text D
6 Texts B/C

Unit 4 | Retailing

B
1. Madrid, Tokyo, London
2. Barcelona
3. more than one thousand
4. customers sit on steps
5. the cuisine is natural – food is prepared in front of customers, bioconstruction
6. images, icons, objects, shoes
7. boxing glove
8. no left or right shoe

Vocabulary Builder

Aims
- TOEIC Part V practice: incomplete sentences
- Vocabulary development: review of separable prefixes – usage and meaning

Before starting this exercise, to take this opportunity to explain that words in English can have two types of prefixes:

- inseparable prefixes cannot be separated from the words that they are a part of:

  <u>be</u>come   <u>con</u>sist   <u>in</u>tend

- separable prefixes can be added to certain words

Note that some prefixes can be both separable and inseparable:

<u>dis</u>tribute   inseparable
<u>dis</u>advantage   separable

You may also want to point out that separable prefixes are associated with specific parts of speech (verbs, nouns, etc.). A list of these is given here.

Answers

A		used with:
1	over	verbs
2	re	verbs
3	bi	adjectives
4	inter	adjectives, verbs
5	under	nouns, verbs
6	up	adjectives, verbs
7	sub	verbs
8	co	verbs, nouns
9	un	adjectives, verbs (especially with past participle forms in -ed)
10	mis	verbs
11	out	verbs
12	dis	verbs

B
1. up   2. over/under   3. mis
4. dis   5. re   6. sub

C
1. *dis*abled
2. *over*charged/*under*charged
3. *re*negotiate
4. *dis*continued
5. *Mis*management
6. *under*estimate
7. *over*size

D
The following is a list of words that take these prefixes:

downgrade	download
*ex-president	ex-member
enforce	enable
enact	extraordinary
extracurricular	inefficient
inoffensive	improbable
impatient	non-profitmaking
nonexistent	hyperactive
hypermarket	superstore
superimpose	

*Note that the prefix *ex* is always followed by a hyphen.

Grammar Check 2

Aims
- TOEIC Part II practice: question/response
- Review of tag question forms

This grammar section explains the uses of tag questions and shows how they are formed. Tag questions are often featured in Parts II and III of the Listening section. It is important to point out that tag questions can be used in two different ways:
- to seek confirmation of information that the speaker is not completely sure of, or that he or she wants to have confirmed.
- to make a comment or give an opinion.

You may want to explain that the intonation varies according to the type of tag question. In the first case (confirmation), the question has a rising tone.

The sales start next week, don't they?

But in the second case (opinion), the question has a falling tone.

She really didn't need to buy a second car, did she?

The listening exercise requires students to focus on appropriate responses to questions.

39

Target Score

Answers
A
1 affirmative
2 negative
B
1 is there
2 doesn't it
3 are they
4 do I
5 will it
6 won't it
7 didn't you
8 could you

● Extension Activity

Distribute the following short summaries of situations to students in pairs. One student should prepare a tag question to ask and the other should make an appropriate response to the question. You can tell the students that they can continue the conversations after the initial question and response, if they wish.

Situations

- You need to buy something from the supermarket but do not have time to go yourself. A friend is going there.
- You are worried that the meeting you have been asked to attend for the first time will last more than one hour. A colleague has attended the two previous ones.
- You have forgotten your credit card and have no money to buy your lunch. A colleague has just asked you if you are planning to have lunch now.
- You have been asked to attend a conference in another country. You are not sure that the organizers will pay for your travel. You are speaking to one of their representatives.
- You would like to invite a colleague out to dinner at a seafood restaurant, but you would like to be sure that he or she likes this sort of food.
- You have heard a rumor that employees in your department will have to work extra hours during the next month. You are with a colleague who usually knows what is going on.

Listening 3

Aims
- TOEIC Part II practice: question/response
- Tag questions and responses

This exercise gives examples of tag questions that seek confirmation of information. This is the most common type of tag question that is used on the test. Ask students to note the answers to the questions that do not begin with a *Yes* or *No*. You may want to give them a selection of the words and phrases and ask them to rephrase the answers.

Answers		
1 E	2 I	3 H
4 B	5 G	6 C
7 J	8 D	

AUDIOSCRIPT

A   We recommend that all drivers perform a routine inspection before they use their vehicles.
B   Yes, that's right. Just leave us the full details of your address and we'll do the rest.
C   No. I'm afraid we are not authorized to sell below list price.
D   That depends. We advise drivers to check with the manager and to obtain permission before driving inside buildings.
E   According to our estimates, it takes only 45 minutes to unpack and put together.
F   Well, all new owners are invited to attend a 30-minute training session.
G   That's right. If any part of the vehicle is defective, we replace it free of charge.
H   Not necessarily. We only carry a limited number of items and we order all others direct from our supplier.

> ⚠ **TOEIC Tip**
> This tip refers to a general characteristic of Part II questions on the test. It is important that students understand that the responses that are given in this section of the test are not mirror responses where the auxiliary verbs in the question are repeated in the answer. Indeed, it is very often the case that a response which does contain the same auxiliary as a question may not be the correct response. It is important for students to understand that there are other ways of responding to a question. Some examples are given in the tip, but others include questions that can be answered by *Yes* or *No*.
> *Yes*
> *quite   exactly   absolutely   indeed*
> *by all means   you're welcome   I think so*
> *I'm afraid so   alright   fine   that's right*
> *of course   naturally   sure*
> *No*
> *no way   I'm afraid not   that's impossible*
> *sorry   I have/had no idea   no chance*
> *not necessarily   not at all*

Communication

> **Aim**
> - Speaking practice: presenting and discussing

For this exercise, students refer to the cards for the two missing products. They should use the information given to prepare a short presentation of the product. Encourage students not just to present the features of their products, but also to focus on the reasons why their product would be a good choice for the catalog. If you want to give students additional practice in doing this, ask them to research other alternative products for homework. They can prepare a description of these and present them in the next class.

● Writing Practice

Ask students to prepare a short description of a product of their choice. They can select an illustration of a product from a magazine or user manual and write a short description to be included in a catalog. Students will need to present both factual information about the products and persuasive arguments to show readers their advantages/benefits.

OR

Ask them to produce a short advertisement for a product. They should first write a short description of the product that they are selling, then prepare a short summary of their advertisement (print ad/TV commercial). They should also create a slogan for their ad.

5 Industry

Unit Focus • Production • Construction • Automation

Unit overview

Unit components	Focus	TOEIC practice	Duration
Snapshot	Manufacturing; industry; construction	Part I	15–25 mins
Grammar Check 1	The passive	Part V	30–40 mins
Listening 1	Jelly Belly factory tour	Part II	15–25 mins
Vocabulary Builder	Synonyms and antonyms	Part V	20–30 mins
Listening 2	Troubleshooting	Parts III/VI	30–40 mins
Viewpoint	Robotics	Part VII	25–35 mins
Grammar Check 2	Causative verbs	Part V	20–30 mins
Listening 3	Save or scrap: building upon the past	Part IV	15–20 mins
Communication	Construction and development vs preservation and heritage		40 mins
		Total	3 hrs 30–4 hrs 45

Snapshot

Aims
- TOEIC Part I practice: picture analysis
- Vocabulary development: manufacturing; industry; construction
- Discussion

The pictures feature a shoe manufacturing assembly line, a refinery, a construction site and a foundry. Focus students' attention on the people, objects, equipment and clothing in a brainstorming activity either as a whole class with you providing vocabulary as needed and organizing the students' input on the board, or in pairs or small groups for students who can work more independently. Ask them to describe the actions that are taking place. Students should be able to come up with several suggested statements to describe what is happening in each picture. This pre-listening strategy will help students predict the statements they will hear in exercise B.

Picture descriptions
Picture 1
This picture shows an *assembly line* in a shoe *manufacturing factory*. The women are using *industrial sewing machines* to *stitch* the shoes. They are all wearing *bonnets*.

Picture 2
This picture shows an *inspector* in a *refinery*. He is standing in front of a large *tank*. He is wearing a *hard hat* or a *helmet* with *goggles*. He appears to be turning a *valve* in order to test the flow of *gas*. There is a *gas* or *vapor exiting* from one of the many *pipes*.

Picture 3
Carpenters or *construction workers* are *building a wooden structure*. They are passing *lumber* (wooden boards) to the upper level of the structure. They are wearing *hard hats* and *tool belts*. We can see a *hammer hanging* from one of the belts.

Picture 4
This scene takes place in a *foundry*. A *foundry worker* is *pouring molten material* into a *mold*. He is wearing *protective eyewear* and *gloves*.

Unit 5 | Industry

Answers
A
Suggested vocabulary

	People	Objects	Actions
Picture 1	line workers	factory assembly line production line shoes sewing machines bonnet	sewing stitching making manu- facturing working
Picture 2	inspector	hard hat helmet goggles tanks pipes gas refinery plant	inspecting testing examining checking looking
Picture 3	carpenters construction workers laborers	tools tool belts hammer hard hats boards lumber	building construct- ing lifting handing
Picture 4	steel worker foundryman	foundry molten steel raw materials gloves protective eyewear goggles	pouring casting

Possible statements
Picture 1
The women are working on an assembly line.
They're making shoes.
They're all wearing bonnets.

Picture 2
The man is working in a refinery.
The inspector is standing in front of a large tank.
He's wearing a hardhat.

Picture 3
The carpenters are building a house out of wood.
The construction workers are wearing hardhats and tool belts.
They're handing a board to the other worker.

Picture 4
The man is working in a foundry.
He is pouring molten steel into a cast/mold.
He is wearing protective eyewear and gloves.
B
1 B, E   2 A, D   3 F, H   4 C, G

AUDIOSCRIPT
B
A The inspector is checking the equipment.
B They're working on an assembly line.
C The hot, molten steel is being poured into the mold.
D The holding tank is being tested.
E Shoes are being manufactured in the factory.
F The carpenters are wearing hardhats.
G The steel worker is wearing protective eyewear.
H The structure is being built out of wood.

Grammar Check 1

Aims
- TOEIC Part V practice: incomplete sentences
- Grammar point: the passive
- Topics: Jelly Belly Factory Tour; manufacturing

Point out that the passive is often used to describe processes and to focus on the action. The emphasis is on *what is being done* rather than *who is doing it*.
Exercises A and B have students determine the grammar rule from the examples.

The passive is a fundamental yet far-reaching grammar point. Passive forms are complex because they occur in a variety of tenses and usage. A good strategy for getting students to understand the way the passive works is to have them change sentences from the active to the passive, and vice versa, as in the examples.
a *The workers **are mixing** the raw materials in large basins.*
b *The raw materials **are being mixed** in large basins (by the workers).*

Answers
A
1 The workers are mixing the raw materials in large basins. (2)
2 The materials are being mixed in large basins. (1)
B Grammar rule
The passive is formed by using the appropriate form of the auxiliary verb *to be* + the past participle form of the main verb.

(43)

Target Score

Exercises C, D and E take students on a factory tour of Jelly Belly jelly beans. Jelly beans are a popular American candy. These colorful sweets have a firm outer shell and soft, chewy centers. Jelly Belly is famous because it produces many delicious flavors. (You can check Jelly Belly's website for more information.)

There are eight steps in the Jelly Belly jelly beans manufacturing process and each one is described using the passive voice. The tour is broken down into three different activities, which lead students from recognition of the passive forms in C, to production of the correct form in D and E.

In manufacturing steps 1–3 (exercise C), students identify the passive form of the verbs. In steps 4–5 (exercise D), students must correctly conjugate the past participle form of the verb to make the passive. In steps 6–8 (exercise E), students must choose the appropriate verb before correctly conjugating it.

You can assign the tour for individual or pair work. Then, when the group is correcting the answers, each student or pair can read the steps out loud as if they were giving a part of the tour.

Answers
C
are blended
are added
is cooked
are dropped
are transferred
D
1 sent
2 sugarcoated
3 given
4 heaped
5 called
6 added
E
7 are poured
8 is sifted
9 is polished
10 are seasoned
11 is inserted
12 is printed
13 are packaged/have been packaged
14 are loaded
15 (are) transported

Listening 1

Aims
- TOEIC Part II practice: question/response
- Jelly Belly Tour FAQs (Frequently-Asked Questions)

As this is a continuation of the Jelly Belly tour, lead into the exercise by asking students: *What questions would you ask at the end of a Jelly Belly tour?* (Listen to see if any of the students use the passive voice form. Write a couple of their questions on the board to have them identify their use of the passive, or have them rephrase a question using an active form into the passive.)

In this exercise, students read five questions commonly asked by visitors at the end of the Jelly Belly tour, then they listen to five answers given by a tour guide. They must match the answers (A–E) to the questions written in the Student's Book.

Answers
1 C   2 D   3 B   4 A   5 E

AUDIOSCRIPT
A Fortunately, delicious Jelly Belly beans are sold in over 35 countries worldwide.
B Jelly Belly beans are made in over 50 amazing and tasty flavors.
C Over one hundred thousand tons are produced every year.
D Our intensely flavored gourmet beans are conceived and tested by our experts in the Jelly Belly Research and Development Division.
E Absolutely! They were sent on the space shuttle in 1983 along with the first American female astronaut, Sally Ride! What a star!

● Extension Activity
After students complete the exercise, ask them to identify the passive forms in the questions and answers.

Unit 5 | Industry

Vocabulary Builder

Aims
- TOEIC Part V practice: incomplete sentences
- Vocabulary development: synonyms and antonyms

This activity encourages students to build upon the words they already know by grouping them with similar meaning words. Part V TOEIC® questions often test students' ability to recognize synonyms and antonyms. In fact, the correct answer to Parts III, IV, V and VII TOEIC® questions is often a synonym or antonym of another word in the test item.

In exercise A, students begin by identifying synonyms and antonyms. In exercise B, they add a synonym to each list.

> ⚠️ **TOEIC Tip**
> Before beginning exercise C, have students read the TOEIC Tip. Students should understand that the correct response is determined by context clues that establish a contrast in each sentence.

Exercise C gives TOEIC® Part V practice. (Note that several answers are possible because students are working with synonyms.)

To consolidate the lesson and the TOEIC® Tip, exercise D has students identify the antonyms in exercise C. For example, in number 1, *modernized* is an antonym of *outmoded*.

Answers

A
1 mended ✓ repaired ✓ damaged ✗
2 maintain ✓ neglect ✗ service ✓
3 modernized ✓ outdated ✗ renovated ✓
4 store ✗ get rid of ✓ throw away ✓

B
1 fixed
2 look after
3 refurbished
4 discard

C
1 modernized/renovated/refurbished
2 neglected/damaged
3 thrown away/gotten rid of/discarded
4 fixed/mended/repaired

D
1 outmoded (antonym of *modernized*)
2 cared for (antonym of *neglected*)
3 kept (antonym of *thrown away*)
4 broken (antonym of *fixed*)

Listening 2

Aims
- TOEIC Part III practice: short conversations
- TOEIC Part VI practice: error recognition
- Topic: troubleshooting and problem-solving

TOEIC® questions frequently involve "troubleshooting" or problem-solving situations where the speakers are discussing a problem and the actions that should be taken. Common TOEIC® questions are:

- *What is the problem?*
- *What is the matter?*
- *What happened?*
- *What is the speaker concerned about?*
- *What is the solution to the problem?*

Before beginning the listening, you may want to teach some technical vocabulary:

safety equipment	spare parts
operation costs	raw materials
to remove	to leak
to be contaminated	

In exercise A, students read the seven industrial problems before listening to the five conversations. Students will then identify five of the industrial problems (two of the problems are not discussed).

In exercise B, students must match one of the seven listed solutions (1–7) to each problem mentioned in the conversation. Students should read the solutions and attempt to match the solutions and problems, relying on their memory, before listening to the five conversations a second time. (Note that two of the solutions are not discussed in the recordings.)

```
Answers
A
1  –        2  B        3  D
4  E        5  –        6  C
7  A
B
1  C        2  D        3  E
4  A        5  B        6  –
7  –
```

AUDIOSCRIPT
A
Woman What seems to be the problem?
Man The pallets were run over by a forklift.
Woman You'd better file a damaged goods report.
B
Man 1 What happened to the safety screen?
Man 2 It was taken off because it slowed production.
Man 1 Have someone replace it immediately. We wouldn't want anyone to have an accident.
C
Woman Excuse me. Hard hats must be worn at all times.
Man Oh, sorry. I seem to have left mine back in the truck.
Woman Here, you can borrow this one while you're on the site.
D
Woman Has the faulty switch been repaired yet?
Man Unfortunately not. The warehouse can't seem to locate a spare part.
Woman Well, have the mechanic express order a new one. The assembly line needs to be up and running by tomorrow morning.
E
Man The plant is not as efficient and cost-effective as it should be. We simply have to reduce labor costs.
Woman Perhaps we should invest in more automation.
Man That's probably the best solution. Robotics on the assembly line would allow us to increase production to 24 hours a day, seven days a week.

You can ask the following questions as a lead-in discussion to exercise C:
- *What other problems might occur in the workplace?*
- *What actions should be taken if these problems occur?*
- *How can such problems be avoided?*

Drawing upon the factory context, this exercise provides direct Part VI practice within the context of a factory inspection. Students are to imagine that they are conducting a site inspection to check the required safety signs. All of the signs contain grammar errors. Most of the mistakes are passive voice errors; however, a few other "classic" Part VI errors are included (participles and prepositions). Have students both identify and correct the errors. Even though students do not have to give the corrections in Part VI of the TOEIC, this tests and reinforces their knowledge of correct forms.

1 ~~wearing~~ – worn
2 ~~conduct~~ – conducted
3 ~~been~~ – be
4 ~~is~~ – are
5 ~~keeping~~ – kept
6 ~~from~~ – by
7 ~~ask~~ – asked

● Extension Activity
Using the classroom, school, or institutional setting in which you are teaching, have your students make signs that include one error like those in exercise C. You may want to encourage them to add some humor to this activity! For example:
- *The whiteboard should be cleaning [cleaned] at the end of every class.*
- *Food and beverages must not be consume [consumed] in the classroom.*
- *Wet umbrellas should be leaving [left] in the stand provided at the front door.*
- *Class attendance sheets must be signed from [by] all students.*

These can be displayed on the wall of the classroom or held up by each student. The class has to identify and correct the error.

Students enjoy writing TOEIC® items to test their colleagues, particularly Part VI statements, which contain an error. The ability to intentionally insert an error into a statement and to be able to correct it demonstrates a high degree of language appropriation. Encourage students to practice writing their own TOEIC® test questions. This develops greater familiarity with the test and helps them to master grammatical and lexical items.

Viewpoint

Aims
- TOEIC Part VII practice: reading comprehension
- Vocabulary development: manufacturing
- Discussion: automation; robotics in industry; technological advances

This Viewpoint provides standard Part VII practice, with a text and two multiple-choice questions. Begin with the

Unit 5 | Industry

two lead-in questions. For the first question, you may want to ask students to list the machines that help them to prepare food, clean and maintain their homes and belongings, etc. For the second question, you can provide them with some clues. Ask if they would like to have their laundry automatically pressed, folded and put away, their home automatically dusted and vacuumed, etc.

As a vocabulary follow-up exercise after students have read the text and answered the questions, have them identify key vocabulary and organize it according to the parts of speech. For example, ask them to make lists of the verbs that refer to automation and automated tasks:
to program, to handle, to weld, to paint, to grip, to transfer, to integrate

Next, have them make lists of the nouns that refer to industrial places, objects and machines:
applications, automation, a load, car plants, a conveyor belt, a packaging line, a flow wrapping machine, vision systems

Finally, have them make lists of adjectives:
heavy, sophisticated, accessible, flexible, randomly-sized, diverse
Extra vocabulary:
improvements, metal giants, quarry products, a croissant

> **Answers**
> 1 a
> 2 d

> **DISCUSSION**
> The discussion questions are intended to stimulate reflection on how advances in technology change our relationship to work and human activity.

Grammar Check 2

> **Aims**
> - TOEIC Part V practice: incomplete sentences
> - Grammar point: causative verbs

Have students look at the examples to see how causative verbs are used in context and to answer the questions in exercise A. Explain how this structure expresses that a person causes or enables another person, animal or machine to do something. Students should be able to come up with the following key points:
- *Have*, *make* and *let*, when used as causatives, are followed by the infinitive without *to*.
- *Have*, *make* and *let* differ in meaning.

> **Answers**
> **A**
> 1 Which causative verbs are followed by:
>   – the direct object + an infinitive with *to*   Type 2
>   – the direct object + an infinitive without *to* Type 1
>   – the direct object + a past participle   Type 3

Suggested answers
2 and 3
Synonyms

	(From the examples)	Other verbs
have	to get	to convince
		to persuade
		to enable
make	to force	to require
		to obligate
		to demand
		to command
		to compel
		to coerce
let	to allow	to permit
		to authorize

Exercise B gives Part V practice with causative verbs. Students are given two choices to best complete the sentence. Have them first identify the primary verb of the sentence and who is involved in the actions in order to determine which type of causative verb is being used. In example sentence 1, the main verb is *is making*; the subject is *the foreman*; the people doing the action are *the crew*. This is a Type 1 causative, so *re-install* (the infinitive without *to*) is the correct choice.

> **Answers**
> **B**
> 1 re-install   2 approved
> 3 inspect   4 by
> 5 take   6 to increase
> 7 have   8 to transfer

Listening 3

> **Aims**
> - TOEIC Part IV practice: short talks
> - Listening for gist and details

This activity establishes the context for the communication activity. Students listen to a news report about the discovery of an ancient settlement during the excavation work for the new Metropolitan industrial park.

Target Score

> ### ⚠ TOEIC Tip
> Before listening, have students read the TOEIC Tip. It recommends that they listen carefully to the beginning of the short talks because this is where information is given about the context of the talk. It is, therefore, important for students to remain alert so they are not caught off-guard when a new listening begins. Students should practice quickly identifying the speaker, the purpose and the main points. Common TOEIC® Part IV questions include: *Who is the speaker? What is the purpose of the talk? What is the main idea of the talk?*

Have students read through the archeologist's page of notes before listening and filling in the missing information.

If necessary, you can pre-teach the following vocabulary. However, students do need to develop skills for filtering difficult vocabulary on the TOEIC®.

a settlement   *to uncover*   *excavations*
dwellings   *remnants*   *burial grounds*
domestic items *to unearth*   *finds*
a boost

> ### Answers
> 1 an industrial park
> 2 domestic items, finely worked gold jewelry, small statues
> 3 construction workers
> 4 local Chamber of Commerce

AUDIOSCRIPT
The mayor announced today that ancient ruins of an important settlement were uncovered two weeks ago by construction workers on the site of the new Metropolitan industrial park. Although an emergency archeological team has only begun exploratory excavations, a network of dwellings, remnants of a ceremonial area and burial grounds have already been located. Many domestic items have been unearthed and finely worked gold jewelry and small statues have also been found. University archeologists are declaring the site by far the most significant ever found in the region.

Not everyone, however, is celebrating. While the discovery has elicited praise from archeologists and local historians, it is also raising serious questions as to whether construction on the new Metropolitan industrial complex should continue. The archeological finds have seriously interrupted the construction of what was promised to be an enormous boost to local business. The planned industrial park would provide manufacturing facilities and office space for dozens of companies bringing in millions of dollars to a slow economy. A planning commission has been created to study all the options. Citizens interested in the future of the site are invited to a public meeting, to be held on Tuesday evening at the local Chamber of Commerce. The one thing that remains clear is that this site has been an attractive building area for hundreds, if not thousands, of years.

Communication

> ### Aim
> • Speaking practice: presenting; discussing; negotiating

Within the context of a planning commission meeting, students must determine the future of the Metropolitan industrial park.

The five roles have opposing visions as to what should be done. On one side is the *land developer* and the *construction superintendent*, who want to proceed with the construction and development of the industrial park. On the other side is the *archeologist* and the *president of the Local Heritage Foundation*, who want to create a heritage site. The mayor is undecided and must determine what is best for the city. Students have to consider not only the cost of construction delays, but also the long-term profitability of an industrial site versus a heritage site. What will bring greater prosperity to the city: industry or tourism?

Students should be given time to prepare their roles. The activity works best if the meeting can be held in a circle. You may want to designate a chairperson to call on each student to speak. Tell students that they must come to a decision within the given class period and that this decision may require a creative compromise to address the challenge!

● Writing Practice
Write a letter to the local newspaper expressing your opinion as to whether the industrial park should be built after the excavations, or whether construction should stop in order to build a museum and cultural center.

6 Trade

Unit Focus · Markets · Shipping · Import and Export

Unit overview

Unit components	Focus	TOEIC practice	Duration
Snapshot	Trade and commerce	Part I	15–25 mins
Listening 1	The international art market	Part III	15–25 mins
Grammar Check 1	Future and forms	Part VI	10–20 mins
Listening 2	The cost of coffee	Part IV	10–15 mins
Viewpoint	The international coffee market; Juan Valdez	Part VII	30–40 mins
Grammar Check 2	Cause and effect	Part V	10–20 mins
Listening 3	Meetings	Part II	15–20 mins
Vocabulary Builder	Idiomatic expressions: *point*	Part V	10–5 mins
Communication	Fair trade or free trade?		40 mins
		Total	2 hrs 35–3 hrs 40

Snapshot

Aims
- TOEIC Part I practice: identifying actions and settings
- Vocabulary development: trade and commerce

The pictures serve both as a general introduction to the unit and as the basis of a series of Part I activities. The pictures show three scenes of international markets (agricultural produce, art, and commodities trading) and one picture of goods being loaded at an international sea port. In A, students should study the pictures to identify the actions that are being performed. Ask students to speculate about the places that are represented in the photos. You may need to explain the meanings of, and explain, the terms in B before asking students to match the photos with the terms. For C, you may need to give students assistance with writing their statements before they listen to identify the statements that describe each picture.

Picture descriptions
Picture 1

This picture presents a *wholesale fruit market* for *agricultural produce*. It shows a worker who is *arranging* or *placing* bunches of bananas in an *outdoor storage area*. The *fruit* has been carefully *laid out* on the *ground* in *rows*.

Picture 2

This picture shows another aspect of international markets: an *art auction* at Sotheby's, the famous *auction house*. In the photo we can see the *auctioneer* who is managing the *sale*, and the potential *buyers/bidders* who are seated in the *auction room*. The auctioneer is inviting buyers *to bid* for the painting that is being displayed by two assistants.

Picture 3

This picture shows another important dimension of trade: the *transportation* of goods. It shows a *dockworker* who is *directing* or *signaling* as a *load* of *crates* or *containers* is lifted by a *crane*. We can see two *ships* whose cargoes are being either *unloaded* or *loaded* at the *docks*.

Picture 4

This picture shows *traders* at work in a crowded room at an *international exchange*. The employees are all wearing the same *uniforms* or *vests*. Some of the traders are *doing business* on the phone, and others are talking together. In exchanges or markets of this type, employees buy and sell both *commodities and services* from around the world.

Answers
A
1 A worker is arranging fruit.
2 An auctioneer is managing an auction.
3 A dockworker is signaling as a container is being moved.
4 Traders are working at an international exchange.

B
1 wholesale food market, fruit and produce
2 auction house, artwork
3 international port, cargo containers
4 financial market, stocks and commodities

Before students read out the statements that they have prepared for exercise C, check them for errors and inappropriate vocabulary use.

Answers
C
Possible statements
Picture 1
The fruit has been laid out (arranged) in rows.
The man is arranging the produce.

Picture 2
The goods are being loaded onto (unloaded from) the ship.
The container is being moved into position.
Cargo is being lifted by a crane.

Picture 3
A painting is being offered for sale.
The people are attending an auction.

Picture 4
The staff are at work in the exchange.
The employees are wearing the same uniforms.

Students should listen to the audio recording and identify the keywords that will enable them to identify which statements refer to which pictures.

Answers

	Keywords
1	fruit, exported, handle, produce
2	bidding, artwork, auction house
3	dockworker, cargo, container, lift
4	orders, phone, traders, vests

D
1 D, H   2 C, F   3 A, G   4 B, E

AUDIOSCRIPT
D
A The dockworker is directing the cargo.
B They're placing orders over the phone.
C They're bidding on the artwork.
D The harvested fruit will be exported.
E The traders are wearing vests.
F The auction house is crowded.
G The shipping container is being lifted.
H He's handling the produce.

Before proceeding to the next section of this unit, you may want to conduct a short question and discussion session. You can focus the discussion on the different forms of international trade and on whether or not trade benefits all the groups involved. Some questions that you could have students discuss are:

Development: *Does trade always benefit all countries involved?*
Trade barriers: *What problems do developing countries face when they seek to export?*
Internet: *How has the Internet changed the way that goods are distributed?*
Commodities: *Which commodities are the most exported/imported by your country/in the world?*
How are goods exported/imported to/from your country? (by road transport/sea/air, etc.)

Listening 1

Aims
- TOEIC Part III practice: short conversations
- Listening for context and keywords

This activity focuses students' attention on the processes involved in exporting goods from one country to another. In this case, the context is the art market, but the procedures are essentially the same for all other commodities. Draw attention to the different steps that are involved in an international transaction. These are presented in the order in which they would normally take place, starting with a purchase and ending with delivery to the customer.

In A, students listen to identify the context that the conversations refer to.

Unit 6 | Trade

Answers
A
1 shipping
2 packing
3 bidding and purchasing
4 clearing customs and paying duty fees and tariffs
5 insuring

In B, students listen for the specific vocabulary that allows them to identify the context. The keywords that will help them to do this are the following:

Answers
B

	Keywords
1	send, sculptures, by air, ocean freight, transit, arrive in time, art fair
2	packing list, container, to inventory, breakable, vases, designated
3	drawing, museum, collection, the reserve price, acquisitions budget, bidding
4	paintings, re-export, duty fees, departure
5	policy, cover, shipment

AUDIOSCRIPT

1
Woman 1 Are we going to send the sculptures by air or ocean freight?
Woman 2 With less than four weeks for transit, they'd better go by air.
Woman 1 Right. That way they'll arrive in time for the art fair.

2
Man Do you need any help with the packing list for this container?
Woman That'd be great, thanks. I was just about to inventory the breakable items.
Man Let's see. Five ceramic vases are designated as very fragile.

3
Man This drawing would make a fine addition to the museum's collection.
Woman And the reserve price is well within our acquisitions budget.
Man Let's begin bidding as soon as the auction opens.

4
Woman Will all the paintings remain in the destination country?
Man Yes, we don't intend to re-export them.
Woman Then you'll have to pay your duty fees before departure.

5
Woman 1 Does this policy cover accidental damage to works of art?
Woman 2 Yes, but you must provide a detailed list of all the pieces and their estimated values.
Woman 1 Of course. We want to be sure that the entire shipment is completely covered.

Grammar Check 1

Aims
- TOEIC Part VI practice: error recognition
- Review of future tenses and forms

This grammar section allows students to review the different tense forms that are used to talk about future time. The examples and explanations cover the main uses of the future. You may want to review more complex forms of the future by referring to the Grammar Reference section on page 133 of the Student's Book. You may need to point out the following vocabulary items:

shipping broker   *trade agreement*   *benefit*
growers   *to go into effect*

Answers
A
1 future arrangements that have already been made
2 schedules and timetables
3 future actions and predictions
4 future plans or intentions

3 *will* + verb
4 *going to* + verb
1 *be* + *-ing* (present continuous)
2 present simple

B
Give the following explanations for the sentences that contain incorrect future forms:

1	handle	– *Will* is only followed by a verb in *ing* when it is preceded by the future continuous form with *be*.
2	to present	– *Going* is always followed by the infinitive *to*.
3	C, are issued	– *As soon as* is followed by a present simple or past tense.
4	begins, C	– Time clauses referring to events that occur regularly are in the present simple.
5	is going	– When referring to a planned future event, we use the present continuous.

51

6 C, receive	– See number 3.
7 is going/will go to	– See number 1.
8 C, arrives	– Clauses with *when* which refer to the timing of future events are always in the present simple.

● Extension Activity

If you have time available, you may want to ask students to prepare a list of the things that they have planned to do in the next few days/weeks. They can then discuss this in pairs.

⚠ *TOEIC Tip*

This tip draws attention to time markers and to the tenses that are used with them in future time clauses, a grammar point that is often tested in questions on Parts V and VI.

Listening 2

Aims
- TOEIC Part IV practice: short talks
- Listening for specific information

This listening requires students to identify the ingredients, materials and services which correspond to a breakdown of the underlying costs of a cup of coffee. It also serves to introduce the topic developed in Viewpoint. You may need to explain the following vocabulary items:

*benchmark   to break down   labor costs   outlet
to account for   middlemen   to grind   harvest*

Before students read the article presented in Viewpoint, ask them if they can suggest ways for coffee growers to improve their financial situation.

Answers
1 $3.75   2 labor at shop
3 $1.29   4 shop owner's profit
5 $0.47   6 grower's share

AUDIOSCRIPT
A recent study of the coffee industry has looked at the actual costs that make up the price of the coffee that the average American buys at the local coffee shop. Taking a cup of Starbuck's latte as the benchmark, the Specialty Coffee Association of America broke down the total retail price of three dollars and 75 cents into its component costs. The most expensive of those were: first the labor costs of staff employed at the outlet – that already takes a one dollar and 35 cent bite – then in second position the one dollar and 29 cents for store rent, marketing, and general administration. Add to that the 18 cents of interest on the shop owner's initial investment and the 25 cents of actual profit on each cup – and that already removes almost 70 percent of the full cost. Of the rest, the cup and the milk account for another 47 cents. So that only leaves 21 cents with 17.5 going to the middlemen: the exporters, the importers, the grinders. The farmers and growers who actually planted and harvested the coffee in the first place – end up with by far the smallest share: 3.5 cents.

Viewpoint

Aims
- TOEIC Part VII practice: reading comprehension
- Speaking practice
- Discussion: Juan Valdez coffee

The text deals with the plans of the Columbia Coffee Federation to open their own Juan Valdez retail outlets in the U.S. in order to increase the returns to coffee growers. The money from the venture, if successful, will be used to finance improvements in infrastructure and marketing in Columbia's coffee-producing regions.

Before doing the reading, focus students' attention on the problems that commodity producers in the developing world face in order to obtain an economic price for their goods on the world markets. Can they suggest any other ways of protecting local producers? (Possible answers could include: subsidies, fair trade, international aid, free trade.)

Answers
B
1 next year
2 $8.4 billion
3 specialty coffee
4 $0.04–0.05
5 roads, schools, health centers, housing

For further vocabulary development, ask students to find the words or expressions in the text that relate to the following things:

Production: *growers, producers, farmers, beans,
                oversupply, surplus*

Unit 6 | Trade

Markets: *share retail shops, consumption, specialty market, price*
Revenue: *losses, to return, ownership stake*

You may need to explain the meanings of the following words:

to brew up
surplus
to urge
oversupply
living wage
brand
analyst
signature character (a person or personification used to promote a product)

per capita consumption
industry trade groups
to return
fair-trade
ownership stake
access roads

Grammar Check 2

Aims
- TOEIC Part V practice: incomplete sentences
- Review of the language of cause and effect

This section provides a review of the verbs, nouns and linking expressions that are used in clauses of reason and result. You should focus attention on the prepositions that are used after certain words and make sure that students are familiar with these. You may need to explain the following vocabulary:

factors   deprive   standards of living   illicit.

Answers
A
1 c
2 d/e
3 a
4 d/e
5 b
B
1 reasons
2 led to/resulted in
3 result
4 effects
5 Since

● Extension Activity
Ask students to work in small groups. Give each group one of the following subjects to work on: traffic congestion, global warming, waste management, alternative energy, noise pollution.

Each group should prepare a simple chart like the one on page 59 of the Student's Book showing the causes and effects for their topic. Two groups can then join together and give the explanations of the causes and effects of the situation/subject they have studied. Alternatively, you may wish to use the board and to do this as an activity involving the whole class.

Listening 3

Aims
- TOEIC Part II practice: question/response
- Vocabulary development

A and B of this activity focus on the language that is used to conduct meetings and on key vocabulary relating to the organization of meetings. Make sure that students are familiar with the following terms:

minutes   agenda   to chair a meeting

Several of the vocabulary items are words that have multiple meanings. You should explain that this is the case for many words in English. Some words may have exactly the same form, but two or more very different meanings:

minutes (noun): unit of sixty seconds
minutes (noun): notes of what is said

Other words may have the same form, but can be used as a different part of speech:

minute (adjective)
chair (noun or verb)

● Extension Activity
If you have dictionaries available, you can ask students to choose words from the following list and check their meanings. Write the list of words on the board and ask students in turn to explain the different meanings the words can have. The following examples are for words with at least one meaning that is related to trade, but you can quite easily make a list of more general words.

check   ship   customs   duty   order
figure   return   deal   pack   clear

Answers
A
1 minutes
2 agenda
3 item
4 views
5 break
6 business
7 chair

B
1. chair
2. business
3. break
4. agenda
5. item
6. views
7. minutes

C
1. b
2. a
3. a
4. b
5. b
6. a
7. b

AUDIOSCRIPT

A
1. Could someone take the minutes, please?
2. Has everyone received a copy of the agenda?
3. Could we move on to the next item?
4. What are your views on this issue?
5. Why don't we take a ten-minute break?
6. Is there any other business?
7. Who would like to chair the next meeting?

C
1. Could someone take the minutes, please?
   A I'm sorry. I left my watch at home.
   B I'd be glad to.
2. Has everyone received a copy of the agenda?
   A You wouldn't have an extra one, would you?
   B I've already had a cup this morning, thank you.
3. Could we move on to the next item?
   A As soon as we've made a decision on the present issue.
   B Relocating the business would be expensive.
4. What are your views on this issue?
   A Yes, all rooms have lovely views of the city.
   B I tend to agree with what Mark said earlier.
5. Why don't we take a ten-minute break?
   A Because it's not broken.
   B That's a good idea.
6. Is there any other business?
   A No, I think we've covered everything.
   B There're plenty of stores just down the street.
7. Who would like to chair the next meeting?
   A I'll be happy to bring an extra one from my office.
   B I'll do it. I think it's my turn.

⚠ TOEIC Tip

This tip talks about distracters. These are questions that are designed to distract the attention of the person who is answering and to make it more difficult for them to identify the correct response. On the TOEIC® test, distracters are often used when a key word in a question has multiple meanings. For example, in the listening exercise C, you heard the following question:

Who would like to chair the meeting?

In this question, *chair* is used as a verb. However, of the two possible responses:

I'll be happy to bring an extra one from my office.
I'll do it. I think it's my turn.

only the second one is appropriate. The first response would only have been appropriate if the question had contained the noun *chair*.

Vocabulary Builder

Aims
- TOEIC Part V practice: incomplete sentences
- Vocabulary development: idiomatic expressions (1) – *point*

This activity focuses on the way a word, in this case *point*, is used to form idiomatic expressions by showing the various collocations, suffixed or prefixed forms. Tell students that developing their vocabulary by learning colloquial language will help them to improve their score.

Answers

A
1. e
2. f
3. a
4. b
5. d
6. c

B
1. beside the point
2. point out
3. point of view
4. pointless
5. to the point
6. makes a point

C

Students need some assistance with this activity as dictionaries will only provide some words and expressions (and not those, for example, where these words appear after another). Here are some suggested answers:

head

verbs:	to head, to head for, to head out, to head home
compounds:	headway, overhead, headstrong, headache
expressions:	head first, to be in over your head, to lose your head

back

verbs:	to back, to back down, to back up, to back out of
compounds:	backpack, backbone, backlash, drawback
expressions:	back to front, to make a comeback

face

verbs:	to face away, to face up to
compounds:	interface, facelift
expressions:	face to face, to face facts, to save face

hand

verbs:	to hand over, to hand out, to hand in, to hand back
compounds:	handheld, handshake, handwriting, beforehand
expressions:	hand to mouth, hands up, out of hand

Communication

Aim
- Speaking practice: presenting arguments and counter-arguments

The context for this activity is a town meeting to decide whether a local community should apply to become a Fairtrade town. Fairtrade towns contribute to the Fairtrade Foundation's objectives of tackling poverty by agreeing to use Fairtrade products and making sure that they are stocked in local stores. (You can find all the details about the Foundation and its various programs at www.fairtrade.org.uk) Ask students to read the text which presents the Foundation's conditions for towns that wish to apply to become Fairtrade towns.

You may need to explain the following words:

to tackle	disadvantaged producers (This is the term used to refer to people whose incomes are extremely low.)
town council	wholefood
awareness	membership

Answers

A
1. to support producers and reduce poverty in developing countries
2. by promoting sales of Fairtrade products

Give students enough time to prepare the roles that they have chosen for the meeting and answer any questions that they may have about vocabulary, etc. The activity has been designed to include a range of viewpoints about whether or not the town should apply for Fairtrade status. Students should therefore try to present their arguments as persuasively as possible.

If you intend to have your students complete the writing assignments, they will need to take notes during the meeting in order to do so.

● Writing Practice
Write up the minutes for the meeting that you attended.
OR
Write a short article for the town's newspaper.
OR
Write a short press release.

Review Test 2 Answer Key

Units 4–6

Listening Comprehension

Part I
Photographs

1 **C** The man's *inspecting* or *checking* the *roll of cloth*, (B) not the *pay roll*. (A) He's not *rolling* up the sleeves of his shirt. (D) He's *working*, but not on a *clock*.

2 **D** The customer's at the *checkout counter*. (A) The *grocery cart* is behind the woman, so she can't be pushing it. (B) The checkout clerk is waiting for the woman to pay for her groceries; he's not *weighing* anything. (C) The customers are *standing*, not *entering* a shopping area.

3 **D** The workers are manufacturing products on an *assembly line* inside a *plant* or factory, (A) not *waiting in line in front* of it. (B) They are not attending a meeting or group gathering such as an *assembly*. (C) They're *working* in a *building*, not *walking* around a new one.

4 **A** A large shipping *container* is being *lifted* or raised by a *crane* on a dock. (B) The *vehicles* are parked on the dock and are not being driven onto a ferry. (C) The shipping container is in the *air*, but it is not being transported by airplane. (D) The *truck* is being loaded or unloaded, not *towed away*.

5 **C** The *sacks* are being placed or *stacked on top of each other*. (A) The man is loading the goods *manually*, or *by hand*, not by *machine*. (B) He's not *packing his bags* or (D) *picking fruit*.

6 **B** The man is *looking at some jewelry* in front of a display case, (C) not *trying on sunglasses*. (A) The *sales clerk* is holding some necklaces, not *taking his measurements*. (D) The jewelry is on *display*, not a mannequin.

Part II
Questions and responses

7 **A** The question asks *when* the permits *will* be signed in the future, but (B) *three days ago* refers to the past. (C) answers a question about *who* will sign the permits.

8 **B** The answer *by midweek* confirms the question about whether *the order* will be delivered by *Wednesday*. The word *order* is repeated in the other answers, but has different meanings than in the question: (A) refers to a sequence and (C) refers to a command or instructions.

9 **C** The question *who* requests the name of the person *in charge of the auction*. (A) provides information about a man who has not been mentioned. (B) gives information about when *a sale will begin*.

10 **B** (B) answers the question *which aisle*. This refers to location. (A) refers to rules about *animals* or pets in *the store*, not *pet food*. (C) mentions *fresh fruit*, which is typically sold in a supermarket, but is not ordinarily used to feed pets.

11 **B** (B) responds to the question about who will *type up the minute*s or notes of the meeting. (A) answers a *Yes/No* question about repairing a *watch*, which relates the meaning of *minutes* as units of time. (C) uses the distracter *tied up*, which sounds similar to *type up*, and *hours*, which relates to time, not the written records of a meeting.

12 **A** The tag question asks whether *batteries* are included with *the toy*. (B) and (C) do not refer to batteries, but to a *service charge* and to the number of people who can play a *game*.

13 **B** The question *Should we …?* asks for advice about *using subcontractors* for a *job*, so this answer is appropriate. The other answers do not refer to *finishing a job* and use similar-sounding words as distracters: (A) the verb *subtract* and (C) a *sublet*.

14 **C** (C) declines the offer *to have the shipment insured*. (A) refers to a purchase, not shipping. The word *insure* sounds similar to *sure*, which could be confused with *certain*. (B) Although *by sea* could refer to a shipment, the reference to safety is not logical.

Part III
Short conversations

15 **B** The keywords *adjourn, committee, chair, agenda* refer to a meeting, not to (A) an interview, (C) an auction or (D) customs.

Review Test 2 | Answer Key

16 **D** The shipment of *fabrics* suffered *water damage*. (A) The man is unhappy about the damage, not the fabrics. (B) The man is asked to provide *copies of the invoices*, not the fabrics. (C) The man asks when he will be *compensated*, which implies that the fabrics were insured.

17 **D** The robots on the assembly line will bring *improved product quality and fewer rejects*. (A) is not correct because the second man mentions increased production. (B) *Control* tests have already been made. (C) There is no mention of an increase in manufacturing time.

18 **A** The man says that the *blouse didn't fit*, which means it's the wrong size. (B) He doesn't mention *damage*, (C) *color*, or (D) anything *missing*.

19 **D** The woman has requested the *weight of each machine*. (B) The man mistakenly thought that only the *serial numbers* were needed. There is no mention of (A) unit price or (C) an invoice number, although they would typically appear on an *invoice*.

20 **B** The woman mentions *buying a new car*. (A) Although she asks about *yesterday's meeting* with *Mr. Walton*, she isn't going to contact him. (C) She is happy about the *news* that employees will receive a bonus. (D) There is no mention of a *call*.

21 **C** The *sale lasts two weeks* = *fourteen days*. There is no mention of a period of (A) *two days* or (B) *ten days*. (D) When the second woman mentions *the end of the month*, she is told that the sale would not last that long.

Part IV
Short talks

22 **A** (A) is the most logical choice. As chair of a meeting, the speaker announces building renovation plans and safety regulations. There could be (B) *researchers* and (C) *lab technicians* in the audience, but they would not be *managing* the *renovations*. (D) A *construction worker* would not be in charge of communicating company policies to the employees and would not refer to the *product research laboratory* as *ours*.

23 **B** The speaker says that the construction site will be restricted *for the next six months*. (A) The six-month construction period will end *early next year*. The construction will *begin* (C) *on Monday* (D) of *next week*.

24 **B** To access the site, authorized personnel *will be required to wear appropriate protective clothing*. A *safety briefing* is also required, but there is no mention of (A) *informing their colleagues*, (C) *reading a safety memo*, or (D) *signing a release form*.

25 **B** There is no mention of *quotas*. No *federation is able to act as an international regulator* and it is *impossible to impose maximum production levels*. There is a crisis in the industry due to (A) coffee being *available at a very low price*, (C) *production of greater quantities*, and (D) a *decline* in *overall demand*.

26 **C** The *Federation* acted as the *regulator* that could *impose maximum production levels*. There is no mention of (A) *financing farmers* or (D) *marketing coffee products*. (B) New *extremely advanced, mechanized production techniques* have been introduced, but not by the International Coffee Federation.

Reading Comprehension

Part V
Incomplete sentences

27 **C** In the passive voice, the auxiliary verb *to be* must be followed by the past participle (*-ed* form) of the main verb. (A) is a noun, an infinitive without *to*, or the present simple, (B) is the third-person singular of the present simple, and (D) includes an extra auxiliary verb.

28 **C** Someone *conforms to regulations*. The other verbs (A), (B) and (D) are not followed by the preposition *to* and do not make sense in the context.

29 **B** The future form *be going* requires the infinitive with *to* of the main verb. (A) is a noun or an infinitive without *to*, (C) is a present participle, and (D) is a noun.

30 **D** The idiomatic expression is *to make a point of doing something*, meaning "to plan on". (A) and (B) are distracters, referring to a *meeting*, but are not usually used with the verb *make*. (C) is a common collocation with the verb *make*, but does not make sense in this context.

31 **C** The present simple tense is used in clauses beginning with *as soon as* that refer to the future. *Bidding period* takes the third-person singular in the present simple. (A) is the passive voice, (B) is the future with *will*, and (D) is either the present simple, but not in the third-person singular, or an infinitive without *to*.

32 **D** *To view something as* means "to consider it to be", "to think of it as". (A), (B) and (C) do not make sense in this context.

33 **A** A *refund* can be given when a customer returns a purchase. (C) Although a purchase might be exchanged for another, *replacement* does not make sense with *purchase price*. (B) and (D) do not fit with the context of retailing/buying a product.

34 **C** In the context of *advertising*, *misleading claim* is a common collocation. (A), (B) and (D) are not commonly used in this way. Common collocations with the other choices are: an *unfulfilled* promise, *insufficient* evidence or information, a *distrustful* person.

35 **B** *Due to* is followed by a noun phrase to indicate a cause. (A) *Since*, when used to express cause, and (D) *because* come at the beginning of clauses (noun + verb). Although *because of* would also be correct, it is not an option. (C) *Consequently* introduces a new sentence that expresses an effect, not a cause.

36 **C** *Mean* is the only word of the four that introduces a *that* clause.

Part VI
Error recognition

37 **A** The verb form *will see* is incorrect because the present simple is used after *when* to indicate the future. The correct form is *see*.

38 **D** The question tag *would it* must be in the negative form after an affirmative statement: *wouldn't it* is correct.

39 **C** The passive voice in the future must be formed with *will* + *be* + the past participle, so *will been* is incorrect and should read *will be prosecuted*.

40 **C** *The manufacture* (of something) refers to the act or way of making something, not to a person. The contractor will talk to *the manufacturer*.

41 **B** The sentence requires a superlative, not the comparative form *lower*. The correct form would be *lowest level*.

42 **C** In this sentence, *let* is a causative verb and is followed by the infinitive without *to*. Therefore, *buy* is the correct form.

43 **A** The comparative *as much than* is incorrect. It should be *as much as*.

44 **C** The causative verb *make* should be followed by the infinitive without *to*. Therefore, *pay* is the correct form.

Part VII
Reading

45 **C** The notice provides general information about transporting goods, presenting several basic issues and options to ensure safe, timely and cost-effective shipping. There is no mention of more specific issues: (A) *weight limitations*, (B) *insurance policies*, or (D) *new safety measures*.

46 **D** *Maritime shipping* is described as being *less expensive*. (A) No option is presented as the best. (B) Although shipping by sea can be less cost-effective, it is said to be *less expensive* and (C) *much slower*.

47 **B** The notice mentions *surface transportation to and from the docks* as a possible *additional cost of sea freight*. (A), (C) and (D) do not appear in the notice.

48 **A** Adeg's new supermarkets have features that are designed to attract *clientele over fifty* years old. (B) There is no mention of *rival stores*. (C) Recruitment is discussed, but only in terms of hiring older employees, not to lower costs. (D) Younger shoppers are attracted to the new stores, but this is presented as an unforeseen and fortunate consequence of their marketing to older clientele.

49 **C** *More than half are under the age of fifty* indicates that the majority is *less than fifty*. Therefore, (A), (B) and (D) are incorrect.

50 **B** There is no mention of *personal shopping assistants*. (A), (C) and (D) are presented as *intriguing innovations*. (A) *Shopping carts* will have seats. (C) *Larger print* on *labels* will be easier to read. (D) *Lower shelves provide easy access*.

AUDIOSCRIPT

Review Test 2 Units 4–6
Part I
1 A He's rolling up his sleeves.
  B He's checking the pay roll.
  C He's inspecting the roll of cloth.
  D He's working on the clock.
2 A She's pushing the grocery cart.
  B He's weighing the vegetables.
  C The customers are entering the mall.
  D She's standing at the checkout counter.
3 A They're waiting in line in front of the plant.
  B They're attending a general assembly.
  C They're walking around the new building.
  D They're working on an assembly line.

Review Test 2 | Answer Key

4 A The container is being lifted by a crane.
   B The vehicles are being driven onto a ferry.
   C The goods are being shipped by air.
   D The truck is being towed away.
5 A The goods are being loaded by machine.
   B The man is packing his bags.
   C The sacks are stacked on top of each other.
   D The man is picking fruit.
6 A The sales clerk is taking the customer's measurements.
   B The man is looking at some jewelry.
   C The man is trying on some sunglasses.
   D The mannequin is on display.

Part II

7 When will the construction permits be signed?
   A Within two weeks' time.
   B Three days ago.
   C By the local official.
8 If I place my order today, can I expect delivery before Wednesday?
   A It's in the wrong order.
   B It should get there by midweek.
   C You should always follow orders.
9 Who'll be in charge of the auction?
   A He's currently not available.
   B Yes. The sale will begin soon.
   C Tom Johnston will be managing it.
10 Which aisle is the pet food located in?
   A I'm afraid animals are not allowed inside the store.
   B At the far end of the store next to the canned goods.
   C All our fresh fruit is locally produced.
11 Are you going to type up the minutes?
   A Yes, I'm taking my watch to be repaired.
   B I'll have my assistant do it.
   C She's been tied up for hours on the other line.
12 This toy comes with batteries, doesn't it?
   A No. I'm afraid they're sold separately.
   B That's right. There is a ten percent service charge.
   C The game can be played by up to four people.
13 Should we get subcontractors to finish the job?
   A Yes, you can subtract the discount from the retail price.
   B We'll save time if we do.
   C The sublet has already been rented.
14 Would you like me to have the shipment insured?
   A Yes. I'm certain I bought it here.
   B Yes, it's much safer by sea.
   C No. I'll take care of that myself.

Part III

15
Woman 1 Before we adjourn, would anyone like to add anything?
Woman 2 We'll have to appoint a new committee chair before the end of the year.
Woman 1 That's right. I'll put it on next week's agenda.
16
Man When the container was opened, I noticed that water had leaked onto the fabrics.
Woman You'll need to provide us with a detailed inventory of the damage and copies of the original invoices.
Man Allright. But how long will it take to get compensated?
17
Man 1 With the new fully-automated line, we plan to manufacture around the clock.
Man 2 But will robotics and increased production affect quality in any way?
Man 1 Initial control tests have shown improved product quality and fewer rejects.
18
Man I'd like to exchange this blouse that I bought here last week.
Woman Certainly sir. What seems to be the problem?
Man Well, when my wife tried it on, it didn't fit.
19
Man Have you finished preparing the export documents for the machines that are going to be shipped to Taiwan?
Woman Not yet. I'm waiting for the production department to tell me how much they each weigh so that I can complete the invoice.
Man I didn't know that was necessary. I just thought the serial numbers would be enough.
20
Woman Hi John. Sorry I missed the meeting with Mr. Walton yesterday. How did it go?
Man Really well. He's going to give all the employees a cash bonus for exceeding the sales target for the last quarter.
Woman That's great news. Now I can think about buying a new car.
21
Woman 1 Have you visited the new fashion boutique down on Seventh Avenue? They've got some great bargains.
Woman 2 Yes. I've heard they're having a huge sale, but I think I'll wait until the end of the month before I go.

59

Woman 1 Oh you'd better go before Saturday. The grand opening sale only lasts two weeks.

Part IV
Questions 22–24:

Now, if we could turn to the next item, which relates to new safety rules. The long-awaited renovation of our product research laboratory is set to begin next week. As of Monday, the north wing of the building will be designated a restricted-access construction site for the next six months. This means that in accordance with company safety regulations, unauthorized personnel will not be allowed into the site until the project is completed early next year. A memorandum has been issued asking company personnel working near the site to follow posted safety instructions.

During the final phases of the renovation, some of you may be granted access to the restricted area in order to oversee the installation of new laboratory equipment. This means that you will be required to attend a safety briefing and to wear appropriate protective clothing. For your own safety and for that of others, please pay careful attention to these new measures.

Questions 25 and 26:

The coffee industry has gone through a radical transformation in the last ten years and this has created some major problems for many coffee-exporting countries. The most important of these is the question of oversupply, which is the direct result of three factors; first, overall demand for coffee has in fact been declining. This is mainly because young people today tend to consume other products than coffee. Second, the International Coffee Federation, which used to guarantee that all producing countries were able to supply the market with sufficient quantities of coffee, is no longer able to act as the international regulator of the industry. And without a regulator it is impossible to impose maximum production levels. Lastly, in recent years, new countries like Vietnam and Brazil, for example, have entered the market, sometimes using extremely advanced, mechanized production techniques and this has led to the production of greater quantities of coffee, available at a very low price.

7 Leisure

Unit Focus ● Entertainment ● Recreation ● Culture

Unit overview

Unit components	Focus	TOEIC practice	Duration
Snapshot	Recreational activities	Part I	15–25 mins
Listening 1	National Pastimes Quiz		10–15 mins
	National leisure trends	Part IV	20–30 mins
Grammar Check 1	Relative pronouns	Part VI	25–35 mins
Viewpoint	Cross golf: polar drive-in	Part VII	40 mins
Grammar Check 2	Indirect questions	Part V	20–30 mins
Listening 2	Indirect questions	Part II	10–15 mins
Vocabulary Builder	Participles used as adjectives	Part V	15–25 mins
Listening 3	Spare time activities	Part III	25–35 mins
Communication	Sales team meeting: outing task force		40 mins
		Total	3 hrs 40–4 hrs 50

Snapshot

Aims
- TOEIC Part I practice: picture analysis
- Vocabulary development: recreational activities
- Discussion

Unit 7 focuses on leisure and recreational activities. Begin the unit by asking pairs of students to come up with a list of leisure and free-time activities. What are their hobbies? What do they like to do for entertainment? What cultural and artistic activities do they enjoy participating in? (Note that more extensive discussion of leisure activities is planned in the Discussion section at the end of Listening 1 on page 70.)

The pictures present four scenes of recreation and leisure: playing board games in a pool, hiking in the wilderness, playing soccer, eating out on a restaurant terrace.

Begin Snapshot by having pairs of students choose one photo and write two statements for it: one correct and the other incorrect. They can then read the statements out loud to their partners or to the class, who then have to identify which statement is the correct one.

Open the class to discussion and brainstorm words for exercise A.

In exercise B, students listen to eight statements and must choose the one that best describes each picture. After the listening, have them read the TOEIC Tip.

> ⚠ **TOEIC Tip**
> This is a good moment to help students understand how some Part I statements may sound correct due to similar-sounding words and homonyms. Have students identify the similar-sounding words and homonyms from the listening. Ask them to explain how statements A, B, C, D in the recording are intended to distract them from the correct statements.

Distracters
A The men are in a *swimming pool*, they are not *playing pool* (billiards).
B The three women are *hiking* (*walking in the outdoors*), not *biking* (*riding bicycles*).
C The *couple* (*man and woman*) is sitting at a table; there are not *a couple* (*two*) *of tables* free on the terrace.
D The soccer *players* are *playing* a game on a field; they are not *on stage performing a play*.

Similar-sounding words:
B *biking* ≠ E *hiking*

Homonyms and words with several meanings:
A *to play pool* (to play the game of billiards) ≠ F *to be in the pool* (a swimming pool)
C *a couple of* (quantity) ≠ H *the couple* (two people)
D to perform *a play* on stage (theatre, drama) ≠ G *to play* on a field (sports)

Picture descriptions
Picture 1
In this picture, people are in a large outdoor *swimming pool*. Several men are *gathered* around two *chess boards*. Some of them are *playing chess*. Steam is rising from the pool.

Picture 2
Three women are *hiking* in the *wilderness*. They are wearing *backpacks* and carrying walking sticks. They are crossing a *stream* (a small river or creek) by walking across a narrow log. Behind them, an *alpine meadow* leads to a line of trees and a forest. In the distance are snow-covered mountains.

Picture 3
In this picture, people are *playing soccer*. Several players are standing around the *goal*. The *soccer ball* is in the air above the goal.

Picture 4
In this picture, two people are sitting at a table outside on a *terrace*. They are *eating out* at a restaurant. The man has his arm raised and he is drinking from a glass. Both the man and the woman are wearing sunglasses. A street slopes upward behind them.

Answers

A
Possible statements
Picture 1
The men are in a swimming pool.
They are playing board games/chess.
The swimming pool is outside.

Picture 2
The three women are walking in the wilderness.
They are backpacking.
They are crossing a stream/river/creek.

Picture 3
They're playing soccer.
The teams are on the playing field.
The ball is above the goal.

Picture 4
The couple is eating at a restaurant.
They're dining on the terrace.
They're enjoying their meal outside.

B
1 F
2 E
3 G
4 H

AUDIOSCRIPT
B
A The men are playing pool.
B They're biking in the forest.
C There are a couple of free tables on the terrace.
D They're on stage performing a play.
E They're hiking in the wilderness.
F The men are playing board games in the pool.
G The players are on the field.
H The couple is dining outside.

Listening 1

Aims
- TOEIC Part IV practice: short talks
- Listening for details
- Discussion

The lead-in activity, a National Pastimes Quiz, can be done as a group or individually. You may want students to extend the quiz by identifying other national/cultural pastimes. Ask students: *Can you think of any pastimes that are associated with other nations or cultures?*

Suggested responses
Belgium – cycling (the most popular sport)
Bhutan – archery
Canada – lacrosse (official summer sport) and ice hockey (official winter sport)
China – table tennis and tai chi
India – yoga
Jamaica – cricket
Japan – sumo wrestling
Mongolia – wrestling and archery
Norway – skiing
Pakistan – field hockey (official sport)
Korea – tae kwon do (traditional): a martial art
Saudi Arabia – falconry and horse racing (traditional)
Turkey – oil wrestling (traditional)
United Arab Emirates – camel racing (traditional)
United States – baseball

Here are a few more traditional pastimes:
Afghanistan – buzkashi (literally "goat-grabbing"): a traditional sport played on horseback
Finland – pesäpallo: a Finnish version of baseball

Hong Kong – dragon boat racing
Iceland – glima: Icelandic wrestling
Uzbekistan – kurash: an ancient style of wrestling
Thailand – muay thai: Thai boxing, a martial art

Exercise B involves an extended listening of a radio program discussing leisure trends in the U.S. Before beginning the recording, have students study the table and guess what the answers will be. You could begin by asking the following questions and writing student answers on the board:

- *What do you think the top four leisure activities are in the United States?*
- *What percentage of Americans watch television every day?*
- *What percentage of Americans watch more than 5 hours of television every day?*

After listening to the recording and completing the table, students can compare the information with their predictions. This leads well into the Discussion section.

> **DISCUSSION**
> Students can compare their own national leisure trends with those of the United States. In addition to this cross-cultural approach, the third question asks students to compare leisure preferences according to gender. How do leisure trends in their country differ between men and women? You can also ask how leisure trends differ according to ages. Ask them what leisure activities they used to do when they were younger. What leisure activities do they imagine doing when they are older?

> **Answers**
> **A**
> 1 e 2 d 3 b 4 g 5 h 6 f 7 a 8 c
> **B**
> 1 watching television
> 2 shopping
> 3 eating out
> 4 81%
> 5 8%
> 6 women
> 7 biking
> 8 men
> 9 golf
> 10 jogging

AUDIOSCRIPT
B
How do Americans spend their free time?
Here are a few facts from LeisureTrak®, which measures the leisure and recreational habits of Americans 16 years old and over.
The top four leisure activities of all Americans are: watching television, reading, socializing and shopping. Using computers, eating out, watching spectator sports, and reading the newspaper also ranked high.
81 percent of Americans enjoy watching television at least once a day.
57 percent watch TV for less than two hours, but eight percent admit watching it for five or more hours per day.
The top five recreational activities for women are walking, aerobics, exercising, biking, and jogging. The top five for men are golf, basketball, walking, jogging, and biking.

Grammar Check 1

> **Aims**
> - TOEIC Part VI practice: error recognition
> - Relative pronouns

Students study the examples to identify the relative pronouns in exercise A. The emphasis here is on the specific meanings of relative pronouns. Although this section does not specifically address the difference between defining and non-defining relative pronouns, it might be useful to briefly explain this to your students. Non-defining relative pronouns and clauses simply add extra information. Defining relative pronouns and clauses add essential information that defines who or what the speaker is referring to.

Non-defining:
His oldest sister (he can only have one *oldest sister*)
1 *His oldest sister,* **who** *is an expert rock climber, recently ascended Mount Everest.*
Defining:
His colleague (which colleague?)
2 *His colleague* **who** *loves to sail recently bought a boat.*

The relative clause in sentence 1 simply adds information, but does not further define the subject of the sentence. Non-defining pronouns and clauses are separated from the sentence with commas.
The relative clause in sentence 2 adds essential information and thus defines *which* colleague the speaker is referring to. Defining pronouns are *not*

separated from the sentence with commas. Generally, *that* is used for defining clauses and *which* can be used for both.

Note that in exercise C, statement 6, the correct answer is *from whom*. Students find the formal, correct usage of *whom* challenging. The general rule is that *whom* is used after a preposition for a person (*to whom*, *from whom*, *with whom*, etc.). Contemporary usage often avoids formal usage of *whom* by placing the preposition at the end of the phrase or by simply using the less formal *who*.

Formal: *The colleague, to whom I loaned my surfboard, was an Olympic swimmer.*
Informal: *The colleague, who I loaned my surfboard to, was an Olympic swimmer.*
Formal: *With whom are you playing tennis this afternoon?*
Informal: *Who are you playing tennis with this afternoon?*

A typical Part VI error that students might encounter on the TOEIC® is the use of an additional pronoun after the relative pronoun:

My friend Brenda, who she is an excellent photographer, recently went to Brazil.
Archery, which it is an ancient martial art, requires great concentration.

> **Answers**
> **A**
> Which relative pronoun(s):
> - are used only for people? *who, whose, (whom)*
> - can be used for objects and people? *that, who, whose, which*
> - is used for possessions? *whose*
> - is used for places? *where*
>
> **B**
> 1 Svetlana, who won the national junior tournament, taught me how to play chess.
> 2 The Olympic Games, which originated in Greece, are held every four years.
> 3 My best friend, whose hobby is magic, can do the most amazing card tricks.
>
> **C**
> 1 ~~who~~ that
> 2 ~~which~~ who
> 3 ~~who~~ which
> 4 ~~which~~ where
> 5 ~~that~~ whose
> 6 ~~which~~ whom

Viewpoint

> **Aims**
> - TOEIC Part VII practice: reading comprehension
> - Discussion: unique recreational activities and their environments; extreme sports

You can approach this topic in several ways, either through the idea that leisure activities are uniquely linked to their environments or through the idea that traditional activities can develop into extreme variations.

Ask students if any of their favorite leisure activities have to occur in specific places. Ask them to imagine doing these activities in the least expected places. Have they heard of "extreme sports"? (Extreme sports are radical variations on traditional sports and are often done in non-traditional, more challenging environments.)

This Viewpoint features two articles presenting two different leisure activities that are uniquely linked to their environments. Both activities could be considered "extreme" variations on their traditional forms. Generally, we see a movie in a theatre. However, the first article presents a drive-in cinema for snowmobiles made entirely out of snow. The second article describes a radical type of golf. It is played indoors, in the middle of cities, anywhere but on traditional golf courses.

In the suggested activity, students practice writing their own Part VII questions. Divide the class into two groups. Have one group read article A and the other group read article B. After they read the article on their own, they should answer the comprehension questions in exercise A.

Exercise B provides students with more active practice of TOEIC® Part VII-type questions. Students write two questions for an article and give them to the other group. You can ask students to simply write the questions or they can write TOEIC® Part VII-style multiple-choice questions.

> **Sample answers**
> **A**
> **Article A**
> 1 This article presents a drive-in cinema for snowmobiles in Norway.
> 2 The people who go to this cinema are the Samis, who are Norway's indigenous people, many of whom are reindeer farmers.
> 3 In northern Norway. In a cold climate where it snows a lot.
> 4 The cinema is made entirely of snow.

Unit 7 | Leisure

Article B
1. The second article describes a type of golf that is not played on traditional golf courses.
2. Cross golfers.
3. Cross golf can be played anywhere – in cities, in hotels, along rivers.
4. There are no official rules. Golfers are free to play wherever they want and they do not have to pay green fees.

B
Sample questions
Article A
How do cinema-goers get to the drive-in theatre?
What is the cinema made of?
What do the people sit on?
Who are the Samis?
What kind of movies do they show?

Article B
What are other names for cross golf?
In what countries is cross golf most popular?
Who started cross golf? Where did he first start playing it?
In a recent tournament, what was the "hole" that players had to hit the golf ball into?

DISCUSSION
Begin by asking students what they think of the two articles. Do they consider these "extreme"? Would they want to experience or participate in either of the activities? Do they know of any other activities that have undergone similar variations?

You may also want to encourage students to talk about recreational activities that are specifically linked to environments and weather conditions. Give them categories such as *water/snow, indoors/outdoors, winter/summer, individual/group*.
For example:

- *What are some sports that require cold or snow?* (skiing, snowboarding, icefishing, ice-skating, etc.)
- *What activities are done in warm weather?*
- *What activities are done on the water?*
- *What activities are done in the mountains?*
- *What activities need courts or playing fields?*

Use thisctivity to revise and expand vocabulary.

Grammar Check 2

Aims
- TOEIC Part V practice: incomplete sentences
- Polite question forms; indirect questions
- Topic: eating out in restaurants

Lead in to the activity by getting students to talk about eating out. Have students look at the business cards on the page. Ask them to imagine what kinds of food are served. What facilities do they provide? Would they want to try any of these restaurants?

Ask students to describe what kinds of foods they like to eat. Do they prefer traditional dishes or modern fast food? What kinds of restaurants do they like to go to in order to get food they can't prepare at home? Do they like to go to more formal, sit-down restaurants where a waiter takes their order? Or do they frequent restaurants where they pick up the food at a counter or along a buffet table? You may want to use indirect questions:

- *I was wondering what kinds of foods you like.*
- *Could you tell me what your favorite kinds of restaurants are?*

Students need to be familiar with the phrases that introduce questions. Indirect questions appear frequently in Parts II and III, and in Parts V and VI. For Parts V and VI, they need to know the rule that in an indirect question the word order of the subject and verb of the original question is not inverted. Have the students determine the indirect question rule inductively by reading the examples in exercise A.

Exercise B provides Part V practice with the indirect question form. Exercise C consolidates the grammar point with a reading of exercise B. Have students brainstorm questions, both direct and indirect, that they would hear in a restaurant.

Answers
A
The order of the subject and the verb is inverted.
Direct question: verb + subject
Indirect question: subject + verb
B
1. Would you happen to know where **we can find** a good restaurant?
2. I was wondering if **we could make** a reservation for two, please.
3. Could you tell us how **the fish is** prepared?
4. I wonder what **today's dessert special is**.

AUDIOSCRIPT

C
1. Would you happen to know where we can find a good restaurant?
2. I was wondering if we could make a reservation for two, please.
3. Could you tell us how the fish is prepared?
4. I wonder what today's dessert special is.

Listening 2

Aims
- TOEIC Part II practice: question/response
- Indirect questions

This Part II listening exercise further consolidates the indirect question forms covered in Grammar 2. Students listen to a question and then hear three responses. They must choose the correct response. The incorrect responses use two types of distracters. They mistakenly refer to the polite question frame and not to the core questions. Or, they mistakenly refer to a similar-sounding word in the question. As in Snapshot, you may ask the students to identify the distracters:

1
Response A mistakenly refers to a word in the polite question frame *happen*.
Response B mistakenly refers to the words in the polite question frame *to know*.

2
Responses B and C misinterpret the word *show*.

3
Response A mistakenly refers to a word in the polite question frame *wonder*.
Response B misinterprets the word *wonder* for *won*.

Answers
1 C
2 A
3 C

ACTIVE PRACTICE
Before you begin the Active Practice activity, brainstorm additional restaurant vocabulary with the class:

to make a reservation	to book a table
a banquet room	a private room
waiter	waitress
chef	cook
steward	to order
a menu	à la carte
today's special	first course
appetizer	dessert
main course	beverage
the check/the bill	a tip
dishes	

Have students imagine that they are planning a farewell dinner party for a friend or colleague. They should prepare a list of questions to ask the restaurant manager who is helping them organize the event. Half the students can play the role of a restaurant manager of one of the restaurants represented by the business cards reproduced in the Student's Book. The students can conduct their interviews in pairs.

AUDIOSCRIPT

1
Would you happen to know what time the café opens?
A No, I don't know what happened.
B Yes, we're aware of that.
C At quarter to twelve.

2
Could you please show me how to use these chopsticks?
A Gladly. You first have to learn how to hold them.
B Yes. We were all very pleased with the show.
C No. She hasn't been able to show her work.

3
I wonder if anyone would like to go out for a drink this evening.
A It's a wonder they're here.
B Nobody won this afternoon.
C We'd love to.

Writing Practice
Write an email to the restaurant manager describing and confirming the farewell dinner party arrangements.
OR
Write a restaurant review of your favorite place to eat.

Vocabulary Builder

Aims
- TOEIC Part V practice: incomplete sentences
- Vocabulary development: present and past participles used as adjectives – *-ing* versus *-ed*
- Discussion: sports and games; competitiveness

Students often confuse present and past participles. TOEIC® Parts V and VI test knowledge of *-ing* and *-ed* endings, particularly when these verb forms are used as adjectives. See the TOEIC Tip for an example.

Unit 7 | Leisure

The paragraphs present a unique game called BrainBall™, which is the opposite of most games. The winner of BrainBall is the person who can remain the most relaxed by being the least interested in winning. Open this activity by asking students if they think they are competitive. What does it take to be a winner? Concentration, focus, drive? Do they always want to win? What would they think of a game where the least *competitive* person would win?

Answers
A
(tired) boring (interested) exciting
surprising (relaxed) (interested)
(relaxed) (excited)
B
1 relaxed
2 surprised
3 bored
4 tiring
5 interesting
6 exciting
7 relaxing

ACTIVE PRACTICE
This section involves pairwork with students interviewing each other about their interests in sports, games and other leisure activities. You may want to brainstorm a list of participle adjectives and write them on the board before doing the interviews.

Suggested adjectives:

exciting	fatiguing
exhilarating	thrilling
stimulating	invigorating
engaging	refreshing
inspiring	fascinating
boring	uninteresting
uninspiring	tiring

Have students give the complementary participle forms of each adjective:
exciting – excited

Encourage students to use as many of the adjectives as possible during the interviews.

Listening 3

Aims
- TOEIC Part III practice: short conversations
- Listening for specific sport and leisure vocabulary

Exercise A is a brainstorming activity that is designed to activate and develop more specific sport and leisure vocabulary. The TOEIC® can feature questions that test students' knowledge of common sport and leisure activity vocabulary.

Have students work in pairs. Each pair can choose several of the listed leisure activities and write a list of words associated with each. Without telling the rest of the class what the activity is, they can then read out their list. The rest of the class has to guess which activity the keywords refer to. More advanced students can choose activities that are not listed in the Student's Book.

In exercise B, students practice identifying keywords and context clues that indicate what the speakers are talking about.

After they complete exercise B, have students read through the audioscripts. More advanced students can write and perform their own Part III dialogues. Ask the rest of the class to answer a few classic TOEIC®-style questions about the performed dialogues:

- Who is the speaker?
- Where does the conversation take place?
- What are they talking about?
- What do they plan to do?

etc.

Answers
A and B

	Keywords	Activity
1	tables with nets, paddles, balls	playing ping-pong
2	show, works, gallery, paintings, sculptures, catalog	going to art exhibitions
3	game, inning, home run, bases, hitter, field player, bat	watching baseball
4	cuisine class, dessert and pastry course, restaurant	cooking
5	keys, classical, improvise, jazz	playing the piano

AUDIOSCRIPT

Man 1 I know a great place to play. The municipal recreation department has set up nice tables with nets in the park.
Man 2 Well, what about paddles and balls?
Man 1 We can rent paddles at the kiosk. We'll have to buy a few balls though.

2
Woman That was an amazing show. Over one hundred works in such a small gallery.
Man I found it very crowded. The paintings were hung so close together and the sculptures were packed into the corners.
Woman We should come back when there are less people. Until then you can read through the catalog that I bought on my way out.

3
Man How about that game last night! It sure was close in the last inning.
Woman You can say that again. If it weren't for Yuchiro's home run with bases loaded, we would have lost the game.
Man What a hitter! Not only is he a solid fielder, he can really swing a bat.

4
Man 1 Hey there. How've you been? Last time we met you had just signed up for an Italian cuisine class.
Man 2 Great to see you. Yeah. I've been taking my life-long hobby very seriously and just finished another six-month dessert and pastry course. It was fabulous!
Man 1 Wow. With all that experience, you'll have your own restaurant in no time!

5
Man What a fine rendition. That was terrific. So how long have you been playing?
Woman I started taking lessons when I turned five. So, counting the conservatory, that makes about 20 years that I've had my fingers on the keys.
Man Do you mostly play classical or sometimes improvise jazz?

Communication

Aim
- Speaking practice: presenting; discussing; negotiating

The students belong to a successful sales team that has been awarded a recreational outing. They must meet in order to choose which activity to do. Referring to ONE of the five activities in the Communication file, they must present an outing to the group, the outing's advantages, the time it will take and how much it will cost. By the end of the meeting, the group must choose one outing for the entire sales team.

For small classes, individuals can present one of the five outings. For larger classes, have students pair up or form small groups and prepare a presentation.

After the activity, ask students what other types of group outings they would enjoy participating in if they had the opportunity.

Writing Practice
Write an email to your sales team reporting on the results of your planning meeting.
OR
Imagine your ideal outing for a sales team and write up a brochure describing the activity.

8 Money

Unit Focus
● Banking ● Budgets ● Investment

Unit overview

Unit components	Focus	TOEIC practice	Duration
Snapshot	Money; personal finance	Part I	15–25 mins
Listening 1	Household expenditure	Part III	15–25 mins
Grammar Check 1	Talking about trends	Parts V/VI	20–30 mins
Listening 2	MoneyTalk radio program	Part II	10–15 mins
Vocabulary Builder	Two-part phrasal verbs	Parts V/VI	15–20 mins
Viewpoint	Cashflow 101 game	Part VII	20–30 mins
Grammar Check 2	Modals of possibility	Part V	15–20 mins
Listening 3	The LETS story	Part IV	10 mins
Communication	Starting a LETS group		40 mins
		Total	2 hrs 40–3 hrs 35

Snapshot

Aims
- TOEIC Part I practice: picture analysis
- Listening for specific information
- Vocabulary development: money; personal finance
- Discussion

Ask students to focus on the settings for these photos and to find the answers to the two questions in exercise A. The pictures show four situations involving money: money-changing, withdrawing money, using banking services, and printing national currencies. A brief description of each is given below.

Picture descriptions
Picture 1
This picture shows the front office of a local *branch of a bank*. The *bank teller* is speaking to a *client*, a *casually-dressed* young man, who is standing at the *counter* of the bank. She is giving him some information and gesturing at the same time. The teller is wearing a *business suit* and she has an *identification badge* on her left *lapel*. We can see another client in the background who is watching a small television screen. Beside the screen there is a slogan which reads: *Explore a world of financial prosperity*.

Picture 2
This picture shows a group of people standing by two *Automated Teller Machines*. (ATMs are machines that clients with *bank cards* can use to *withdraw cash*.) The couple on the left are either preparing to withdraw cash or are *putting away* the cash that they have just *taken out*. On the right-hand side of the picture, there is a line of people who are *queuing up* to use the machines. Two young women are looking closely at the screen of an ATM.

Picture 3
The picture shows a *money changer*, who is seated with her back to the mirror, and a client who is *leaning* with his *elbows* on the *counter*. The woman is holding a wad of *banknotes* or *bills* in her uplifted left hand. She is *examining* one of the notes by holding it up to the light. In front of her she has a *calculator* and a roll of tape.

Picture 4
This picture shows an employee of the U.S. federal reserve*, which is responsible for *printing* and distributing *paper money*. The woman is working in a *printing plant*. We can see *sheets* of freshly-printed *banknotes* on two *conveyor belts*, one in front and one behind her. She has taken several sheets which are *spread out* around her and she is *checking* them for printing errors. The sheets have not yet been cut into individual banknotes.

*Only coins are produced by the U.S. Mint.

> **Answers**
> **A**
> **Possible statements**
> **Picture 1**
> In the front office of a bank.
> The bank teller is giving a customer some information.
> A customer is making an enquiry.
>
> **Picture 2**
> Beside two Automated Teller Machines.
> They are taking out/withdrawing money.
> They are standing next to the machine.
> They are waiting to take out/withdraw money.
>
> **Picture 3**
> In the office of a money changer.
> The woman is holding up some banknotes.
> She is inspecting some banknotes.
> The customer is leaning on the counter.
> He is holding some notes in his hands.
>
> **Picture 4**
> At the printing office of the federal reserve.
> The woman is checking sheets of newly-printed dollar bills.

The statements focus on the actions that are being performed in each picture. Remind students that in this section of the test they will often hear words that are synonyms of more common terms. Developing vocabulary by learning synonyms for simple actions will help them to recognize the correct answers. A suggested list of synonyms is given beside the answers below.

> **Answers**
> **B and C**
> | | Verb | Synonym |
> |---|------|---------|
> | 1 A | assisting | helping |
> | 2 B | withdrawing | taking out |
> | 3 C | converting | changing, exchanging |
> | 4 D | checking | verifying, inspecting, looking over, scanning |

You may wish to hold a short discussion after completing the listening in exercise B. Focus the discussion on the practical side of money and banking and avoid talking about how people/students manage their finances, which will be dealt with later in the unit. Suggestions for additional discussion questions focusing on the practical aspects of banking and personal finances could include the following:

- *How do people in your country generally pay for their purchases? (by card, by check or in cash?)*
- *What banking services do people use?*
- *When are the opening hours of banks?*
- *Have you ever had to change money into another currency?*

AUDIOSCRIPT
B and C
A   He's converting some money into another currency.
B   They're withdrawing cash from an ATM.
C   She's checking some sheets of dollar bills.
D   The bank teller is assisting a customer.

> ⚠ **TOEIC Tip**
> This tip draws attention to some of the most common abbreviations that students may encounter on the test. The test does not include less common abbreviations, but you may want to point some of these out to.
>
> **Positions in a company hierarchy**
> CFO   Chief financial officer
> COO   Chief operations officer
> CIO   Chief information officer
> VP   Vice-president
>
> **Businesses**
> Inc.   Incorporated
> Corp. Corporation (company)
> Ltd   Limited (company)
>
> **Measurements**
> kg   kilogram
> mph   miles per hour
> kph   kilometers per hour
>
> **Countries and communities**
> US   United States of America
> EU   European Union
> UK   United Kingdom
>
> **International organizations**
> WTO   World Trade Organisation
> UN   United Nations
> NGO   Non-governmental Organization

Listening 1

> **Aims**
> - TOEIC Part III practice: short conversations
> - Vocabulary development

In exercise A, students complete a diagram showing the main sources of expenditure for a typical U.S. household. You may want to pre-teach the following vocabulary:

footwear   tuition   mortgage   utility bills   tolls allowance   prescription medicine   club membership

Unit 8 | Money

Once students have completed A, you may want to ask how the diagram compares with their own sources of expenditure. You can ask simple questions:

- *What are the main categories of expenditure for your household?*
- *How does your pattern of expenditure differ from that of a U.S. household?*
- *Are there any other items that you regularly spend money on, but which are not mentioned in the chart/diagram?*

Answers	
A	
footwear	7/8
vehicle insurance	1/2
school tuition	9/10
mortgage	3/4
utility bills	3/4
tolls	1/2
medical coverage	5/6
groceries	7/8
allowance	9/10
club membership	11/12
prescription medicine	5/6
concert tickets	11/12

Exercise B features four Part III dialogues where students are to identify the category of expenditure that they relate to. Ask students to focus first on the situations and to identify the keywords that allow them to identify the exact subject of the discussion in each case. An explanation of the context is given next to the answers below.

Answers		
B		
1	transport	A couple are discussing the cost of the repairs that will be made to their car.
2	entertainment	A couple are talking about the cost of buying tickets for the opera.
3	housing	Two people are discussing the price of rental accommodation.
4	utility bills	Two people are discussing the price of electricity.

In exercise C, students are asked to identify the following vocabulary:

charge   estimate   cost   afford   rent

Other vocabulary that students may have difficulty with includes:

brake (system) (1)   *vacate* (3)   *sports complex* (3)
switch (4)   *solar energy* (4)

AUDIOSCRIPT

1
Woman The garage called this morning. They said they've found a problem with the brake system on the car, which means they're going to charge us more.
Man Did they give you an estimate?
Woman Around two hundred dollars, including labor.

2
Man Why don't we get tickets for the opera festival next week?
Woman Have you seen what they cost? There's no way we can afford that much.
Man I guess you're right. Maybe we should just go to a jazz concert instead.

3
Man I'm looking for a small two-bedroom apartment.
Woman Well, we have one that's just been vacated. It's on Jermyn Avenue near the new sports complex.
Man That sounds great. How much is the rent?

4
Woman Can you believe that electricity has gone up again?
Man I figure it's increased by almost seven percent since last year.
Woman Yeah. I'm seriously considering switching to solar energy.

Grammar Check 1

Aims
- TOEIC Parts V/VI practice
- Review of the language of trends: verb and noun forms; prepositions

This grammar sections deals with the language that is used to describe trends and to talk about changes in levels or quantities over a period of time. Many of the audio recordings, documents and questions on the test contain language that refers to trends.

Exercise A reviews the principal verbs that are used to express upward and downward movement in relation to numbers, figures and trends. he following are some examples of words that express an extreme upward or downward movement.

71

Upward: *soar   skyrocket   shoot up   surge*
Downward: *plummet   collapse   plunge*

It is a good idea to remind students that extreme trends are more usually referred to using the verbs in exercise A, followed by adverbs such as:

significantly   slightly   moderately

Answers	
A	
↑	↓
1 increase	1 lower
2 raise	2 reduce
3 grow	
go up	fall
rise	go down
	decrease
	drop
	decline

Students may find it difficult to use some of these verbs and not know which are transitive and which are intransitive. This is an area of grammar that is commonly tested on Parts V and VI. Explain that transitive verbs take an object and intransitive verbs do not. You can use the following examples:

*Taxes **rose** by five percent.* (intransitive)
*The government **raised** taxes by five percent.* (transitive)

Explain that the verbs in the list belong in three categories:

a   verbs that can be used both transitively and intransitively:
    decrease   increase   grow*
b   verbs that can only be used transitively:
    raise   lower   reduce
c   verbs that can only be used intransitively:
    go up   go down   fall
    rise   drop   decline

* The verb *grow* is usually considered to be intransitive, but in modern English usage it is often used in a transitive form.

Exercise B focuses on the noun forms that are associated with these verbs. All of the noun forms are identical to the verbs, except for the suffixed form *reduction*. You should point out that these nouns are also very often qualified by the adjectives:

slight   significant   huge

Answers	
B	
increase	decrease
raise	reduction
growth	fall
rise	drop
	decline

In exercise C, students are asked to identify the prepositions *from* and *to* which are used to mark the beginning and end of a period. The preposition *by* is used to show the extent of a change.

Answers
1   *from ... to*
2   *by*

The bar chart and the graph in exercise D are presented to give students an opportunity to practice talking about trends. You can ask students to choose one and make a short summary of the trends that it illustrates. They can refer back to these charts and use them as models for the Active Practice activity at the end of the grammar section.

Answers
D
Bar chart illustrates downward trend.
Graph illustrates upward trend.

ACTIVE PRACTICE
Provide students with charts or graphs that you have clipped from a business magazine, or you can ask them to draw their own. If you choose to do the latter, make it clear to students that they can invent the figures in their chart. In both cases, before students give their commentaries, they should explain what it is that they will be describing, i.e.

This chart shows the evolution of car sales from 2001–2003.

The TOEIC Tip gives a list of words that are used to refer to numbers, figures and units.

Before students complete the text in exercise E, remind them that they will have to use a selection of nouns, verbs and prepositions.

Answers
E
1   Reducing
2   fell/decreased/declined/went down/dropped
3   from ... to

4 rise/increase/grow/go up
5 increasing
6 raise/increase
7 has grown/has increased
8 by
9 reduction
10 increase

●Extension Activity

Before doing this activity, you will need to prepare a selection of documents to use in class!

Put up a short list of numbers and figures from the documents you have prepared (see below for advice on how to do this) on the board. This should include a variety of types of numbers and figures, for example:

Prices:	$2.75
	two dollars and seventy-five cents
Numbers:	1.95
	one point nine five
Percentages:	7.5%
	seven point five percent
Fractions:	$\frac{1}{2}$
	half, one third, one fourth, etc.
Ratios:	1:3
	one in three
Square and cubic numbers:	42 m^2
	forty-two square meters
	13 m^3
	thirteen cubic meters

Quickly review pronunciation and usage.

Ask students to form pairs. Distribute one of the authentic documents that you have prepared to each pair. The documents can be of different types: product descriptions, user instructions, short articles, publicity materials, etc. Each text should contain several numbers and/or figures. After giving the pairs five minutes to study their documents, write a number (that appears in one of the documents) on the board. The pair that has the document containing that number has to pronounce it correctly, then explain what it corresponds to in their document.

Listening 2

Aims
- TOEIC Part II practice: question/response
- Listening for specific information

Ask students to listen for specific vocabulary that will help them to identify which extract on the recording corresponds to each topic.

Answers
A
1 the stock market   D
2 inheritance   E
3 retirement   C
4 selling a property A
5 pay   B

In section B, students should listen for specific vocabulary related to income:

*to appreciate   salary   raise   pension fund   stocks
to invest   inherited   investment   return*

●Extension Activity

Ask students to form groups and to prepare answers to each of the questions. This can be done individually or in pairs. Once they have prepared the answers, students take it in turns to read a question for another student to answer.

AUDIOSCRIPT
A and B
A My home is already worth about 140,000 dollars. Would you advise me to sell it now or would it be better to wait for it to appreciate?
B I've been at the same salary level for the last two years. How should I go about asking my boss for a raise?
C Is there an annual limit on the amount of money I can put into my pension fund?
D I'm interested in buying stocks. How should I choose which companies to invest in?
E I recently inherited some money. What type of investment would give me the best return?

Target Score

Vocabulary Builder

Aims
- TOEIC Parts V/VI practice
- Phrasal verbs (I): two-part

Questions that feature two-part phrasal verbs are often included in Parts V and VI of the test. This exercise is designed to show the variety of phrasal verbs that can be generated by adding prepositions to some common verbs. For exercise C, students should be encouraged to find their own examples before consulting a dictionary.

Answers

A
1. broken down — had mechanical problems
2. carry out — make
3. take out — purchase
4. deal with — handle
5. go through — discuss/explain

B
1. take out
2. took up
3. work out
4. looks after
5. bringing out
6. look up
7. bring forward
8. turned down
9. set out
10. set up

C
check	out/up/in
come	down/forward/out
cut	down/out/up
fall	down/out
get	down/out/up/over/through
go	after/forward/out/up/over/through
look	after/forward (to)/out/up/into
make	out/up
pay	out/up
put	down/forward/up
run	down/out (of)/up/into
settle	down/up

Viewpoint

Aims
- TOEIC Part VII practice: reading comprehension
- Discussion: Cashflow 101

This reading text is about Cashflow 101, a board game created by Robert Kiyosaki in order to help people to better understand and manage their personal finances. The article explains why the game has become so popular, and explains how it is played. It also gives a short profile of a Cashflow 101 player.

Begin by discussing the lead-in questions in A. You can either pre-teach the following words or have students guess their meanings from the context after reading and answering the questions about the article:

to roll dice	wealth	to earn income
nine to five	pet-grooming	to play host
get-rich-quick	big break	rat race
fast track	paycheck	real estate
leaky		

Answers

B
1. d, opened a restaurant
2. c, leave the rat race
3. a, salesman
4. c, he left his job

For more TOEIC® reading comprehension practice, students can work in pairs to prepare a multiple-choice question about one of the following aspects of the game.

- The number of players
- The duration of the game
- The people who play the game
- Why the game was created

They can then ask and answer each other's questions.

The Money Quiz

How good are you at managing your personal finances? Take the money quiz!

Note down your answers, then check with a partner to see how well you each handle your finances.

1. You see that the bank has made an error on your statement of 500 dollars in your favor. Are you most likely to:
   a Say nothing and use the money?
   b Inform your bank immediately?
   c Put the money aside and wait?

2. A close friend asks you to lend them some money urgently? How do you react?
   a Lend them the money immediately.
   b Tell them that you don't have enough ready cash.
   c Give them part of the amount and get them to agree on a repayment date.

3. When you go shopping, do you:
   a Buy on impulse?
   b Only shop for things that are already on your list?
   c Occasionally let yourself be tempted to buy something you really don't need?

4. You win a large sum on the lottery. How would you like the money to be paid to you?
   a Receive the money in installments.
   b Receive all the money now.
   c Receive half now and the rest in installments.

5. You have just bought a new mobile phone. What would you do with the old one?
   a Give it to a friend.
   b Sell it second hand.
   c Keep it just in case.

6. You received an unexpected payment of 1,000 dollars six weeks ago. Where is the money now?
   a Long gone.
   b Invested in the stock market.
   c In your checking account.

7. You've just taken out some money from an ATM. What do you do with the receipt?
   a Throw it away.
   b Put it carefully into your wallet.
   c Leave it in the machine.

8. Your overdraft has reached its limit. What will you do?
   a Borrow more money.
   b Decide to reduce your budget.
   c Get a weekend job.

9. How often do you meet with your bank advisor?
   a Haven't met him/her so far.
   b At least three times a year.
   c Whenever he/she asks me to meet.

Calculate your score:
Give yourself: five points for every **b** answer
three points for every **a** answer
one point for every **c** answer

If you scored:

between 31 and 45
You have no difficulty in managing your finances. You are well organized and have the discipline to plan for the future and to adjust your spending when necessary. You know how to make your money work for you to maximum advantage.

between 16 and 30
You need to spend more time organizing your finances. It's only by calculating exactly how much money you have available and how much you can afford to spend that you will be able to avoid making decisions that will ultimately cost you.

between 1 and 15
You need to review your whole approach to dealing with money. Start with the basics and learn how to prepare a budget and record your expenditure. It may be best for you to seek professional advice about how best to do this.

Grammar Check 2

Aims
- TOEIC Part V practice: incomplete sentences
- Review of modal verbs

This grammar section explains how modal verbs are used to talk about the probability of something happening. You may need to review the use of modal verbs, or have students refer to pages 134 and 135 of the Grammar Reference section in the Student's Book.

Answers
A
1 b 2 a 3 c 4 a 5 a 6 c 7 a 8 b/c
B
1 b 2 a 3 a 4 a 5 a 6 b

Listening 3

Aims
- TOEIC Part IV practice: short talks
- Listening for specific information

The audio recording describes how the LETS system was created. Students have to listen for three specific pieces of information, then answer one general question, which helps them to develop the listening strategies required for this part of the TOEIC®. The information that students listen for also provides background facts to introduce the topic of the Communication activity.

Before continuing to the Communication activity, ask students if they have ever heard of any similar systems. In some European countries, similar trading networks exist such as the "sel" network in France. All of these systems replace cash with a unit that has no value outside the trading network. Ask students if they know (or can imagine) how the system works in practice.

Answers
1 Local Exchange Trading System
2 In Canada.
3 extremely successful
4 You exchange goods and/or services without using money.

AUDIOSCRIPT
LETS, which stands for "local exchange trading system", is the brainchild of Michael Linton, a Canadian business graduate with a keen sense of observation. Back in 1983, when he first came up with the idea, he was living on Vancouver Island in Canada. There he noticed that while the local community had significant resources and plenty of skills and products to offer, little trading was taking place. Why not? Simply because there wasn't enough money circulating to make that possible. The solution? Create an economy where money would be replaced by a simple credit system. And so that's exactly what he did. How does it work? Nothing could be simpler. First you create an association of members who want to trade goods and services amongst themselves. Next you set up a virtual currency unit, "noodles", "cowries", or whatever, and then each member receives a credit when they sell something and a debit when they make a purchase. All the transactions are negotiated directly between buyer and seller and centrally recorded. And all members have open access to the group's accounts. Sounds simple and it is – which may well explain why today you can find LETS groups in over 38 countries around the globe.

Communication

Aim
- Speaking practice: negotiating

This activity has several stages and involves both group discussion and individual work, pairwork or group negotiation. There are several ways to manage the activity in class, which can be done:

- as one complete class with the teacher playing a central role
- in several interactive groups
- in paired groups

Whatever format is chosen, start the activity by giving a short briefing to the class to make sure that students understand exactly what they will be asked to do at each stage of the activity.

Explain that the class will be experimenting with a LETS-type system. Choose a name for the currency that will be used (i.e. one unit of currency equals one noodle). Explain that each group (or individual participant, if done as a complete class) will need a clean sheet of paper on which to record the transactions that they will conduct.

This "balance sheet" should have two columns one to record sales and one to record purchases. At the end of the activity, they will be able to use this document to calculate their credit or debit balance.

Make sure that you give students a time limit for each stage of the activity.

- Ten minutes to prepare and list the items for sale.
- Ten minutes to write up the complete list of items for sale on the board.
- Five minutes for groups (or individuals) to decide what items they would be interested in buying.
- Fifteen minutes to conduct negotiations between buyers and sellers.
- Ten minutes to calculate the balance of the transactions.

Writing Practice

You have decided to open a LETS group in your community. Write a short text explaining what this will involve and inviting people to an information session. Your text will be posted on noticeboards in your community.

9 Travel

Unit Focus — Tourism — Transport — Accommodation

Unit overview

Unit components	Focus	TOEIC practice	Duration
Snapshot	Taking a trip	Part I	15–25 mins
Listening 1	Travel announcements	Part IV	25–35 mins
Grammar Check 1	The language of obligation	Part V	25–35 mins
Listening 2	Airport enquiries	Part III	20–30 mins
Vocabulary Builder	Adjectives and adverbs	Part VI	30 mins
Viewpoint	Eco-tourism	Part VII	30 mins
Grammar Check 2	Conditionals: negotiations	Part V	30 mins
Listening 3	Conditionals: negotiations	Part II	10 mins
Communication	Eco-tourism development		50 mins
		Total	3 hrs 55–4 hrs 35

Snapshot

Aims
- TOEIC Part I practice: picture analysis – identifying settings, actions, objects
- Vocabulary development: travel and tourism
- Discussion

Unit 9 provides a good forum for classroom discussion. Students generally like to exchange travel stories and experiences. Begin this unit by asking them about their most recent trips.

- *How do you like to travel? By bus, train, car, plane, cruise ship?*
- *What would be your ideal vacation?*
- *Where would you go and how would you get there?*
- *What tourist activities do you most enjoy?*
- *Which ones do you avoid? What has been your best travel experience?*
- *What has been the worst?*

For larger classes, you can have students work in pairs, interviewing each other about their travel experiences and preferences.

The pictures present four travel and tourism-related scenes: clearing airport security, visiting a museum, riding in a taxi, checking in at an airport. Have the students first read through the list of eight situations and match each picture to a situation.

Extension Activity

In this unit, have individual or pairs of students write their own Part I statements for each of the pictures. Get them to imagine what kind of statements they might hear on the TOEIC®. Have students choose one photo and write two statements about it: one correct and the other incorrect. They can then read the statements out loud to their partners or to the class, who then have to identify which statement is the correct one.

You can also have them imagine what kind of conversation would take place in each of the pictured scenes and in the list of situations. Elicit their ideas by asking questions such as:

- *What would you say to a taxi cab driver if you wanted a ride?*
- *What do you say at an airport check-in counter?*
- *What do you say when registering at a hotel?*

With more advanced students, have them write and perform Part III conversations.

Picture descriptions
Picture 1
The scene takes place in an *airport security* area. The male *passenger* on the right is going through a *security screening* process. He has placed his *personal belongings* (a belt, watch, a cellular phone, keys, etc.) into the *plastic bins*, which will be sent through an *X-ray machine*. The *security officer* is handling a bin with a *carry-on bag*,

shoes, and possibly a coat. Sanitary gloves are hanging from the security officer's pocket.

Picture 2
This scene takes place in a *museum*. A group of three people are looking at a *sculpture* in a *sculpture gallery*. There are windows on either side of the gallery. One woman is wearing a small backpack. She is raising her arm, possibly pointing out some feature on the sculpture. The sculptures appear to be made of marble.

Picture 3
This scene takes place in the street. Two *tourists* are *riding* in the back of a three-wheeled motorized *taxi cab*. We can see the *driver* and the *passengers* clearly because the taxi does not have any doors.

Picture 4
This scene takes place at an *airport check-in counter*. The two airline check-in employees are standing behind the counter, *checking in* the *travelers* and *checking their luggage*. Between the two men on the left, there is a *suitcase* waiting to be checked. The two travelers on the right are checking in, showing their *plane tickets*, *ID* (*identification papers*) and possibly their *passports*, getting their *boarding passes* for the *airplane* with *their seat assignments*. A board behind the counter indicates the *flight numbers*, destinations, etc.

Possible statements
Picture 1
He's clearing airport security.
The security personnel is screening the passenger's bag.
His belongings are in the bins.
He's putting his passport and tickets in his coat pocket.
Incorrect: He's buying items at the duty-free.

Picture 2
They're visiting an art museum.
They're looking at the sculptures.
They're in a sculpture gallery.
Incorrect: She's painting a work of art.

Picture 3
The taxi is driving down the street.
They're riding in a taxi cab.
Incorrect: The taxi is parked in front of the hotel.

Picture 4
They're checking in for their flight.
The airline service representative is issuing their boarding passes.
Incorrect: They're waiting at the baggage claim.
Incorrect: They're driving to the airport.

Answers
B
1 Clearing airport security
2 Visiting a museum
3 Taking a cab
4 Checking in at an airport

Listening 1

Aims
- TOEIC Part IV practice: short talks
- Identifying settings, actions, objects

Students practice identifying the speaker and what type of announcement is being made in three travel and tourism-related settings: on a boat tour through a city, in a train station, on a ferry boat. In exercise B, students complete the missing information on three documents: a boat tour map, a refund claim form, and a sign indicating the food services on the ferry.

Announcement descriptions
1 The first announcement is a commentary made by a tour guide on a river boat cruise in a major city. The tour guide is pointing out the various monuments that the tourist can see as they travel along the river.
2 The second announcement, made in a European train station, is informing train passengers of delays due to mechanical errors (the signaling system is malfunctioning). Some train lines guarantee their passengers that the trains will arrive on time. If the trains are late, the passengers can receive money back if they fill out reimbursement claim forms.
3 This announcement is made on a large ferry boat, informing passengers of the two types of food and restaurant services on board. The *Sea Breeze* is a self-service restaurant, where passengers pick up their own meals along a buffet line and bring their food to tables in a seating area. *The Wheelhouse* is a more formal, *à la carte* restaurant where waiters and/or waitresses take the diners' orders at their table.

Answers
A

Announcement	Speaker	Message type
1	a tour guide	a commentary
2	a conductor	an apology
3	a catering manager	an invitation

> **B**
> 1 Museum 2 2 hours 3 11 p.m. 4 the upper

AUDIOSCRIPT
A and B
1. The first part of today's cruise will take us down the river and through the heart of the old city. Once we have passed the cathedral, which you can now see on your right, we will continue downstream past the Royal Palace and the National Gallery. If you look over to your left, you will be able to see the façade of the Maritime Museum. The bridge that we are just about to pass under is one of the city's most famous landmarks.
2. We regret to inform passengers that today's service to London Waterloo will be subject to delays due to a malfunction of the signaling systems. Our arrival time will now be 11:45, two hours later than scheduled. On behalf of Eurotrains we would like to apologize for the inconvenience and we would like to remind passengers that they are entitled to a partial refund of their fares on completion of the forms that our personnel will distribute on arrival at the station.
3. We would like to inform all passengers sailing with Sea/Ocean Ferries that our self-service and à la carte restaurants are now open for dining. Our self-service restaurant, which is located on B deck, offers a wide selection of local and international dishes. It closes at 11 p.m. Our à la carte restaurant, *The Wheelhouse*, is situated on the upper deck and offers a gourmet dining experience with spectacular sea views. Reservations will be accepted until 10 p.m.

Grammar Check 1

Aims
- TOEIC Part V practice: incomplete sentences
- Language of obligation
- Discussion: traveling abroad; air travel requirements and restrictions

This grammar section presents verbs of obligation, which are featured on all parts of the test (except Part I). You may want to open the activity by asking students the following questions:

- *When you travel, what things do you have to do before you leave?*
- *What things must you do when you travel on an airplane?*
- *Do you need to do anything different when you travel to a foreign country?*

In exercise A, students identify the verbs of obligation, then group them according to their use. It is important that students understand the difference in meanings between the affirmative and the negative forms of each verb of obligation.

Before doing exercise B, it might be helpful to consult the Grammar Reference section on page 135.

In exercise B, students practice using the most common verbs of obligation that are featured in Part V by completing an instruction brochure for passengers.

> **Answers**
> **A**
> have to, require, need to, don't … have to, must, must not
> 1 must, have to, require, need
> 2 don't have to
> 3 must not
> **B**
> 1 need/require
> 2 must/have to/need to
> 3 don't have to
> 4 have to
> 5 must not
> 6 must/has to
> 7 must/have to
> 8 have to
> 9 required
> 10 need to/have to

Listening 2

Aims
- TOEIC Part III practice: short conversations
- Discussion: modern airports; airport services

Travelers often have to spend a lot of time in airports, checking in, clearing airport security, and going through customs. Sometimes travelers have to wait several hours for lay-overs. Modern airports have responded by providing many services to travelers. Ask students if they can think of any airport services, for example: restaurants, cafés, newspaper and magazine shops, bookstores, gift shops, clothing stores, music shops, duty-free shopping, mail services, pharmacies, etc. Some airports have private gyms and fitness areas for travelers who want to get some exercise during a lay-over. Massage therapists have opened stands in some airports in order to offer back and shoulder massages to travel-weary passengers. In exercise A, students locate on the map where they

Unit 9 | Travel

would go if they needed to do a common travel-related activity or action. Students should be encouraged to read the phrases aloud. For example: *If I had to change some money, I would go to the bank*. These statements are also preparing students to revise the conditional forms in Grammar Check 2 on page 91.

Answers
A
1 (Bank)
2 (Check-in)
3 (Medical office/First Aid)
4 (Car rental)
5 (Lost and Found)
6 (CTourist information)

In exercise B, students listen to three dialogues and determine where they would take place in the airport. In the first, a traveler is requesting a recommendation for a hotel at the Tourist information center. The second takes place at the airport's Lost and Found, where a traveler is asking about an address book that he may have misplaced at a telephone booth. In the third, a car rental agent is explaining the rental conditions to a traveler. Car rental agencies often offer rates that include unlimited mileage and various insurance options.

Answers
B

	Location	Enquiry
1	Tourist information	looking for a hotel
2	Lost and Found	looking for a personal item
3	Car rental	getting car rental information

● Extension Activity

After listening to the recordings, students can improvise what the speakers would say next.
OR
Have pairs of students choose one of the places in an airport. They should imagine a situation and write a short dialogue for it. For example, one of them could be working in a car rental agency and one of them is a traveler. After they practice the dialogue, they can perform it for the other students, who must guess where the dialogue takes place.

AUDIOSCRIPT
B
1
Woman Could you recommend a nice hotel near the convention center?
Man Try the Hyatt Regency. It's only one stop from the conference center by subway.
Woman Oh, great. That's perfect.
2
Man Has anyone turned in a small black leather address book?
Woman Do you have any idea where you might have left it?
Man I'm not sure exactly, but I think it must have been at the telephone booth, next to the newsstand.
3
Man The basic charge is $475 for one week.
Woman Does that include unlimited mileage?
Man Yes. But full insurance coverage is on top of that.

Vocabulary Builder

Aims
- TOEIC Part VI practice: error recognition
- Vocabulary development: adjectives and adverbs; suffixes
- Discussion: conferences

This section presents an extended word family exercise involving adjectives and adverbs. TOEIC® Parts V and VI often test a student's ability to recognize the correct adjectival or adverbial form of a word.

Students add suffixes to stem words to build adjectives in exercise A, then adverbs in exercise B. In exercise C, they practice Part VI error correction within a letter from the International Federation of Travel. The letter is inviting Ms. Cronofsky, an expert in global tourism, to be the keynote speaker at the annual conference.

Make sure students understand that adjectives usually come before a noun. Adverbs can come before or after a verb, or before a noun or past participle or an adjective. You may wish to point out the following vocabulary in exercise C.

Conference-related vocabulary: *keynote speaker to chair   panel discussions   participants*

Other: *ground-breaking   to shed new light on*

Answers

A
1. careless
2. primary (primal)
3. persuasive
4. reasonable
5. original
6. familiar
7. different
8. republican
9. electronic
10. passionate
11. accessible
12. observant

B
1. careless – carelessly
2. primary (primal) – primarily
3. persuasive – persuasively
4. reasonable – reasonably
5. original – originally
6. familiar – familiarly
7. different – differently
8. republican – –
9. electronic – electronically
10. passionate – passionately
11. accessible – –
12. observant – –

C
1. annual
2. conveniently
3. finally
4. complete
5. C
6. C
7. kindly
8. personally
9. C
10. certainly
11. Sincerely

⚠ TOEIC Tip

This tip points out some exceptions to the general rules presented in this section. Draw students' attention to the last example, in particular *hardly*. Students often mistake *hardly* as having the same meaning as the adjective/adverb *hard*. The meaning of the adjectival and adverbial forms of a word can radically differ. Other commonly confused words of this type are *nearly, pretty, fairly, barely, far*.

We **hardly** travel. = We **rarely** travel.
We **nearly** missed the train. = We **almost** missed the train (but we got on it).
The view is **pretty** unattractive. = The view is (**somewhat**) unattractive.
They are **fairly** strict about cancellations. = They are (**somewhat**) strict.
We **barely** have any space in this crowded hotel room. = We do **not** have **very much** space.
He took the photo **far** too close. = **much** too close

Viewpoint

Aims
- TOEIC Part VII practice: reading comprehension
- Topic: eco-tourism
- Discussion: alternative tourism

The Viewpoint establishes the context for the unit's Communication activity. The newspaper article presents an alternative type of tourism: eco-tourism.

Eco-tourism is one of the fastest-growing sectors of the international tourist industry. Travel agencies promote eco-tourism as environmentally- and socially-responsible travel. Eco-tourists visit relatively undisturbed natural areas in order to enjoy and appreciate nature and the local cultures and peoples. Eco-tourism projects share a four-point mission: to promote conservation of landscapes and cultures, to have low visitor impact, to actively involve local populations and to provide them with sustainable socio-economic benefits.

After students skim the article and answer the questions, you may want to point out the following adjectives and adverbs:

nonprofit   pristine   worthy causes
environmentally-conscious   socially-minded
passionate   lucrative
to experience something *firsthand*.

You may want to ask the following questions:

- What adjective means "deserving respect, admiration or support"? (worthy)
- Can you define "socially-minded" or "environmentally-conscious"?
- Which word is the opposite of "nonprofit"? (lucrative)
- What is a synonym of "pure", "unspoiled"? (pristine)

Answers
1. c
2. b

Ask students to read the cartoon. Ask:

- *Why are the animals running away?*
- *Are there any problems or drawbacks with eco-tourism?*
- *How does tourism negatively impact a place, either in nature or in the city?*

> **DISCUSSION**
> Have your students imagine how they might develop a volunteer vacation in their country, region, or local area. What specific environmental or social feature or issues in your country, region, or local area might interest people from other countries?
> - Preservation of unique cultures?
> - Animal protection?
> - Re-forestation?
> - Literacy?
> - The desire to learn foreign languages?

Grammar Check 2

> **Aims**
> - TOEIC Part V practice: incomplete sentences
> - Conditionals: 0–2
> - Negotiating phrases

Conditional forms appear frequently in Parts II–VII of the TOEIC®. You can introduce conditionals as two-part sentences that are most often *if …, then …* statements. (See the TOEIC Tip for other forms of the conditional.)

In exercise A, students should first think about the differences in meaning – in terms of probability – between the three grammatical forms. Which conditional form expresses an event that generally occurs, a future event that is likely to happen, or a future event that is not likely to happen? Then, draw students' attention to the two parts of each example and to the conditional phrases (beginning with *If, When*) that "condition" or determine the main actions. Then ask them to identify the verb tenses in both parts of the sentences. Point out the three verb tense combinations:

- present simple with present simple
- present simple with future
- past with *would* + present simple

You may want to consult the Grammar Reference with them to consolidate their understanding of these forms before doing exercise B.

> **Answers**
> **A**
> a future event that is not likely to happen 3
> a future event that is likely to happen 1
> a general state that is always true 2
> 1 present simple, future   1st conditional
> 2 present simple, present simple   0 conditional
> 3 past, *would* + present simple   2nd conditional

Exercise B provides Part V practice with 0–2nd conditionals within the context of a negotiation between a travel agent and a hotel manager. Point out that conditionals can take the form of statements and questions.

> ⚠ **TOEIC Tip**
> This tip introduces other words and phrases other than *if …, then* that express conditions. For extra practice, you can ask students to re-write sentences in exercise B by replacing the *if …, then* phrase with *provided that, as long as*. Also make sure they understand *unless* and *in case of*. These two conditional forms often appear on the TOEIC®.
> - *unless = except if*
>   We will go outside **unless** it rains. (… **except if** *it rains.*)
> - *in case of = if there is a*
>   **In case of emergency**, please call the manager. (**If there is** *an emergency, …*)

> **Answers**
> **B**
> 1 requested
> 2 includes
> 3 would/could you offer
> 4 will receive
> 5 occupy
> 6 will/'ll be able to
> 7 will/'ll give
> 8 doubled
> 9 would offer

Listening 3

> **Aims**
> - TOEIC Part II practice: question/response
> - Negotiation phrases

This section is a continuation of the negotiation in Grammar Check 2, but here students listen to four questions and must choose the correct response. After

Target Score

completing the exercise, ask students to identify the conditional phrases, sentences and questions in numbers 2–4.

Answers
1 b
2 b
3 a
4 b

AUDIOSCRIPT
1 Do you offer a shuttle service from the airport?
   A Yes, 24-hour room service is available.
   B We can arrange that for a small fee.
2 If one of our guests wanted to play golf, would you be able to arrange that for us?
   A Yes, they want to.
   B We could do that.
3 In the case of a cancellation, would you return our deposit?
   A As long as you notify us at least 48 hours in advance.
   B I'm sorry. No briefcases have been turned in.
4 What can we offer our clients if they're interested in eco-tourist activities?
   A We're very interested.
   B They can choose from a range of exciting options.

● Extension Activity
Brainstorm hotel vocabulary with the class:
   make a reservation
   book a room
   a single room
   a double room
   a suite
   a room with a view
   receptionist
   bellhop
   concierge
   front desk
   room service
   maid service
   check-out time
   wake-up call

Have students work in pairs. One student plays a traveler who needs to book a room in a hotel. The other student plays a hotel receptionist. Have them prepare dialogues using the vocabulary. They can then perform them for the rest of the class.

Communication

Aims
- Speaking practice: negotiating
- Skills focus: negotiations
- Discussion: eco-tourism

The negotiation involves an eco-tourism developer, an eco-tourism financial investor, a local community leader whose region will be the site of the eco-tourism development, and a non-governmental organization (NGO) representative, who is interested in seeing that a fair agreement is reached. Students should understand that their role cards indicate what terms they would *ideally* like to obtain. However, they will have to negotiate these terms and make compromises in order to reach an agreement since their colleagues' cards present different and conflicting information. Students should negotiate each item on the agenda. Tell them that they *must* come to an agreement by the end of the class period.

Give students 15 minutes or more to prepare their roles before they come together around the negotiating table. Remind them that the language of negotiation involves conditional phrases. The sentences in Grammar Check 2 provide good examples for the students to follow when preparing their Communication activity negotiations.

Here are some more examples:

- *If you allow too many visitors,* **then** *the site will be too commercial and it will lose all its pristine, natural beauty.*
- *If we received ten percent of the profits,* **then** *we would commit ourselves to a three-year contract.*
- *We will give you twenty percent of the profits* **provided** *that we limit the number of eco-tourists to thirty per month.*
- *We will sign a ten-year contract* **as long as** *we can have fifty percent of the profits.*

● Writing Practice
Create an eco-tourism brochure, promoting your ideal eco-tour. Describe all the adventures that your clients will be able to experience.

Review Test 3 Answer Key

Units 7–9

Listening Comprehension

Part I
Photographs

1 **D** The tables are outside on the *sidewalk* so (A) the people are not sitting indoors. (C) There is no *waiter* in the picture and (B) the restaurant terrace is not near a *pool*.

2 **A** The bank employee is a *teller* and she is *counting out* bills for a customer. (B) Although the individual counter space in a bank is called a *window*, the woman is not closing it. (C) The *teller* is a person, not a machine. (D) She's at the *counter*, but not *clearing* it.

3 **C** A *tour group* is posing for a *photographer* who is in front of them. (A) The people are not *applauding*, or watching a *performance*. (B) There are several tourists, not just one, and they are looking at the *photographer*, not at a *photograph*. (D) They *appear* in the *picture*, but are not *framing* one.

4 **D** The man is walking up some steps towards an *exchange booth*. (A) The booth, which is open, sells foreign *currency*, not company *stocks*. (B) There is no *vending machine*, although we can see a *vendor* or sales person. (C) The man is probably going to *change* money, but not his clothes.

5 **B** The man is hitting the ball back or *returning* the ball. (A) He's holding his *racket*, he has not *dropped* it. He's playing, not (C) *repairing the net* or (D) *waiting* for a court.

6 **D** The people are *standing* and waiting to recover their luggage at the *baggage claim*. (A) Their *plane* has arrived, so they cannot be *boarding*. (B) Their *bags* are already *packed*. (C) They are looking at the carousel, not at a *display*.

Part II
Questions and responses

7 **C** The question *How much?* is asking about the cost of the fare, not (A) the method of payment (*How*). (B) answers the question *How far?*

8 **B** The question *How long?* is asking for the length of time to *transfer* money into the *account*. (A) The idiomatic expression *to take something into account* means "to consider something", and is not related to banking. (C) *Fifteen minutes* answers the question *How long does it take?*, but refers to public transport, not to a *bank transfer*.

9 **B** The speaker asks if the person has finished reimbursing (*paying off*) a real estate loan or *mortgage* which still has *six months* left. (A) includes the words *pay* and *more*, which could be confused with *mortgage*. (C) repeats the verb *paid off*, which means "to be successful" in this context, not "to reimburse".

10 **A** (A) is the appropriate response to the request that an item be added to the check or bill. (B) has the distracter *built*, not *bill*. (C) refers to the name *Bill*, not to a *bill*.

11 **C** The question is an invitation or suggestion to *play tennis*, which is accepted in this response. (A) *I'd prefer* expresses a choice, but not one related to a sport. (B) uses the words *run into* and *tenant*, which sound similar to *running* and *tennis* in the question.

12 **A** The tag question seeks agreement with the opinion expressed about the *tour guide*. (B) refers to *guidelines* or instructions, not to a *tour guide*. (C) mentions the word *tour*, but not *guide*.

13 **C** The indirect question requests information about when the *next ferry* leaves, so the answer *right now* is appropriate. (A) uses the words *happen* and *sail* in a different context to the question. (B) includes the homonym *sale*, but not *sail*.

14 **A** The question asks about the normal opening hours of the *arts center*. (B) and (C) refer to *art supplies* and to an *arts center*.

Part III
Short conversations

15 **D** In response to the woman's question about *where to go swimming*, the man suggests *a lake at the state park*, which is located *west of town*, not (A) in the next town. (B) He mentions a *pool*, but says it is *closed*. (C) He does not answer her question about whether there is a *picnic area* at *the park*.

16 **C** The woman says that she will take the bus to the beach, so she will not (A) *take a taxi*, (B) *walk there*, nor (D) *go by bicycle*.

17 **A** The man is asking *a stockbroker* for professional advice about when to *sell* his *stocks*, not (B) *a technician* or (C) *a reporter*. (D) A *sales clerk sells* merchandise in a store, not on the stock market.

18 **C** The woman wants to know if the *hotel* provides a *shuttle* service *from the airport*. She wants to reserve *three places*, (A) not *three nights*. She does not mention (B) making a *dinner reservation* or (D) obtaining *flight information*.

19 **C** The speakers can only visit the museum *later today* since it (A/D) is closed on Wednesday, which is *tomorrow*. (B) They cannot visit in the *morning* because the only morning they have left is *tomorrow* morning, i.e. Wednesday morning.

20 **B** They are discussing where to *change money* when they *arrive*. (A) They are going to *take a taxi downtown*, not *to the station*. They are not going to (C) *exchange goods* or (D) *change their clothes*.

21 **C** The woman cannot pay by credit card because the *machine* in the store *isn't working*. There is no mention of a (A) *damaged* or (D) *expired* card. (B) There is no indication that the *nearest ATM (Automated Teller Machine) is out of order* although she offers to get cash from one.

Part IV
Short talks

22 **C** The announcement informs *air travelers* that a *flight* is ready to begin *boarding* prior to *departure*, so it wouldn't be made in (A) a *train station*. Only arriving passengers would be at (B) the *baggage claim*, and the *travelers* are not (D) *on board the plane* yet.

23 **C** The flight is *boarding* from Gate 3 which is where passengers are advised to *report* to. Other numbers given are (A) *forty-four* and (B) *thirty-two*, referring to rows of seats, and (D) flight *five seventeen*.

24 **B** The audio guide recording welcomes *visitors* to the *museum* and provides information about the *collections*, but is not reserved for use by (A) *tour guides* or (D) *gallery owners*. (C) Although the *instructions* mention the museum *staff*, the guide is not intended for *security staff*.

25 **D** The commentaries are about *paintings* in the *permanent collection*, not (C) *temporary exhibits*. The visit takes place in a museum, not in (B) a company or (A) around the city where *historical monuments* are located.

26 **B** The way to *set* the *volume* is by using the *arrow keys*, not (A) which is for *pause*. (C) and (D) refer to other procedures.

Reading Comprehension

Part V
Incomplete sentences

27 **D** In this context, *to take out* means "to obtain" (usually used for *money*, a *loan*). The other verbs have the following meanings: (A) "to assume control", (B) "to start a new activity", (C) "to leave the ground in an aircraft".

28 **C** Only an adverb can be used between a modal verb and the verb that follows it. (A) is either a verb or an adjective, (B) is a present participle (adjective) or a gerund (noun), and (D) is an adjective.

29 **C** The passive voice is formed by the auxiliary verb *to be* followed by the past participle (*-ed* form) of the main verb. (A) is a noun or an infinitive, (B) a present participle, and (D) the third-person singular form of the present tense, or a plural noun.

30 **D** The relative pronoun *which* is the only one that can refer to an object (*system*). (A) *What* is not a relative pronoun, (B) *whom* refers to a person, and (C) *where* refers to a place.

31 **D** The second conditional *would take* requires the past simple in the *if* clause. (A) and (B) are the present simple tense, and (C) is a present participle.

32 **A** The passive voice can only be completed by the past participle form of the verb. (B) is the present participle, (C) is the noun form, and (D) is the third-person singular form of the present simple.

33 **B** The preposition *by* indicates the degree or extent of the change. (A) indicates a position at a specific time, (C) indicates the initial position of a trend. (D) is incorrect.

34 **C** The sentence requires an adjective to describe the state or condition of the stadium which was full of people, or *crowded*. (A) cannot be used as an adjective. (B) is a noun or infinitive and (D) is a plural noun or the third-person of the verb *crowd*.

35 **C** *Should* can be used in place of *if* in a first conditional sentence. None of the other modal forms (A/B/D) can be used in this way.

36 **B** The context *will be provided* indicates that no *special equipment* is necessary. (A) and (C) both refer to requirements. (D) cannot be used before an infinitive with *to*.

Part VI
Error correction

37 **B** The adjective *interesting* is incorrect because it refers to the *program* rather than to the *passenger* who *was interested in the program*.
38 **A** The modal *can* is never followed by the infinitive with *to*.
39 **D** The phrasal verb *turn out* is incorrect in the context of this sentence. The correct verb is *turn down*, which means "to refuse" or "to reject an offer".
40 **A** The modal form *must have* is incorrect before the infinitive *to adjust*. The future modal form *will have* or the past form *have had* would both be appropriate.
41 **B** The pronoun *he* is incorrect and redundant after the relative pronoun *who,* which is the subject of the verb *led*.
42 **D** The word order is incorrect. In an indirect question form, the main verb should be in the affirmative.
43 **B** The future tense is incorrect in the *if* clause (introduced by *unless* here) of a first conditional sentence. The correct verb form is *builds*.
44 **D** The adjective *significant* is incorrect after the verb *risen*. The adverb *significantly* should be used.

Part VII
Reading

45 **D** The letter accompanies a customer's n*ew credit card*. (A) The previous card has been *replaced*, but not because it was lost. (B) The customer is not new because their *current card* is about to *expire*. (C) The customer's *PIN* has not changed and is not communicated in the letter.
46 **A** This is the only *transaction* that is not mentioned in the letter and therefore we can assume that it cannot be *carried out*. Customers can use their bank cards to do (B), (C) and (D).
47 **C** *About half* means "approximately 50 percent", which is the proportion of air travel forecast for Pacific Asia, not for (A), (B) or (D).
48 **C** The airport is located on *landfill* along the *Pacific Ocean*, which means it is *on the coast*, not (B) *inland*. It is *situated between* two capitals, not (A) *in the capital. Far from residential areas* is not (D) *in the suburbs*.
49 **A** The only possible problem mentioned in the article concerns *development potential*, so *getting sufficient business* may be difficult. No problems are mentioned in the article concerning either (B), (C) or (D).

50 **D** The cost of the project is not *low* since it has been estimated at $5.6 billion. Answers (A), (B) and (C) refer to outstanding or significant features of Incheon Airport.

AUDIOSCRIPT
Review Test 3 Units 7–9
Part I

1 A The people are sitting indoors.
   B Dinner is being served by the pool.
   C The waiter is taking their orders.
   D The tables are set up on the sidewalk.
2 A The teller's counting out the money.
   B The woman is closing the window.
   C The customer's using an automated teller machine.
   D She's clearing the counter.
3 A The audience is applauding the performance.
   B The tourist's looking at the photograph.
   C The tour group is facing the photographer.
   D They're framing a picture.
4 A The Stock Exchange is closed.
   B The vending machine doesn't give change.
   C The man's changing into his work clothes.
   D He's stepping up to the currency exchange booth.
5 A He's dropped the racket.
   B He's returning the ball.
   C He's repairing the net.
   D He's waiting for a court.
6 A The passengers are boarding the plane.
   B They're packing their bags.
   C The tourists are looking at the display.
   D They're standing in the baggage claim area.

Part II

7 How much is the one-way fare?
   A You can pay by credit card.
   B It's very far.
   C That depends when you travel.
8 Can you tell me how long it will take to transfer the funds to my account?
   A Yes. I've taken that into account.
   B You should be credited within the next three days.
   C It only takes fifteen minutes by subway.
9 Have you paid off your mortgage yet?
   A Yes, I know. I really should pay them more.
   B No. I still have six more months to go.
   C Our hard work has really paid off.
10 Could you put that on my bill, please?
   A Certainly. If you'd just sign the check.
   B Actually, I built it myself.
   C I'm sorry but Bill is not on duty today.

11 Are you going running this afternoon or would you rather play tennis?
   A I'd prefer not to arrive too late.
   B Unfortunately, we've run into a few problems with the new tenant.
   C Sounds like fun. I'll meet you down at the court, say, around three.
12 The tour guide was outstanding, don't you think?
   A Her comments were both entertaining and informative.
   B Yes. The guidelines seem to be very complete.
   C Well, I think the next tour starts in an hour.
13 Would you happen to know when the next ferry sails to the mainland?
   A It happened when they were sailing.
   B Our entire stock goes on sale tomorrow.
   C It's boarding right now from Dock 5.
14 Isn't the art center open on Mondays?
   A It usually is, but they're setting up a special exhibition this week.
   B Yes, the registration fee covers all art supplies.
   C No, I sent her the artwork on Tuesday.

Part III

15
Woman If we want to go swimming, where can we go?
Man Unfortunately the public pool is closed this month for repairs, but there's a real nice lake at the state park just a few miles west of town.
Woman A park with a lake? Perfect. They wouldn't have a picnic area too, would they?

16
Woman 1 How far is the beach from the hotel?
Woman 2 About a 20-minute walk or there's a bus that runs every half hour.
Woman 1 I think I'll wait for the bus. It's too hot to walk.

17
Man Do you think that I should sell now or would it be wiser to wait until the quarterly reports are published next month?
Woman I'd advise you to hold on to your stocks until the market stabilizes.
Man Fine. I'll count on you to place a sell order when the time is right.

18
Woman Does the hotel offer a courtesy shuttle from the airport?
Man Yes, it does. Pick-up is from Arrivals at Terminal 1.
Woman Could you reserve us three places for 4 o'clock?

19
Woman Maybe we could fit in a visit to the national museum before we catch our train tomorrow.
Man The guidebook says it's closed on Wednesdays so why don't we go this afternoon instead?
Woman Perfect. I can't wait to see their Italian collection.

20
Woman The first thing we should do when we arrive is to change some money.
Man OK. But we shouldn't do it at the station. They charge too much.
Woman I have enough to pay for a cab to get downtown. I'm sure we'll get a better exchange rate there.

21
Woman I'd like to pay for these items by credit card.
Man I'm afraid I can't accept credit cards today because our machine isn't working. Can you pay by cash or check?
Woman I don't have a checkbook with me, but I can go to the nearest ATM and take out some money.

Part IV

Questions 22 and 23:
Flight five-seventeen to Houston will now begin boarding from Gate three. As we will be boarding from the rear of the aircraft, we ask passengers sitting in rows forty-four to thirty-two to report to Gate three immediately. Please have your boarding passes ready to present to airline personnel. Passengers are reminded that federal regulations currently limit air travelers to one carry-on item per passenger.

Questions 24–26:
Welcome to the Museum of Modern Art and thank you for choosing our audio guide to accompany you on your visit. The audio guide provides commentaries about some of the paintings in our permanent collection. Before you start your visit, please listen carefully to the following instructions.

Beside selected paintings, there is a white sticker with a corresponding audio guide number. To hear a commentary, enter the number displayed next to the painting. If you wish to interrupt the recording, you can press the red pause button. To restart, push the green play button. Use the arrow keys to set the volume.

Should you have any questions about the audio guide or if you experience difficulties using it, please ask the staff to help you.

Before leaving the gallery, please remember to return your audio guide to our staff. We hope that you will enjoy the Museum collections.

10 Environment

Unit Focus • Weather • Natural Resources • Architecture

Unit overview

Unit components	Focus	TOEIC practice	Duration
Snapshot	Environments and living spaces	Part I	15–25 mins
Listening 1	The weather	Part IV	15–25 mins
Grammar Check 1	Indirect speech	Part VI	30–40 mins
Viewpoint	City limits	Part VII	40 mins
Grammar Check 2	Reporting verbs	Parts III/IV	10–20 mins
Listening 2	Reporting conversations	Part III	10–15 mins
Vocabulary Builder	*make* and *do*	Part V	15–25 mins
Listening 3	Living spaces for the future: Freedom Ship	Part II	15–25 mins
Communication	Winds of change		40 mins
		Total	3 hrs 10–4 hrs 15

Snapshot

Aims
- TOEIC Part I practice: picture analysis
- Vocabulary development: environments/living spaces
- Discussion

The pictures in this section present four different environments: rural, urban, industrial and residential, which familiarize students with a particular type of picture that is often used in Part I: landscapes, buildings and other exterior spaces. Students should identify the elements in the picture and describe their positions in relation to each other. For exercise A, a list of suggested key words is provided opposite. The photos can also be used as a basis for a short discussion after students have completed listening exercise B. They can reflect on how the different environments shown in the pictures might affect the lifestyles of people living there. Students can also compare these environments with the places where they live and point out some of the differences.

Picture descriptions
Picture 1
The picture shows an area of *farmland* where some *cattle* are *grazing*. In the background, we can see a *petroleum refinery* with *industrial installations* and a tower with flames coming out.

Picture 2
This is a picture of a *residential street* in Argentina. It shows a group of small *homes* and *apartments*. The *houses* are built with *wood* and have two *stories*. The house in the center of the picture has two *balconies*, one above the other.

Picture 3
The picture is of a city center. A *multi-lane freeway* can be seen in the foreground, with an *overpass* leading towards the *high-rise buildings* in the background.

Picture 4
The picture shows a small *one-story cottage* on the *coast*. The building is isolated and there are no other *dwellings*/habitations nearby. There is very little vegetation and the *land* is not cultivated.

Answers
A
Suggested vocabulary

Picture 1	cattle, field, refinery, farmland, flame, smoke
Picture 2	house, balcony, window, rooftop, wall, story, facade
Picture 3	skyscraper, freeway, traffic, vehicle, building
Picture 4	cottage, coast, coastline, shore, sea, wave

B	
Statement A	inaccurate
Statement B	accurate
Statement C	accurate
Statement D	inaccurate
Statement E	accurate
Statement F	inaccurate
Statement G	inaccurate
Statement H	accurate

AUDIOSCRIPT

B
A Palm trees grow along the coast.
B The cottage overlooks the sea.
C The freeway runs past the skyscrapers.
D The high-rise buildings are on opposite sides of the river.
E Cattle are grazing in a field next to the refinery.
F The farmland is being plowed for planting.
G The laundry is hanging from the balcony.
H The houses are only three stories high.

> ⚠ **TOEIC Tip**
> This tip focuses on how Part I statements are sometimes worded to distract attention from the correct answer by including statements that are partially true. Students should be aware of this and should expect to hear potentially confusing statements to choose from on this part of the test.

The words that are referred to in a different context from the one shown in the pictures are the following:
A coast
D high-rise buildings
F farmland
G balcony

Listening 1

> **Aims**
> - TOEIC Part IV practice: short talks
> - Vocabulary development/acquisition
> - Discussion

Exercixses A and B provide practice with Part IV listening and introduce the vocabulary related to meteorology and weather forecasting. The selection of weather symbols presented in B is not exhaustive. You may want to add to this by referring to other terms and to other adjectives that could be used to talk about weather conditions such as:

clear skies
rainy periods
light rain
drizzle
thick fog
mist
light/moderate winds
heavy snow
snowstorms
high/low pressure
high/low temperatures
warm/cold spell

In Exercise C, you may wish to draw attention to the following vocabulary items:

prolonged   mild   weather front   weather office   gusting

Point out that temperatures can be referred to in either Celsius/Centigrade or Fahrenheit degrees.

> **DISCUSSION**
> This section can be used to activate the vocabulary by asking students to talk about the weather in their home countries.

● **Extension Activity**
You may wish to bring in a selection of weather maps, clipped from newspapers (ideally these maps should be for different seasons). You can distribute these to students in pairs and ask them to prepare a transcript of the weather report for a particular region. Alternatively, this can be done as a homework assignment.

> **Answers**
> **B**
> 2 bright sunshine
> 4 overcast skies
> 1 sunny intervals with scattered showers
> 5 heavy rain
> 6 fog
> 3 thunderstorms
> 9 strong winds
> 7 moderate snowfall
> 8 high pressure
> 10 mild temperatures
> **C**
> 1 heavy rain
> 2 snow
> 3 46°
> 4 strong winds
> 5 thunderstorms
> 6 bright sunshine

Unit 10 | Environment

AUDIOSCRIPT
C
Welcome to the European weather forecast for Friday September 7th. Well, there's certainly been a lot of wet weather around for most of northern Europe over the last few days and that looks set to continue over the weekend. We have an area of low pressure moving across from southern England into continental Europe and that's bringing some very heavy rain indeed. So, much of Germany and France can expect prolonged rain during today and tomorrow which will be falling as light snow at higher altitudes as it moves through to the Swiss Alps. Temperatures quite mild, but slightly below the seasonal average; around 46 degrees in London, but definitely a little warmer in Brussels with 50 degrees. That weather front is also bringing strong winds with it and the weather office has issued a storm warning for western Austria where winds are expected to be gusting at over 120 kilometers per hour. A very different picture in southern Europe where high pressure over central Spain and Portugal is creating some unusually warm weather for this time of year. Bright sunshine over most of the Mediterranean with temperatures well up in the seventies in Lisbon and an expected high of 75 degrees in Barcelona later today. Moving further east to Turkey. Mostly overcast in this part of the continent, but there is a risk of some thunderstorms around the Black Sea coast.

Grammar Check 1

Aims
- TOEIC Part VI practice: error recognition
- Review of indirect speech

This grammar section presents the rules for the use of indirect speech. Reported statements are featured on all parts of the test (except Part I). In exercise C, students practice identifying the most common forms of reporting errors that are featured in Part VI error recognition. The TOEIC Tip reinforces student awareness of these types of errors. Before students complete the Active Practice section, you may need to give them assistance with the preparation of appropriate questions. If necessary, they can refer to the Grammar Reference section on page 129 of the Student's Book for help with question forms.

Answers
C
1 said/C
2 C/would be
3 told/C
4 (no correction necessary)
5 C/had
6 asked/C

ACTIVE PRACTICE
Some suggested questions for the questionnaire are given below.
- *Do you believe that climate change will have a direct effect on your life? (If so, how?)*
- *Have you already made any modifications to your lifestyle or behavior that could help to reduce global warming? (If so, what?)*
- *What measures would you be willing to take to reduce the threat?*
- *Would you be prepared to pay more for gas or for air travel?*
- *What factors do you think are mainly responsible for climate change?*
- *What do you think will be the most serious consequences of climate change?*

Viewpoint

Aims
- TOEIC Part VII practice: reading comprehension
- Discussion: urban sprawl

This newspaper article presents a Part VII reading text which summarizes the results of a WorldWatch survey of the impact of urban sprawl on the quality of life. It draws attention to the deterioration of living conditions in urban environments due to urbanization and the increase in vehicle traffic and car-related infrastructures such as surfaced roads and parking lots. WorldWatch is a non-profit organization that publishes research on a number of environmental issues. You can obtain further information about WorldWatch from their website at www.worldwatch.org

For the discussion question in A, focus students' attention on how the capital cities of their countries have evolved in recent years. You will be able to refer back to this at the end of the Viewpoint section by asking students if they consider that the problems mentioned in the article are also present in their capital cities. The final question in the Discussion section focuses on the complex issue of how to find solutions to improve the lives of city dwellers. You can extend this discussion into a debate and ask students to present the arguments for and against having car-less cities.

Once students have completed exercise B, focus attention on the word *sprawling* in the last sentence of the first paragraph. Ask them if they know the meaning of this word. Do they think it is an important word to know in order to understand the sentence? You can then write on the board the four definitions below, taken from the *Cambridge Advanced Learners Dictionary*, or have students look up the word *sprawl* in their own dictionaries.

1. sprawl (CITY) *v* [I usually + adv or prep] *disapproving* (esp. of a city) to cover a large area of land with buildings which have been added at different times so that it looks untidy
2. sprawl *n* [C usually sing] *disapproving*
   the **urban** sprawl *of south Florida*
3. sprawl (BODY) *v* [I] *disapproving*
   to spread the arms and legs out carelessly and untidily while sitting or lying down
4. sprawl *n* [U] *disapproving*

Ask students to identify the definition that is appropriate in the context of the sentence. If you have dictionaries available, you may want to do further dictionary work as preparation for the reading. You can do this by giving one of the following words to a pair or group of students:

concern   shift   ahead   roughly
transit   dedicated

Students should check the meaning of the word they have been given, in the dictionary. Each group can then present the various possible definitions for their word. The class as a whole has to decide which definition is the most appropriate in the context of the article.

Other vocabulary items that students may find difficult could include the following terms:

clogged   cut short   deprive   dwellers
de-emphasizing   outstanding   busways
zoned   thoroughfares

Answers
B
1. global warming
2. urban areas
3. road transportation
4. carbon emissions
5. new technologies
6. air pollution
7. parking lots
8. recent research
9. traffic accidents
10. physical exercise

C
1. wind turbines, new technology, urban design, parks
2. air pollution, traffic accidents, illness, clogged roads, deteriorating neighborhoods

D
1. 1 million
2. China
3. 1 billion tons of carbon emissions will be released.
4. Curitiba

The following comprehension questions provide additional practice for Part VII.
- Which country will have a population of over 752 million people?
- How many lives are lost every year as a result of air pollution?

Grammar Check 2

Aims
- TOEIC Parts III/IV practice
- Review of reporting verbs

This grammar section presents another aspect of indirect speech: the use of reporting verbs. This is a complex area of grammar, but one that is particularly important for the test as it is often featured in questions in Part III and in Part IV. It is important that students understand that when people are reporting what has been said, they tend to paraphrase rather than give the exact words that were used by the speaker or speakers. In terms of grammar, the difficulty is that reporting verbs are not all used in the same way. The main differences in usage are outlined below:

- verbs followed by either *that* or *to*:
  to admit   to agree   to claim
  to promise   to warn

- verbs followed by either *that* or a preposition:
  to confirm   to disagree (with)
  to recommend   to announce
  to complain (about) to predict

- verbs that can be followed by a direct object (*you/him/us/them*):
  to admit   to advise   to agree
  to claim   to instruct   to invite
  to promise to recommend   to warn

Answers
Type a: admit to, (dis)agree with, apologize for, complain about
Type b: advise, (dis)agree, claim. instruct, invite, promise, propose
Type c: admit, advise, (dis)agree, announce, claim, complain, confirm, predict, promise, warn, propose

Unit 10 | Environment

Listening 2

Aims
- TOEIC Part III practice: short conversations
- Vocabulary development: reporting verbs

This Part III listening activity focuses on how conversations are summarized by using verbs of this type.

Answers
1 The man warned/predicted that the bus drivers would go on strike.
2 The woman invited the man to join the car pool.
3 The man advised the woman to take some warm clothing.
4 The woman apologized to the man for canceling the appointment and suggested they fix another.

AUDIOSCRIPT
1
Man I've just been looking at the figures that the mayor announced for the new city budget.
Woman I heard the interview he gave on the radio. I can't believe that he's going to cut the mass transit budget again.
Man Me neither. He's really asking for trouble by doing that. I wouldn't be surprised if the bus drivers decide to go on strike.

2
Woman Would you be interested in joining our car pool?
Man Why not? Sounds like a good idea. How does it work?
Woman Well, we each take turns driving. So you'd only have to use your car once a week.

3
Man Are you going to be home this weekend?
Woman No actually, we're planning to go hiking, up in the mountains.
Man Well, make sure you take some warm clothing. The weather report said there will be frost on Saturday.

4
Woman I'm calling about the appointment that we made for you to visit the three-bedroom apartment on Central Avenue.
Man That's tomorrow at ten, right?
Woman Well, I'm very sorry but I'm afraid we'll have to switch that to another date. The owner has just told me he won't be available then.

Vocabulary Builder

Aims
- TOEIC Part V practice: incomplete sentences
- Review of idiomatic expressions (II): *make* and *do*

The vocabulary exercise explains the idiomatic uses of the verbs *do* and *make* and presents a selection of the collocations that are used with the two verbs.

You may wish to point out the following vocabulary in exercise B:

array   sensors   devices   vacuum cleaning
robotic servants   home operating system
smart   utensils   sink

If you have time, you may want to finish by asking students to describe the types of household chores that they do at home. Do they use machines to help them to do these? Would they like to live in a fully automated house?

Answers
A
1 make
2 do
3 do
4 make
5 do (carry out), make (create)
6 make
7 do
8 make
9 do (also make a deal)
10 make
11 make
12 make

B
1 make a change/difference
2 making use
3 do, work
4 make, easy, possible
5 doing, housework, cooking, ironing
6 doing, programming
7 do, rest
8 doing, damage
9 do, shopping
10 make, most
11 made, miscalculations

Listening 3

Aims
- TOEIC Part II practice: question/response
- Listening for specific information
- Discussion

This section presents a listening activity where students have to complete the question forms, then match these with the appropriate responses on the audioscript. The subject of the recording is the Freedom Ship, a project to build a floating city where people will be able to live outside national territorial waters.

Answers
A
1 When 2 What 3 How much/What 4 What
5 Which/How many 6 How 7 What 8 How many
B
1 B 2 G 3 F 4 H 5 C 6 D 7 E 8 A

AUDIOSCRIPT
B
A Well, there should be about 100,000 on board at any one time but only 40,000 of them will actually be residents. There will also be a crew of 20,000 and the rest will be visitors.

B The construction phase hasn't actually started yet. But some specialists are suggesting that it could be launched within three years.

C Well there's really no limit on where it can go. So probably it will travel regularly around the world, calling at many of the major cities with seaports.

D It'll have a fully operational airport on the top deck – so planes will be able to fly in and out rather like on an aircraft carrier. And there will also be a marina so that smaller ships can dock with it.

E It's been designed as a city not just as a ship. So you'll have a full range of commercial activities going on inside with trade centers and so on – just like in any normal city. And, of course, you'll have schools for the children who are living on board and a fully equipped hospital.

F There's a whole selection of real estate investment opportunities. These range from luxury suites to much more simple "living units". The starting price should be about 180,000 dollars and the top price will probably be around 40 million dollars.

G It's a project that's attracting a lot of interest from potential residents, and that group includes not only people who are looking for a secure environment for their retirement but also business people who are interested in living and working in a city that's not part of any one nation.

H I think that convenience is certainly one of the main factors. The idea is that this will be like a compact city and you'll have everything you need within easy reach. So there will be no need to take public transportation and, of course, the weather is another factor. The ship will be able to position itself in warm weather all year round – and that's certainly a major advantage.

DISCUSSION
The question asks students to give their reactions to this project and to talk about whether or not they would choose to live in an environment like this. You may want to extend this activity and include discussion of *gated communities*. These are residential areas with restricted access for non-residents. You can ask students whether they think it is acceptable for groups of affluent people to live together in relative luxury with little or no contact with other sections of the population.

Communication

Aim
- Speaking practice: presenting arguments and counter-arguments

The Communication activity focuses on a case study of the project to build a wind farm off the coast of Cape Cod in New England. You may want to make a brief introduction to the subject by referring to other projects to develop wind energy. Ask students if they know of projects to develop this kind of alternative energy supply in their countries. How would they react if a wind farm were proposed for the area where they live? You may wish to point out the following vocabulary items:

maritime heritage   dunes   sought-after   offshore

● Writing Practice
Students can prepare a short article for the local newspaper, summarizing the points of view that were expressed at the discussion forum.

OR

They can present a written summary of what happened, to be included in a newsletter that will be communicated to the supporters of the group that they represented during the discussion.

11 Health

Unit **Focus** · Nutrition · Medicine · Fitness

Unit overview

Unit components	Focus	TOEIC practice	Duration
Snapshot	Body positions	Part I	15–20 mins
Grammar Check 1	Gerund and infinitive forms	Part VI	20–30 mins
Listening 1	Health professionals	Part III	25–35 mins
Viewpoint	Living the Longer Life	Part VII	25–35 mins
Listening 2	The United Okinawa Association: radio announcement	Part IV	20–30 mins
Grammar Check 2	Third conditional	Part V	25–35 mins
Listening 3	Giving advice/making suggestions	Part II	20–30 mins
Vocabulary Builder	Three-part phrasal verbs	Part V	20–30 mins
Communication	Keeping the company healthy		40 mins
		Total	3 hrs 30–4 hrs 45

Snapshot

Aims
- TOEIC Part I practice: identifying actions and body positions in pictures
- Vocabulary: body movements and positions

The pictures present four scenes related to health and the medical profession: a doctor examining a patient, relief workers giving food to a woman, three people practicing tai chi (he ancient art of Chinese exercise), and physical therapist working with a patient. Some TOEIC® Part I photos require students to be able to identify body positions and movements. A correct statement on Part I could be: *The worker is bending over to pick up the tool.* In this Snapshot, students are asked to identify the actions and body positions from the list provided. You might also want to teach other verbs that describe body positions and movements: *lifting, folding, twisting, turning, raising, pointing, touching, grasping, handing,* etc.

Picture descriptions
Picture 1
In this picture, a *doctor* is examining a *patient*. They are in an *examination room* in a *medical clinic* or in a *hospital*. The doctor is *leaning* forward and holding a *stethoscope* to the patient's *chest* in order to listen to his *heartbeat* and *breathing*. The doctor is wearing a white medical coat and glasses. The patient is sitting, looking downwards with his shirt unbuttoned.

Picture 2
In this picture, there are several *relief aid workers* who are all wearing white shirts with red crosses on them. They are *distributing* food from the back of a vehicle. One relief worker is *handing* food to a woman who is *bending* over slightly and looking down at what she has *in her hands*. She is *carrying* in her arms several loaves of bread.

Picture 3
In this picture, three people are *standing* in the middle of a field. They are *practicing* the ancient Chinese art of tai chi. They are all *balancing* on one leg. The left leg is firmly on the ground and the right leg is slightly *raised*. Their right arms are *extended* forward while the left arms are raised, but *bent* at the *elbow*. They are all looking forward. Behind them are several large bales of hay and *a line of trees*.

Picture 4
This picture shows a scene in a *physical therapy* room. In the *foreground*, a *physical therapist* is *kneeling* next to a man who is *lying* on his *back* with his *arms folded* behind his head. The therapist is *lifting* the man's left leg in order

95

to stretch the muscles and to develop *flexibility* in the *joints*. Behind them, another therapist is sitting and talking to another patient who is also lying on his back on a mat. Behind them, a man is *exercising, pulling* himself up on a bar.

Answers
A
Suggested vocabulary

Picture 1	sitting, holding, placing
Picture 2	clutching, holding, standing, handing
Picture 3	balancing, standing, lifting
Picture 4	lying down, kneeling, stretching, bending, lifting, holding, bracing

Possible statements
Picture 1
The patient is sitting in the examination room.
The doctor is holding a stethoscope to the patient's chest.
He is standing next to the patient.

Picture 2
The worker is handing the woman some food.
She is holding/clutching/carrying the food.
She is leaning forward and looking down at what she is carrying.

Picture 3
They're balancing on one leg.
They're standing in a field.
They're raising their arms.
They're lifting one leg.
They're stretching out their arms.

Picture 4
The man is lying on the mat.
The man's arms are folded behind his head.
The therapist is kneeling next to him.
The therapist is stretching the patient's leg.
He's holding/lifting/bracing the man's leg.
B
1   F
2   H
3   E
4   B

AUDIOSCRIPT
B
A   They're exercising on the beach.
B   He's kneeling next to the patient.
C   They're lifting weights in the gym.
D   The physical therapist is stretching the patient's arm.
E   They're balancing on one leg.
F   The doctor's examining the man's chest.
G   They're holding hands.
H   The relief workers are handing out food.

Grammar Check 1

Aims
- TOEIC Part VI practice: error recogntion
- Gerund and infinitive forms

Grammar Check 1 provides practice with gerund and infinitives, which is commonly tested on the TOEIC® and is particularly challenging for students because there are no set rules to follow. This means that students must memorize the verbs that take a gerund and those that are followed by an infinitive.

The Part VI error recognition exercise is presented in the context of a promotional letter from a health club. The letter introduces the services and advantages of the club in order to solicit new memberships. Private health clubs offer a wide range of sports and exercise facilities for paying members. Some universities and companies provide discounts on memberships for their students and employees.

Students can work in pairs for exercise B in order to prepare them for the Active Practice section afterwards.

ACTIVE PRACTICE
Students can work in pairs: one of them works at the Madison Health and Racquet Club as a membership sales representative. The other is interested in joining the club. The sales rep could interview the potential club member about his or her sports and exercise interests.

⚠ TOEIC Tip
This tip draws students' attention to the use of gerunds after prepositions. The TOEIC® tests this item in Parts V and VI. For higher-level students, you can extend the grammar explanation by teaching the verbs that can take either, but have different meanings: *stop, try, forget, remember, regret*. See the Grammar Reference section for further information.

> **Answers**
> **A**
> 1 gerund
> 2 infinitive
>
> **B**
> 1 playing
> 2 to attend
> 3 becoming
> 4 taking
> 5 being
> 6 to join
> 7 C
> 8 waiting
> 9 to become
> 10 to extend
> 11 C
>
> **TOEIC Tip answers**
> 1 without having to
> 2 of receiving
> 3 to hearing

Listening 1

Aims
- TOEIC Part III practice: short conversations
- Listening for keywords

Students might find the following dialogues challenging if they are not familiar with any basic medical vocabulary in English. In exercise A, have students brainstorm word lists for several of the listed health professionals:

Dentist: *teeth, molars, wisdom teeth, check-up, teeth cleaning, fillings, cavities,* etc.

Pharmacist: *pharmacy, drugstore, drugs, medicines, medications, prescription, pills, tablets, syrups, to fill a prescription, refills,* etc.

Veterinarian: *animal doctor, pets, check-ups, vaccinations, shots,* etc.

Exercise B has them focus on the keywords that give clues to the context of the recorded conversations.

Short conversations
1 This conversation occurs between a dentist and his patient in a dentist's office. The patient has come for an annual check-up and teeth cleaning. The patient also mentions that one molar has been giving him pain. The doctor suggests taking an X-ray.
2 This conversation occurs between a doctor and a patient who are discussing when the patient had his last complete physical (medical check-up/general health examination).
3 This conversation occurs in a pharmacy between a client who would like a prescription filled and the pharmacist. The pharmacist asks whether the client would like brand name medicine or less expensive generic drugs. Note that medicine is often sold under the brand name of the pharmaceutical company that has produced the drug or as a less expensive "generic", whereby the chemical composition of the drug is the same, but the producer is not listed and therefore does not have to spend money on advertising.
4 This conversation occurs between a patient and an eye doctor (optometrist). The patient is receiving "corrective lenses" in order to read more easily in the evening. "Corrective lenses" could be glasses or contact lenses.
5 This conversation occurs between a health insurance advisor in a company and a new employee. The advisor explains what the company's health insurance benefits package covers. The new employee asks whether prescription drugs will be covered. Note that in some countries, the federal government does not offer medical and dental insurance. Companies can offer their employees medical insurance as part of their benefit packages.

Answers
B

	Keywords	Person	Place
1	check-up cleaning molars chew X-ray	dentist	dentist's office
2	complete physical see a doctor check-up	doctor	doctor's office
3	prescription filled medicines drugs prescribed	pharmacist	pharmacy
4	corrective lenses eyesight prescription vision read	eye doctor optometrist	optometrist's office
5	health insurance benefits package covers medical and dental policy reimburses	health insurance advisor	in a company

Target Score

AUDIOSCRIPT

B

1
Man 1 So you're in for your annual check-up and cleaning, is that it?
Man 2 Yes. And I was wondering if you could take a look at one of my molars on the top left. It's been sore lately, especially when I chew.
Man 1 OK, I'll have a look and then take an X-ray. Open wide, please.

2
Woman Do you remember when you had your last complete physical?
Man Actually, it was some time ago. Eight, maybe, ten years.
Woman You know, even if you're in good health, you should see a doctor every two or three years for a check-up.

3
Man Hi. I'd like to have this prescription filled, please.
Woman Certainly. Which would you prefer: brand name medicine or the less expensive generic drugs?
Man Hmm. I think I'll go with the brand name, since that's what my doctor's prescribed.

4
Man 1 Will I have to wear corrective lenses all the time?
Man 2 No, no. You have very good eyesight. This prescription will correct your vision so that you can read comfortably at night.
Man 1 That's good news.

5
Woman 1 The health insurance benefits package we offer our employees includes full medical and dental coverage.
Woman 2 Will my policy include prescription drugs?
Woman 1 Yes, it does. It reimburses 90% of all doctor-prescribed medications.

Viewpoint

Aims
- TOEIC Part VII practice: reading comprehension
- Vocabulary: diet; fitness; longevity
- Discussion: healthy lifestyles

In this Viewpoint activity, students read an article, then work on four presentation slides that have incorrect and missing information. The activity provides a good opportunity to compare and contrast different cultural approaches to health, exercise, and eating habits. You may want to introduce the general lead-in question in the Student's Book as pairwork. Students can work in pairs to draw up a list of elements that they think are important for a healthy lifestyle before reading the article. Ask them to consider issues such as eating habits, diet, nutrition, exercise, work, rest, relaxation, sleep, regular visits to the doctor, etc. Pairs can also correct and complete the presentation slides in exercise B. Here is some useful vocabulary:

generation   exercise   a sharp mind   centenarian
consumption   rigorous activity   low-stress lifestyle
to endanger   to urge   to return to your roots
longevity   a warning   local dishes   to be scorned
a treasure   old folks

● Extension Activity
You can have students do mini-presentations. Students can either use the corrected slides in the Student's Book to do a mini-presentation of the Okinawa community and dietary practices.
OR
They can make their own slides and do a mini-presentation about the dietary practices or another health-related issue within their own cultures.

Answers
B
Slide 1   i   wrong – <u>low</u> levels of cholesterol
Slide 2   i   wrong – tofu
Slide 3   ii   wrong – <u>more</u> stressful
         iii   wrong – <u>less</u> exercise
Slide 4

Suggested answers
i   newspapers are providing advice for healthier living
ii   schools are introducing traditional foods
iii   doctors and the government are encouraging people to return to the traditional lifestyle

Listening 2

Aims
- TOEIC Part IV practice: short talks
- Listening for specific information

Listening 2 follows on from the Viewpoint article. The listening is a press release, announcing a book presentation by the authors of *The Okinawa Diet Plan*. Have students scan the invitation before listening to the radio announcement and completing the missing information. Here is some useful vocabulary:
to entitle   hardback copy   seating is limited

Unit 11 | Health

> **Answers**
> 1 authors
> 2 recipes
> 3 community center
> 4 6 p.m.
> 5 9 p.m.
> 6 40

AUDIOSCRIPT
Now for those of you who may be thinking that it's high time to switch to a new healthier diet, we've got just the thing. On May 15th, the United Okinawa Association is organizing a special evening event where you'll have the opportunity to meet two of the authors of the best-selling *Okinawa Diet Plan*. Doctors Craig and Bradley Willcox will be giving a short presentation of their research on the Okinawa community and explaining what makes it so unique. Don't forget, that's May 15th from six to nine at the community center in Waikiki. Seating is limited so you'd better book early. Tickets to the event are on sale for 40 dollars and that includes the price of your personal hardcover copy of the book that could help you to get leaner, live longer and never feel hungry. Sample Okinawan recipes will be available for tasting after the presentation. For further information about the event and to make a telephone reservation, call 215-658-4321.

Grammar Check 2

> **Aims**
> - TOEIC Part V practice: incomplete sentences
> - Third conditional

This section reviews the third conditional within the context of folk medicines and remedies that were used in the past. The central idea here is to have the students imagine the following context (expressed using the third conditional). You should either read the following question to the class or write it on the board.

If you had lived in the past and had suffered from a particular ailment, such as a fever, what remedy would you have used?

Remind students that conditionals are most often expressed in two parts (*If ..., then ...*). Also draw students' attention to the past perfect form of *have* (*had had*), which is frequently tested on the TOEIC®.
In A, students identify the verb forms in both parts of example sentences. In B, students complete a Part V "fill in the blank" using the third conditional.

In pairs, students can ask each other questions using the information in the Folk Medicine quiz. Make sure they practice constructing third conditional sentences. For example:
Student 1: *If you had had a fever, what remedy would you have used?*
Student 2: *If I had had a fever, I would have applied an ice-pack.*

● Extension Activity
Here are two additional ailments and their folk remedies. Ask students to imagine what remedy someone in the past would have used if he or she had had a toothache or a burn?

Ailment **Remedy**
Toothache   a chew tobacco
            b rub your tooth with snakeskin
            c apply a mixture of alcohol and chloroform
Burns   a rub with cold tea
            b apply flour
            c pour on cold water

> **DISCUSSION**
> Ask students if they know of any local traditional folk remedies that people used in the past. You can lead this into a discussion of old remedies versus modern medicine.

> **Answers**
> **A**
> 1 first part: past perfect; second part: third conditional
> 2 first part: third conditional; second part: past perfect
> **B**
> 1 had lived
> 2 wouldn't have had
> 3 wouldn't have been able
> 4 would have had
> 5 would have done
> 6 would have worked
> 7 wouldn't have been

Listening 3

> **Aims**
> - TOEIC Part II practice: question/response
> - Giving advice and making suggestions

In this exercise, students practice identifying advice and suggestion phrases in the context of a health

99

organization's meeting, scheduled in order to plan a vaccination week campaign.

Ask students if they know what the words *vaccinations* and *immunization* mean. They need to understand that these words refer to protective shots, injections, or inoculations that give people resistance to certain diseases, such as polio, etc. Health organizations around the world plan annual vaccination campaigns to vaccinate people, particularly children.

Have students study the examples. You may want to offer a few examples: *Why don't we practice making suggestions? How about practicing a few suggestion phrases with a partner?* It is important that students understand that these phrases are idiomatic and they indicate that the speaker is making a suggestion. The TOEIC Tip box is particularly helpful here.

Have students read through the memorandum. Before beginning the listening, you may want to do some Part VII reading comprehension practice by asking them some questions.

- *What is the purpose of this memo?*
- *Why is Saskia Lindstrom calling a meeting?*
- *When is the meeting scheduled?*
- *Which item on the agenda would include advertising?*

After students have matched the listening extracts with the agenda items, ask them to identify the suggestion phrases in each extract.

a   *How about targeting …?*
b   *We should provide/And how about developing …?*
c   *We ought to approach/Why don't we approach …?*
d   *How should we* (asking for advice)/ *Why don't we …?*
e   *What about posters?/Couldn't we also get …?*

These expressions provide useful language as students will practice giving advice and making suggestions in the Communication activity at the end of the unit.

Answers	
A	
I	A
II	C
III	B
IV	E
V	D

AUDIOSCRIPT
A
Woman How about targeting schools?
Man Excellent idea. We can be sure that every child in school would have the opportunity to be vaccinated.
B
Man We should provide mayors with information that will help them support vaccination programs for their communities.
Woman I agree. And how about developing neighborhood vaccination workshops to involve people on a local level?
C
Man We ought to approach companies that market children's products.
Woman That's not a bad idea. Why not approach the President's wife, too? She's a great supporter of public health issues.
D
Man 1 How should we evaluate the success of the Vaccination Week campaign?
Man 2 Why don't we conduct a public awareness survey afterward?
E
Woman 1 What about posters? They're inexpensive and can be widely distributed.
Woman 2 Great idea. Couldn't we also get national television stations to donate air time for our commercials?

Vocabulary Builder

Aims
- Phrasal verbs (II): three-part
- Dictionary practice

Phrasal verbs are used throughout the TOEIC® and can appear in Part V and VI questions. This section familiarizes students with phrasal verbs that contain three parts. In this exercise, students read a paragraph presenting on-the-job physical therapy. Many industries that involve physical labor are incorporating preventive measures to reduce job-related injuries. Begin by asking students: *What can companies do to prevent work-related injuries?*

Have students read the paragraph and ask them to define the six underlined terms based on context clues within the sentences. Ask them to give a synonym for each word. They should then match the words with the correct dictionary definition. You can ask them to identify two two-part phrasal verbs in the paragraph:

to look into = to investigate
to cut down = to reduce

Ask students if they know of any other three-part phrasal verbs that begin with *to get*.

Suggested answers
get away with something/doing something = to do something without assuming the consequences
get back into something = to begin to do an activity that you used to do
get back to somebody = to re-contact someone; to call them back
get back to something = to resume doing something that you were doing after a break
get down to something/doing something = to start doing something; to begin a project
get out of something/doing something = to escape from or avoid doing something
get something over with = to finish something

Students can research more three-part phrasal verbs with *come, run, make, take, go*. Have them consult the *Cambridge International Dictionary of Phrasal Verbs* on-line: http://dictionary.cambridge.org/default.asp?dict=P

You may also want to teach the additional health-related vocabulary in the article. Ask students to identify the word that refers to:
- a health professional who treats job-related injuries (*occupational therapist*)
- absence from work because of illness (*sick leave*)
- an injury to a part of the body caused by overuse (*strain-related injury*)

Other vocabulary items that can be taught in this way are *physical condition, strenuous job requirements, stretching program, injury and compensation claims, injury-free*.

Answers
1 e
2 f
3 a
4 d
5 c
6 b

Communication

Aim
- Speaking practice: presenting findings; decision-making

In this activity, students are part of a planning team that must design a new health and wellness program for their company, MacroMix.

Before students break down into planning teams, it might be helpful if you lead a brief group review session of the health topics and areas covered in the unit. This provides a review of useful vocabulary and helps students to generate ideas in preparation for the activity:
- exercise facilities
- nutritional programs
- vaccinations and possibly annual flu shots
- on-the-job stretching and physical therapy programs

For larger classes, you can have two or more teams. For smaller classes, you can have one team meeting. Depending on the size of the class, have individuals or pairs prepare the areas covered in the role cards for 10–15 minutes before convening the team meeting(s). Students should be encouraged to practice using the phrases for giving advice and making suggestions from Listening 3.

If you intend to assign a follow-up writing assignment, have students take notes of all the suggestions for the health program made during the meeting.

Writing Practice
Drawing on the suggestions that come up in the Communication activity, students can design a company brochure that gives advice and suggestions on how employees can improve their overall health. General categories could be:
- Exercise and physical activity
- Nutritional advice
- Comfortable working conditions (ergonomics)
- Work/life balance

12 Society

Unit Focus • Elections • Education • Law

Unit overview

Unit components	Focus	TOEIC practice	Duration
Snapshot	Law courts; voting; school; police	Part I	15–25 mins
Grammar Check 1	Words expressing contrast	Part VI	30 mins
Listening 1	Civic conversations	Part III	20–30 mins
Vocabulary Builder	Collocations	Part V	15–20 mins
Listening 2	Tribal law	Part IV	15–25 mins
Grammar Check 2	Subjunctives: formal language in the U.S.	Part V	30 mins
Viewpoint	To Kill an Avatar	Part VII	30 mins
Listening 3	Debating phrases	Part II	15–20 mins
Communication	Debate: virtual violence		40 mins
		Total	3 hrs 30–4 hrs 10

Snapshot

Aims
- TOEIC Part I practice: picture analysis
- Vocabulary development: law courts; voting; education; law enforcement
- Discussion

The pictures present a few examples of legal and civil institutions within society: a law court, voting at a polling station, students in a classroom, policemen.

Picture descriptions
Picture 1
The picture shows an "Open *Court*" in Rangpur, India. The Open Court is an *alternative system of justice* that *settles* local *disputes* and provides *legal council* to people living in rural areas. Two court *officials* are sitting at a table facing a group of people who appear to be sitting on the ground. Behind the men, there is a large tree from which is hanging a sign that reads "Open Court, Rangpur".

Picture 2
In this picture, we see people *registering* to *vote* at a *polling station* in a Spanish-speaking region. Several people are around a table that is covered with paper. On the right, a woman is *filling out a form* while a young girl looks on. Next to them, several men are leaning on the table. Behind them is a large poster showing a hand holding what might be a voter's *ballot*.

Picture 3
This picture shows a school *classroom*. The young students are sitting at their *desks* with their books open. Some of them are *raising their hands* in order *to be called on* by the teacher/instructor, who is standing next to a *blackboard*.

Picture 4
In this picture, we see two *police officers* on *bicycles* at a *public market* in Seattle in the U.S.. Police in this region *patrol* public areas on bicycles, on foot, and sometimes on horses. They *ensure security*, *enforce the law* and *provide assistance* to the *public*. They are *in uniform* and are wearing helmets and sunglasses.

Answers
A
1 People are attending a court session outdoors.
2 People are registering to vote in a polling station.
3 Young students are attending school.
4 Two police officers are on bicycle patrol near a market.

B
1 E, J
2 D, H
3 I, L
4 B, K

AUDIOSCRIPT
B
A The schoolchildren are clapping their hands.
B The law enforcement officers are on patrol.
C The candidate is making a speech.
D The people are registering to vote.
E The court session is held outside.
F The police are writing out a traffic ticket.
G The lawyers are meeting in the court house.
H A woman is filling out a form.
I The instructor is calling on the students.
J The court officials are facing the people.
K The policemen are riding bicycles.
L Some students are raising their hands.

Grammar Check 1

Aims
- TOEIC Part VI practice: error recognition
- Grammar point: complex sentences
- Vocabulary development: words expressing contrast
- Discussion

This section begins with an inductive presentation of words expressing contrast. In exercise A, students identify the contrast words and the way they are used in different types of sentences. In exercise B, students use contrast words to form sentences. In exercise C, students then practice a Part VI error recognition and correction exercise.

There are three basic categories of words that express contrast:

- *Although*, *even though*, *while*, *whereas* begin dependent clauses that must be linked to an independent clause in order to make a complete sentence.
- *In spite of*, *despite* begin noun phrases that must be linked to an independent clause.
- *But*, *yet*, *however* begin independent clauses. They can form compound sentences (two linked independent clauses) and they can show contrast between two separate sentences.

In Part V, TOEIC® will often test a student's ability to determine which contrast word is needed to form a complete sentence. Students need to determine whether the section of the sentence is a clause or a phrase.

Although/Even though **it was raining**, *we had a picnic in the park.*

Despite/In spite of **the rain**, *we had a picnic in the park.*

In the first sentence, the two-part sentence begins with a clause (noun + verb).
The second sentence begins with a noun phrase.

The theme of the activity is voting and elections. In the U.S., voters can cast their ballots either in person or by mail. In order to vote by mail, a voter must first be registered to vote and must obtain an absentee ballot. In other countries, a voter who cannot go to the polls will sign over his vote to another voter, who will vote for him. This is called *voting by procuration*.

Students might find the following topic-related vocabulary useful:

citizen	the right to vote
to register (to vote)	election
a newcomer	legislators
laws	police
to enforce	referendum
at the polls	candidate
absentee ballot	observers
to monitor	citizenship
(someone's) voice	guidelines
application	witness
notary	widespread corruption

Answers
A
1 but, in spite of, although, despite, even though, yet, whereas
2 in spite of, despite
3 however, but, yet
B
1 **Even though** the new candidate has less experience, I've decided to vote for her.
2 Some people like to vote in person, **whereas** others prefer using an absentee ballot.
3 **Despite** (the) many observers monitoring the elections, there was widespread corruption.
4 (1) Although (2) while (3) In spite of
C
1 Although
2 Even though
3 However
4 While, Even though, Although
5 whereas

Listening 1

Aims
- TOEIC Part III practice: short conversations
- Listening for keywords in order to identify context
- Vocabulary development: registering to vote; policing; filing taxes; campaigning for an elected office; continuing education and training

The section begins with a review of vocabulary in exercises A and B that prepares students for five TOEIC® Part III short conversations, which involve:

1. A man registering to vote.
2. A police officer checking a motorist's driving license because a brake light on the car is not working.
3. Two people discussing filling out the income tax declaration forms.
4. A conversation with a candidate for mayor as to what he would do if elected.
5. Two professional, working people talking about taking continuing education courses.
   Note that Higher Education institutions, such as universities and colleges, offer continuing education courses and degree programs for working professionals who would like to pursue more training.

The focus here is to get students to concentrate on listening for specific keywords that indicate the context of the conversation. After completing exercise C, you may want to have students read through the audioscripts and perform the conversations in pairs.

Extension questions for discussion
- What questions would a police officer ask a driver?
- What questions would a voter ask a candidate for mayor?
- Do you find filling out income tax forms difficult or complicated? Do you have someone help you file your taxes?
- Do you know anyone who had entered professional life and then returned to school part-time to pursue further training or another degree? Is this a common practice in your country?

Answers
A
Suggested answers
voting – polling place
educating people – classroom
law-making – police station
enforcing laws – courtroom, police station
governing people – city hall/capitol building
reporting income and paying taxes – taxation bureau

B
Suggested vocabulary
Voting: vote, ballot, ballot box, list of candidates, voter, registration, registration card
Educating people: school, college, university, students, teachers, instructors, professors
Law-making: legislation, rules, laws, regulations, ordinance
Enforcing laws: courts, judges, lawyers, defenders, prosecutors, police, sheriff, federal agents, soldiers, military, army, navy
Reporting income: tax forms, to file taxes, income tax, sales tax, payments, deductions

C

	Keywords	Activity
1	register, eligible to vote, elections, voter registration, polling place	voting
2	driver's license, vehicle registration, officer, speeding, pulled over	law enforcement
3	filling out, income tax returns, due, to file	filing and reporting income taxes
4	elected, in office, mayor, city, raise local taxes	elections, campaigning for office
5	course catalog, semester, classes, credits, MBA, university	education

AUDIOSCRIPT
1
Woman Do you have a currently valid form of photo ID, your birth certificate, and proof of residence?
Man Yes, I do. By the way, if I register today, will I be eligible to vote in the upcoming elections?
Woman Yes. You'll receive your official voter registration card indicating your local polling place in the mail within a few days.

2
Man 1 Good morning, sir. May I see your driver's license and vehicle registration, please?
Man 2 Certainly, here you are. Is there something wrong, officer? Was I speeding?
Man 1 Not to worry, sir. We pulled you over because we noticed that your left brake light is out. You'll need to get that fixed as soon as possible.

Unit 12 | Society

3
Woman 2 What a weekend! I spent the whole time filling out my income tax returns.
Woman 2 Oh, that's right! I totally forgot. When are they due again?
Woman 3 You have until midnight Wednesday to file. Hope yours are less complicated than mine!

4
Man 1 If elected, what will be your top priority during your first six months in office?
Man 2 If I become mayor of this city, I would devote time and effort to improving the local public school system. We need to upgrade our educational facilities.
Man 1 Would that mean that you would raise local taxes?

5
Man Have you seen the continuing education course catalog for next semester?
Woman I think I saw one in the HR office yesterday. Were you considering taking some classes?
Man Yes. In fact, I'm only six credits away from completing my executive MBA in the university's professional business program.

Vocabulary Builder

Aims
- TOEIC Part V practice: incomplete sentences
- Vocabulary development: collocations (adjective + noun; adverb + adjective)
- Topic: education; life-long learning; literacy

This exercise reviews collocations (idiomatic word-pairings) often tested in Part V. The topic of "life-long learning" refers to the idea that people can pursue further education at any age. The activity features an article about a book co-written by George Dawson, *Life is So Good*. Mr. Dawson lived most of his life without being able to read and write, but at the age of 98 he returned to school.

Suggested discussion questions
- *What do you think of Mr. Dawson's achievement?*
- *When do people complete their education in your country?*
- *Can a person return to university after having worked for several years? If yes, is this common?*

For professional students, you might ask:
- *If you were to return to school, what training, education, or degree would you pursue?*
- *How important is "life-long learning" in your culture?*
- *Are there age limits?*

You may also have students consider the importance of literacy or, more specifically, the importance of continuing to learn and develop foreign language skills, for example.

Answers
A
1 d
2 a
3 f
4 e
5 c
6 b
B
1 b
2 c
3 a
C
1 highly unlikely
2 hugely successful
3 close collaboration
4 valuable lessons
5 positive outlook
6 Critically acclaimed
7 major contribution

Listening 2

Aims
- TOEIC Part IV practice: short talks
- Skimming comprehension questions before listening
- Discussion: indigenous peoples; culture and tradition; law

This short talk is addressed to lawyers who are attending a seminar in order to work as volunteers giving legal council. The Hopi Indians live according to their own traditions and laws. The aim of the seminar is to present the cultural and legal differences between the Hopi Indian Reservation system of government and the U.S. government. In short, how do Hopi tribal laws differ from state and federal laws and from the U.S. constitution?

You may want to lead the students into this section with the following general questions:
- *Can you think of an example of a "nation" existing within a larger political entity?*
- *Does this "nation" live autonomously, that is, independently of the dominant culture?*

Students may want to consider some of the issues involved in the formation of the European Union, where countries of different cultures, languages and traditions form a single economic and political entity.

The Hopi Indian Reservation Key Facts provide some background information. Additionally, you may want to assign to your students some Internet research on the Hopi Indians.

> ⚠️ **TOEIC Tip**
> Before doing exercise B, have students read the TOEIC Tip. Students should be aware that questions pertain to either general information (context, setting, purpose, speaker, audience) or specific information (dates, times, numbers, names, locations, etc.). By skimming the comprehension questions beforehand, they can better focus their attention while listening.

B
1 general
2 general
3 specific

C
1 d
2 b
3 c

AUDIOSCRIPT
B
I would like to thank you for showing interest in our Legal Aid Volunteer Program here on the Hopi Reservation. As you know, the Hopi Tribal Council is looking for lawyers to volunteer their time to provide legal advice to Hopi tribal members. This is important because although Native American Reservations are within the borders of the United States, the tribes have independent governments whose legal policies and practices differ from state and federal law. For example, did you know that within the Hopi Reservation, laws are enforced, not by federal, state, or county police, but by Hopi Tribal Rangers? This three-day seminar will introduce you to the basic governmental and legal differences between Hopi culture and the surrounding United States. This knowledge will enable you to better inform tribal members of their legal rights regarding such important issues as reclaiming lands belonging to the tribe, securing the right to manage the natural resources within tribal property and, more generally, expanding Native American autonomy in order to preserve Hopi language, culture and traditions.

Grammar Check 2

Aims
- TOEIC Part V practice: incomplete sentences
- Revision of the U.S. English use of the subjunctive
- Vocabulary development: citizenship requirements
- Discussion: immigration and naturalization policies

This is a simple but often unexpected grammar point that appears regularly on the TOEIC®. Students have generally been so trained in conjugating the third-person singular (-s) that they are surprised when they encounter the English subjunctive.

> ⚠️ **TOEIC Tip**
> The tip emphasizes the use of the subjunctive in U.S. English.

Have students study the examples. Draw their attention to the verbs in bold. Normally we would think that we would have to conjugate the verb, for example, *the governor resigns*, *quotas are*. However, in *that*-clauses after certain verbs and adjectives that express necessity, U.S. English leaves the verb in the simple infinitive without *to*: *that the governor **resign**, that immigration quotas **be***. (Note that in non-U.S. English, the sentence would read: *that the governor **should** resign*.)

The topic is intended to stimulate students' awareness and discussion of immigration and naturalization requirements and policies. Ask them to define "proficiency in the national language". What, if any, level of language should a person be required to attain in order to become a citizen of a country? You may ask students to reflect upon the challenges of developing their language skills. Do certain levels of language proficiency allow someone to gain membership to a particular group or community? How might a language proficiency requirement be used as a form of "linguistic discrimination"?

Several answers are possible in the exercise, but students must correctly conjugate the verb they choose into its subjunctive form.

Answers
1 reside
2 speak
3 understand
4 be
5 show; demonstrate
6 show; demonstrate

Unit 12 | Society

Viewpoint

Aims
- TOEIC Part VII practice: reading comprehension
- Vocabulary development
- Discussion: to kill an avatar

Computer graphics technology is now able to produce fairly "realistic" worlds, in which a player can either create a private virtual world on his computer or can subscribe to and then participate in an on-line, Internet world with many other players. One of the most popular virtual world games is "The Sims". For further background information, visit The Sims on-line website, produced by the company Electronic Arts.

This article presents a controversial topic dealing with ethical practices in on-line, virtual worlds. The article explores the question as to whether *avatars* (virtual world characters) should have the power to *eliminate* or *kill* other avatars (other players). Many on-line game producers say subscribers want to be able to have total freedom to do what they want in virtual worlds. Game producers argue that they have to allow such virtual crimes to exist in order to keep their profits up. The topic is controversial because it touches on ethical and moral issues, particularly in relation to technology.

The article contains many interesting words for vocabulary development. After they have read the article, you may want to have students identify words according to different categories, for example:

Crime and law enforcement:
to kill   crime   fraud   theft   harassment   to murder   federal prosecutors   to establish laws   to enforce laws   policing   to police

Computers, the Internet and the people involved in on-line games:
avatar (a computer-generated representation of a person)   *subscribers   virtual world   digital   on-line game designers   to code out of the program*

Elements and issues within civil society:
citizenry   to stress equality   freedom   to offend   restriction   newcomers

Economic terms:
the bottom line   to drive up costs

Additional vocabulary:
to strike the wrong balance
to be mindful of   appeal   allure   to undermine   prevalent   time-consuming   complain   banish

Answers
1. Freedom to decide
2. For: it's like the real world.
   Against: it's costly for the players who have been eliminated.
3. Subscribers would be dissatisfied.
4. They make decisions about the virtual world, its laws and how they are enforced.

Listening 3

Aims
- TOEIC Part II practice: question/response
- Vocabulary development: idiomatic debating phrases; expressing agreement/disagreement

Draw students' attention to the box with some of the language functions that are commonly used in a debate. Ask them to think of different ways of "asking for an opinion", "requesting clarification" or expressing "agreement" or "disagreement". Then have them read the sentences to determine the function of the underlined expressions. Here are some extra phrases that you may want to teach:

Agreeing:
I agree with you.
I agree in principle.
I think you're right.

Disagreeing (tactfully):
By and large, I would agree with what you say, but …
Although I agree with most of what you've said about that …
I understand your point, but I think that …

Disagreeing (strongly):
I don't agree.
I cannot accept your point of view.
I can't say that I share your view.
I take issue with the idea that …
What you're saying is not feasible.

Students should become familiar with common idiomatic phrases that can appear on the TOEIC®, such as *to take issue with* (*to disagree with*) and phrases that ask for opinions: *Where do you stand on this issue?* and *What is your position on this?*, etc.

After completing exercise B, have students identify the distracters in the incorrect responses.

Target Score

Distracters:
1 A is incorrect: *position* is asking for an opinion, not for a specific spatial location.
2 B is incorrect: *expand* is asking for greater clarification; not for more physical space.
3 B is incorrect because it is not a logical response; *greeted* is a distracter because it sounds similiar to *agreed*.
4 A is incorrect because it is not a logical response; *to come* is a distracter because it sounds similiar to *companies*.

Answers
A
1 disagreeing
2 asking for an opinion
3 presenting an argument
4 agreeing
5 requesting clarification
B
1 B
2 A
3 A
4 B

AUDIOSCRIPT
B
1 What's your position on this issue?
   A We're standing near the exit.
   B By and large, I share the same opinion as Sally.
2 Could you expand on that, please?
   A I'd be glad to go into greater depth.
   B Yes. Let's move to a larger room.
3 Wouldn't you agree that video games are completely harmless?
   A Well, I wouldn't go that far.
   B Yes. We greeted them at the door.
4 Do you realize that companies would lose subscribers?
   A Yes. We'd really like to come.
   B That won't necessarily happen.

Communication

Aims
- Speaking practice: debating
- Topics: law; government; justice; civics; virtual worlds; violence in society

The Communication activity draws upon the ideas presented in the Viewpoint article. It focuses on governance in virtual, Internet worlds. The language focus is debating, and students should be encouraged to use the debating phrases from Listening 3.

Students are asked to imagine that they are active members of a virtual world. The specific question to be discussed is:

- *Should avatars in virtual worlds* (virtual world characters) *have the power to "eliminate" or kill other avatars* (other players)?

The topic is controversial because it touches on ethical and moral issues. Students should be encouraged to consider what laws should be established and enforced in order to govern their imagined virtual world. More broadly, the discussion may be expanded in order to consider larger questions, such as:

- *Should players apply the real-world values in virtual worlds?*
- *What freedoms should an avatar have?*
- *Is virtual violence the same as real violence?*
- *Does (computer) technology allow us to escape from our real-world values?*

Writing Practice
The company that has created the virtual on-line world has decided to take a vote next month on two important issues. Should "avatars" have the power to "eliminate" or "kill" other avatars? If not, then should we "program out" (remove) the possibility of committing any crimes in our virtual world?

The company has posted the questions on its website and is asking each virtual world subscriber to post a public response expressing his or her opinion.
Have students write a response and present it to the class.

Review Test 4 Answer Key

Units 10–12

Listening Comprehension

Part I
Photographs

1 **D** The *optometrist* is *checking* the *patient's eyes*. (A) His arm is not visible, but *she* is *wearing* a *watch*. (B) She's *reading* dials on a machine, not a *manual*. (C) He's not *looking for his glasses*. He's looking into the machine to have his eyes checked.

2 **A** The man is *clearing* the *snow away* with a *snow shovel*. (B) He's not *showing* anything. *Showing* is a distracter that sounds similar to *snowing*. (C) The *street* has been *cleared*. (D) He's *shoveling snow*, not dirt.

3 **B** The *road* that *passes over the freeway* is an *overpass*. (A) The *freeway* is quite *full*. This is not a *parking lot*. (C) The *cars* in the *lanes* on the right are well spaced apart and *traffic* appears to be moving. (D) Although there may be *commuters riding* in the cars, no *buses* can be seen.

4 **C** The man is standing in the street, *pointing his arm to direct the cyclists*. He is not (A) *waving* to them and his arm is not *raised* (B) *above his head*. The man is *pointing* in a *direction*, but not (D) *pointing out a problem*.

5 **B** The people are sitting and *studying* in a *library*. (A) There are *books on the shelves*, but no books are *on sale*. (C) There are many people working, so it must be open. (D) They are not *booking* or reserving a table at a restaurant. The words *booking* and *table* are distracters.

6 **C** He is *voting* by placing his *ballot* into the *ballot box* at a *polling station*. (A) He only has *one ballot* in his hand. He is not *counting* the votes. (B) The signs indicate a *ballot box* in a *polling station*, so he is not *mailing a letter*. (D) The *ballot box* is on the table, not *under* it.

Part II
Questions and responses

7 **C** This idiomatic question asks for the person's opinion (*stance*) on a subject (*issue*), not about physical location (A/B).

8 **B** The question *How about* is suggesting a day for the person's yearly examination (*annual check-up*). It is neither asking (A) *what* it is about, nor (C) *how often* something occurs. (A) includes the distracters *checking account* that sound similar to *check-up* and *about*.

9 **B** The question *Wouldn't it be better* is making a suggestion. The response confirms and then defines the suggestion. (A) is an illogical response, which first confirms the suggestion, but then negates it using the distracter *it wouldn't help*. (C) is not a logical response that plays upon the word *better* in the question with *not improved* in the answer.

10 **B** (B) is an appropriate response to the request for items on a medical *prescription*. (A) and (B) both try to distract by referring to or using the word *fill*. In (A), the phrase *there's no more room* means that the space or reservations are full. (C) uses the adjective *filling*, which refers to food.

11 **C** The question seeks information about the weather. (A) refers incorrectly to a *delay* and to an *announcement*, not to a *weather report*. (B) uses the words *whether* and *hers*, which sound similar to *weather* and *heard* in the question.

12 **A** The response politely declines the invitation to *join* the exercise *group*. (B) The word *fit*, which sounds similar to *fitness*, refers to trying on clothes. (C) The word *joint*, which sounds similar to *joining*, refers to opening an account.

13 **B** The question requests information about *when* the car lanes for *commuters will reopen*. (A) does not respond to the question *when*. (C) The word *late* relates to time, but the answer does not refer to *commuter lanes*.

14 **A** The question seeks confirmation of an opinion. The response agrees that the apartment was too small and adds new information about the cost. (B) uses the distracters *thinking* and *mall*, which refer to a shopping center, not an *apartment*. (C) refers to duration, not size, using the distracters *lasted* and *thought*.

109

Part III
Short conversations

15 **B** She is leaving the city and *moving to the suburbs* where housing is more affordable. (A) *She couldn't afford to buy a place in the city*. They discuss *high real estate prices, buying a place*, and the increase in *housing costs*, without mentioning (C) *commuting* or (D) a *landlord* or *rent*.

16 **D** Nancy is *running for Mayor*. (A) uses the distracter *jogging* for *running*. (B) She must already be with the firm because they *would miss her if she were elected*. (C) There is no mention of her *taking time off*, only the future possibility of her leaving.

17 **C** The woman says that she *is going to try the new Japanese restaurant*. (A) The *man* says that he has *brought a salad from home*. They do not talk about (B) the *office* or (D) the *cafeteria*.

18 **B** The man *would like to make an appointment with Dr. Stevens*. He is not requesting to see (A), (C) or (D).

19 **A** Although pre-registration was scheduled to open *today at noon*, it has been rescheduled for *eight a.m. on Monday morning*. Thus, (B), (C) and (D) are not possible.

20 **C** The woman says that a *relative, her sister-in-law, who's an accountant, fills out her taxes for her*. (A) Therefore, she does not do it herself. (B) uses the distracter *lawyer*, referring to *in-law*. (D) uses the distracter *foreman*, which sounds like *for me*.

21 **D** The man suggests using *posters*. There is no mention of (A) *brochures*, (B) *Internet* or (C) *radio commercials*.

Part IV
Short talks

22 **B** The speaker addresses *you* as someone who has employees (*your employees*) and implies that *you* can *develop corporate programs* for *your company*. Although (C) and (D) could have employees and direct a company, as health professionals, they would not be the most likely target audience for this seminar.

23 **C** The speaker recommends *developing a corporate fitness program* to *reduce health insurance costs*, not (A) *increase* them. (B) There is no mention of *healthy food*. (D) *Greater corporate loyalty* would be a *benefit* of what the speaker is recommending.

24 **D** This *weather advisory* broadcast is meant to alert people to heavy *snowfall*. Although the *state, roads* and *schools* are mentioned, there is no reference to (A) *state elections*, (B) *road repairs* or (C) *school programs*.

25 **A** The *advisory* specifically addresses drivers or *motorists*, not specifically (B) school children, (C) road crews, or (D) advisors, even though they could drive a car.

26 **C** The advisory announces that *school will begin one hour later than normal*, which is the same as *sixty minutes*. Another announcement could be made (B) at 6 a.m. (D) to *cancel classes*. For now, they will be held, but not (A) at the normal time.

Reading Comprehension

Part V
Incomplete sentences

27 **D** After the verb *avoid*, the gerund form (*-ing*) is used. (A) is the past participle, (B) is the infinitive without *to*, and (C) is the infinitive.

28 **C** In reported speech, the future is expressed with *would* and the main verb. (A) is the present continuous, (B) the present simple, and (D) the subjunctive.

29 **C** *Strictly enforced* is a common collocation. (A), (B), and (D) are not commonly employed as adverbs with *enforced*.

30 **A** *Progress* is commonly collocated with the verb *to make*. (A), (B), and (D) are incorrect.

31 **C** The subordinating conjunction *even though* is needed to complete the dependent clause of a complex sentence. (A), (B), and (D) are incorrect.

32 **B** Gerund forms (*-ing*) follow prepositions, in this case *to*. (A) is the past participle, (C) the third-person singular form of the present simple, and (D) the infinitive without *to*.

33 **D** The *if* clause of a third conditional requires the past perfect, which is formed with *had* and the past participle form of the main verb, in this case *had*. (A) is the third-person singular of the present simple and (B) the present perfect. (C) is the third conditional form used in the *then* clause.

34 **A** (A) is the subjunctive form. Verbs in *that* clauses that are introduced with *require* take the infinitive form without *to*. (B) is the third-person singular of the present simple, (C) the emphatic past tense form, and (D) the present perfect tense.

35 **B** *To come up with* is a three-part phrasal verb meaning "to produce". (A), (C), and (D) do not form phrasal verbs with *up with*.

36 **C** Only *ought* is followed by the infinitive form. (A), (B), and (D) cannot be used before an infinitive with *to*.

Part VI
Error recognition

37 **B** The preposition *to* is incorrect. The correct form is *to ask someone to do something*.

38 **B** The verb *consider* is followed by a gerund. Therefore, *postponing* is the correct form.

39 **A** The gerund form is used after prepositions. Therefore, *leaving* is the correct form.

40 **B** Verbs in *that* clauses that are introduced with *recommend* take the subjunctive, which is the infinitive form without *to*. Therefore, *exercise* is the correct form.

41 **D** The past perfect *had had* is correct in the *if* clause of the third conditional, but not in the *then* clause, which requires the past perfect form of *would*. Therefore, *would have received* is the correct form.

42 **A** The verb *agree* is conjugated in the same way as other verbs in the simple present; the auxiliary verb *to do*, not *to be*, is used in the negative. Therefore, *does not agree* is the correct form.

43 **A** The preposition *despite* comes at the beginning of a noun phrase. This complex sentence begins with a dependent clause that requires a subordinating conjunction, such as *although* or *even though*.

44 **A** The verb *to tell* must be followed by a person or an object, whereas the verb *to say* does not. *They told us …* or *They said* would both be correct.

Part VII
Reading

45 **D** This is a *renewal* notice, reminding *drivers* to renew their *license* before it *expires*. (A) *Renewal* implies that the drivers already have their license. (B) Nothing is mentioned about having a license *suspended*. (C) The notice only warns drivers about the possibility of receiving a ticket if they drive *without a valid license*.

46 **B** The *fee* for *license renewal* is $25.

47 **C** Drivers receive a *five-year license* when they renew it.

48 **B** The website informs companies about *waste reduction techniques* or *practices*. The site mentions *generating less trash*, but does not mention (A) *increasing business*, (C) *electricity* or (D) *hiring*.

49 **C** Waste reduction practices save (*your*) *company money*. (A) and (B) are not logical, because the website only says that such practices *conserve landfill space* and *preserve natural resources*. (D) There is no mention of *office equipment*.

50 **D** There is no mention of *using less energy*. (A)

Companies can *call to schedule a visit* by a *Business Recycling consultant*. The site directs companies (B) to the *Best Practices* page to *help them reduce trash* and (C) *to use the Recycler Finder* to locate a recycler.

AUDIOSCRIPT
Review Test 4 Units 10–12
Part I
1. A   The patient is wearing a watch.
   B   She's reading the manual.
   C   He's looking for his glasses.
   D   She's checking the patient's eyes.
2. A   He's clearing the snow away.
   B   He's showing his house.
   C   The street is covered with snow.
   D   He's shoveling the soil in his garden.
3. A   The parking lot is full.
   B   There's an overpass across the freeway.
   C   Traffic is stopped in both directions.
   D   The commuters are riding the bus.
4. A   The man is waving to the cyclists.
   B   He's raising his arm above his head.
   C   The man is directing traffic.
   D   He's pointing out the problem.
5. A   The books are on sale.
   B   They're studying in a library.
   C   The library is closed for repairs.
   D   They're booking a table at the restaurant.
6. A   He's counting the votes.
   B   He's mailing a letter.
   C   He's dropping his ballot in the slot.
   D   The ballot box is under the table.

Part II
7. Where do you stand on this issue?
   A   Yes, we're near the elevator.
   B   Over there, next to the photocopier.
   C   I share Don's point of view.
8. How about next Tuesday for your annual check-up?
   A   It's about the checking account.
   B   That would be fine.
   C   About twice a week.
9. Wouldn't it be better to get a second opinion?
   A   You're right. It wouldn't help at all.
   B   Good idea. Let's ask Toshiro.
   C   Unfortunately, the results haven't improved.
10. May I have this prescription filled, please?
    A   I'm sorry. There's no more room.
    B   I'll need to order this. You can pick it up this afternoon.
    C   It certainly is very filling.

11 Have you heard the weather report?
   A Yes, the announcement was delayed.
   B I'm not sure whether it's hers.
   C The forecast is for clear, sunny skies.
12 Would you be interested in joining our fitness group?
   A Thank you for asking, but I already have a membership at the gym.
   B Could you get me a larger size? This one doesn't fit.
   C Yes, we can open a joint account.
13 When will the commuter lanes re-open?
   A We'd be more than happy to pass on the message.
   B Not before next week. Until then we'll just have to leave earlier.
   C You can come as late as you want.
14 Didn't you think that last apartment was too small?
   A But considering the location, it's a great deal.
   B We were thinking about going to the mall.
   C Yes, it lasted longer than I thought it would.

Part III

15
Man John said you were moving to the suburbs. Is that right?
Woman Yes. Real estate prices are so high that we can't afford to buy a place in the city.
Man I know what you mean. Housing costs have skyrocketed in the last year.

16
Man 1 Hey Bill. Have you heard that Nancy's running for mayor?
Man 2 Really? She certainly has the experience to do a terrific job.
Man 1 Yes. But we'd sure miss her here at the firm if she were elected.

17
Woman We're going to try the new Japanese restaurant on the corner. Would you care to join us?
Man Oh I'd love to, but I just started my new diet and brought a salad from home.
Woman I'm watching what I eat too. My nutritionist has advised me to cut down on red meat, so I'm trying to eat more fish.

18
Man Hello. I'd like to make an appointment with Dr. Stevens, please.
Woman OK. Are you one of his regular patients or will this be your first visit?
Man This will be the first. But I've been referred to him by Dr. Avery, who's already sent my records.

19
Man Wasn't pre-registration for next semester beginning today at noon?
Woman Yes, but the administration had to make so many last-minute changes to the course listing that they've postponed it until 8 a.m. Monday.
Man I sure hope none of the classes I wanted to take is cancelled.

20
Man Do you fill out your income tax forms yourself?
Woman Actually, my sister-in-law, who's an accountant, does them for me.
Man I wish I knew someone who could help me. I find them so complicated.

21
Woman What would be the best, most cost-effective way of promoting our clean city campaign?
Man How about posters? We could put them in schools and supermarkets.
Woman Good idea. That way we would reach people of all ages.

Part IV

Questions 22 and 23:
Hi, my name's Steve Zachery and I'll be leading today's seminar entitled "On-the-job Fitness". We will be looking at how and why your company should consider developing a corporate fitness program. But let's begin with the bottom line; what are the real, tangible benefits of a corporate fitness program? Human resources directors that have implemented complete health plans have reported many positive outcomes. These benefits range from fewer worker absences to better attitudes, greater corporate loyalty, and less stress. Companies have also found such fitness programs to be a valuable recruiting tool that improves employee retention. One of the most significant long-term advantages is reduced health insurance costs for you and your employees. These are just a few of the points we'll be covering today in greater detail. So turning to…

Questions 24–26:
The National Weather Service has issued a winter weather advisory for tonight. Temperatures over the state will remain cold enough to produce steady snow through at least midnight. Snow is expected to accumulate from three to five inches across Jefferson County, while four to six inches are likely in Madison County. Motorists are urged to exercise caution while driving. Many roads across the advisory area will be snow-covered and icey. Due to the heavy amounts of

snow, schools in Jefferson and Madison Counties have announced a "Delayed opening" tomorrow. School will begin one hour later than normal in order to allow road crews to clear roads and highways. In the event that heavy snow makes it dangerous to hold regular classes and forces closure of school, an announcement will be made by the school district and broadcast tomorrow morning at 6 a.m. on this and other radio stations. Stay tuned for further information.

Classroom Activities for the TOEIC®

Each of the following interactive classroom activities for TOEIC® preparation focus on one of the seven parts of the test and are designed to enhance students' understanding of the format and the question types that are specific to each part. The activities can be done either in groups of varying sizes or in pairs.

Activity 1 (Part I: photographs)
Material: selection of TOEIC®-type photos
Duration: 30–40 minutes depending on the number of students

Instructions
- Select enough photos so that there is at least one photo for every pair. The photos should reflect the types of pictures that are used in the first part of the test (i.e. indoor or outdoor scenes relating to work, leisure, transport, travel, etc.). You can use the ones provided on the CUP website or clip suitable photos from magazines.
- Assign one photo to each pair and get students to brainstorm it for suitable vocabulary.
- Ask them to prepare one statement about their photo. (You can provide corrections if necessary.) Remind students that their statements should not be too straightforward as this is not the case on the test.
- Redistribute the photos so that each pair has a different one.
- Each pair takes turns reading out the statements that they have prepared. The pair who now has the photo that the statement refers to has to recognize it!

Activity 2 (Part I: photographs)
Material: 1 photo for each pair of students
Duration: 30–40 minutes

Instructions
- Assign one photo to each pair.
- Ask them to focus on the actions and body positions of the people in the picture, then on the positions of the people in relation to each other.
- Get students to write two statements about each photo, which are not entirely true. The statements should include references to people or objects that can be seen in the photo, but should contain an incorrect description of either the body positions of the people or of the positions of the people and objects in relation to each other.
- The pairs exchange statements and photos with another pair.
- Each pair modifies the statements to make them true, then returns them to the others.

Activity 3 (Part I: photographs)
Material: 1 photo for each pair of students
Duration: 30–40 minutes

Instructions
- Assign one photo to each pair.
- Each pair takes turns asking another pair a series of closed questions until they have a clear idea what is pictured. (*Is there more than one person in the photo? Are they playing a game?*, etc.)

This activity can also be done with a complete group. Each pair takes turns answering the questions of the group.

Activity 4 (Part II: questions)
Material: slips of paper with answers
separate slips of paper with questions
Duration: 30–40 minutes

Instructions
- Prepare a series of Part II questions with the corresponding correct answers on separate slips of paper. There should be enough for each student to have two questions and two answers.
- Distribute at least two answers per student and place the questions in a hat.
- Students take turns picking a question out of the hat and reading it out to the rest of the class.
- The student who thinks that he/she has the right answer to the question reads it out.

Classroom Activities

Extra activity (Part II: questions)
Material: slips of paper with questions and answers from Part II exchanges
Duration: 25 minutes

Instructions
- Divide the class into two groups. The students in one group each receive one question while those in the second group receive one answer.
- Students memorize their questions and answers, then mix together.
- Students with questions pronounce their questions. Students with answers respond until they have identified the person who has the matching question or answer.

Activity 5 (Part III: short conversations)
Material: individual slips of paper, each with 1 exchange (line of dialogue) from several short conversations (the 3 parts of each conversation should be on separate pieces of paper)
Duration: 40–60 minutes

Instructions
- Distribute one line from a dialogue to each student or pair of students. For a class of ten students, you will require 15 slips of paper for each of the exchanges from five short conversations. One student will have the first line from the conversation and another will have the second. The slips of paper with the third exchange from each conversation will be placed on a table.
- Students memorize their "lines", then move around the classroom speaking them to other students until they have found the partner whose lines fit with theirs.
- Pairs of students then identify the missing line from their conversation from the slips of paper on the table.
- Each pair then practices acting out the complete dialogue before performing it in front of the class.

Extra activity (Part III: short conversations)
Material: Jumbled exchanges for 3 Part III conversations.

Instructions
- Working in pairs, students have to reconstitute the correct sequence for each conversation.

OR
- Students are given two exchanges from Part III conversations, then have to write the missing exchange which must include a selection of words that they have been given.

Activity 6 (Part IV: short talks)
Material: bingo cards with keywords taken from a selection of Part IV short talks
Duration: 30 minutes

Instructions
- Each group or pair receives a different bingo card with 12 words. Each card features three keywords from each of three short talks and three distracters (words which do not appear in any of the talks, but which may be similar in sound to words that do appear).
- Students listen to the three short talks and circle the words as they hear them. The first group to recognize the nine keywords on their card is the winner.

Extra activity (Part IV: short talks)

Instructions
- This game is played in teams. Play a Part IV short talk, then read out each question.
- The first team to score five correct answers is the winner.

Activity 7 (Part V: incomplete sentences)
Material: photocopies of 20 sentences from Part V. Each sentence is presented with a bland and no suggested answer.
Duration: 25–30 minutes

Instructions
- Distribute photocopies and give each team ten minutes to agree on one suitable word to complete each sentence.
- Ask one team to supply the answer to the first sentence and award a score.

> Scoring system:
> 1 point for correctly completing the sentence
> 1 point for challenging an incorrect answer and providing a correct one
> 0 points for an incorrect answer or no answer
> -1 point for challenging a correct answer

- Distribute a photocopy with a jumbled list of the original correct answers. The first team to insert the correct answer into each sentence wins a bonus of three points.

Activity 8 (Part VI: error recognition)
Material: 2 sets of photocopies of 20 sentences with errors
Duration: 30 minutes

Instructions
- Each pair of students receives a photocopy with 20 sentences which each contain one error. Pair A receives a photocopy where sentences 1–10 are unmarked – there is no indication of where the error might be. In sentences 11–20, the error in each sentence has been circled. Pair B receives a photocopy with the circled errors for sentences 1–10 and unmarked sentences for 11–20.
- Each pair identifies and circles the errors in each of the unmarked sentences.
- The pairs meet and compare their answers.

Activity 9 (Part VII: reading comprehension)
Material: sets of 4 texts and a selection of comprehension questions on individual slips of paper
Duration: 30 minutes

Instructions
- A set of three or four texts and eight to ten comprehension questions is distributed to each group.
- Students read the texts, then match each question to one of the texts.
- The first group to successfully match and answer the questions is the winner.

Target Score Student's Book Answer Sheet

Be sure to completely fill in the circle that corresponds to your answer choice. Completely erase errors or stray marks.

EXAMPLE: CORRECT Ⓐ Ⓑ ● Ⓓ WRONG Ⓐ Ⓑ ⌀ Ⓓ WRONG Ⓐ Ⓑ ⊗ Ⓓ WRONG Ⓐ Ⓑ ⊙ Ⓓ WRONG Ⓐ Ⓑ Ⓒ Ⓓ

LISTENING SECTION

1. Ⓐ Ⓑ Ⓒ Ⓓ
2. Ⓐ Ⓑ Ⓒ Ⓓ
3. Ⓐ Ⓑ Ⓒ Ⓓ
4. Ⓐ Ⓑ Ⓒ Ⓓ
5. Ⓐ Ⓑ Ⓒ Ⓓ
6. Ⓐ Ⓑ Ⓒ Ⓓ
7. Ⓐ Ⓑ Ⓒ Ⓓ
8. Ⓐ Ⓑ Ⓒ Ⓓ
9. Ⓐ Ⓑ Ⓒ Ⓓ
10. Ⓐ Ⓑ Ⓒ Ⓓ
11. Ⓐ Ⓑ Ⓒ Ⓓ
12. Ⓐ Ⓑ Ⓒ Ⓓ
13. Ⓐ Ⓑ Ⓒ Ⓓ
14. Ⓐ Ⓑ Ⓒ Ⓓ
15. Ⓐ Ⓑ Ⓒ Ⓓ
16. Ⓐ Ⓑ Ⓒ Ⓓ
17. Ⓐ Ⓑ Ⓒ Ⓓ
18. Ⓐ Ⓑ Ⓒ Ⓓ
19. Ⓐ Ⓑ Ⓒ Ⓓ
20. Ⓐ Ⓑ Ⓒ Ⓓ
21. Ⓐ Ⓑ Ⓒ
22. Ⓐ Ⓑ Ⓒ
23. Ⓐ Ⓑ Ⓒ
24. Ⓐ Ⓑ Ⓒ
25. Ⓐ Ⓑ Ⓒ

26. Ⓐ Ⓑ Ⓒ
27. Ⓐ Ⓑ Ⓒ
28. Ⓐ Ⓑ Ⓒ
29. Ⓐ Ⓑ Ⓒ
30. Ⓐ Ⓑ Ⓒ
31. Ⓐ Ⓑ Ⓒ
32. Ⓐ Ⓑ Ⓒ
33. Ⓐ Ⓑ Ⓒ
34. Ⓐ Ⓑ Ⓒ
35. Ⓐ Ⓑ Ⓒ
36. Ⓐ Ⓑ Ⓒ
37. Ⓐ Ⓑ Ⓒ
38. Ⓐ Ⓑ Ⓒ
39. Ⓐ Ⓑ Ⓒ
40. Ⓐ Ⓑ Ⓒ
41. Ⓐ Ⓑ Ⓒ
42. Ⓐ Ⓑ Ⓒ
43. Ⓐ Ⓑ Ⓒ
44. Ⓐ Ⓑ Ⓒ
45. Ⓐ Ⓑ Ⓒ
46. Ⓐ Ⓑ Ⓒ
47. Ⓐ Ⓑ Ⓒ
48. Ⓐ Ⓑ Ⓒ
49. Ⓐ Ⓑ Ⓒ
50. Ⓐ Ⓑ Ⓒ

51. Ⓐ Ⓑ Ⓒ Ⓓ
52. Ⓐ Ⓑ Ⓒ Ⓓ
53. Ⓐ Ⓑ Ⓒ Ⓓ
54. Ⓐ Ⓑ Ⓒ Ⓓ
55. Ⓐ Ⓑ Ⓒ Ⓓ
56. Ⓐ Ⓑ Ⓒ Ⓓ
57. Ⓐ Ⓑ Ⓒ Ⓓ
58. Ⓐ Ⓑ Ⓒ Ⓓ
59. Ⓐ Ⓑ Ⓒ Ⓓ
60. Ⓐ Ⓑ Ⓒ Ⓓ
61. Ⓐ Ⓑ Ⓒ Ⓓ
62. Ⓐ Ⓑ Ⓒ Ⓓ
63. Ⓐ Ⓑ Ⓒ Ⓓ
64. Ⓐ Ⓑ Ⓒ Ⓓ
65. Ⓐ Ⓑ Ⓒ Ⓓ
66. Ⓐ Ⓑ Ⓒ Ⓓ
67. Ⓐ Ⓑ Ⓒ Ⓓ
68. Ⓐ Ⓑ Ⓒ Ⓓ
69. Ⓐ Ⓑ Ⓒ Ⓓ
70. Ⓐ Ⓑ Ⓒ Ⓓ
71. Ⓐ Ⓑ Ⓒ Ⓓ
72. Ⓐ Ⓑ Ⓒ Ⓓ
73. Ⓐ Ⓑ Ⓒ Ⓓ
74. Ⓐ Ⓑ Ⓒ Ⓓ
75. Ⓐ Ⓑ Ⓒ Ⓓ

76. Ⓐ Ⓑ Ⓒ Ⓓ
77. Ⓐ Ⓑ Ⓒ Ⓓ
78. Ⓐ Ⓑ Ⓒ Ⓓ
79. Ⓐ Ⓑ Ⓒ Ⓓ
80. Ⓐ Ⓑ Ⓒ Ⓓ
81. Ⓐ Ⓑ Ⓒ Ⓓ
82. Ⓐ Ⓑ Ⓒ Ⓓ
83. Ⓐ Ⓑ Ⓒ Ⓓ
84. Ⓐ Ⓑ Ⓒ Ⓓ
85. Ⓐ Ⓑ Ⓒ Ⓓ
86. Ⓐ Ⓑ Ⓒ Ⓓ
87. Ⓐ Ⓑ Ⓒ Ⓓ
88. Ⓐ Ⓑ Ⓒ Ⓓ
89. Ⓐ Ⓑ Ⓒ Ⓓ
90. Ⓐ Ⓑ Ⓒ Ⓓ
91. Ⓐ Ⓑ Ⓒ Ⓓ
92. Ⓐ Ⓑ Ⓒ Ⓓ
93. Ⓐ Ⓑ Ⓒ Ⓓ
94. Ⓐ Ⓑ Ⓒ Ⓓ
95. Ⓐ Ⓑ Ⓒ Ⓓ
96. Ⓐ Ⓑ Ⓒ Ⓓ
97. Ⓐ Ⓑ Ⓒ Ⓓ
98. Ⓐ Ⓑ Ⓒ Ⓓ
99. Ⓐ Ⓑ Ⓒ Ⓓ
100. Ⓐ Ⓑ Ⓒ Ⓓ

READING SECTION

101. Ⓐ Ⓑ Ⓒ Ⓓ
102. Ⓐ Ⓑ Ⓒ Ⓓ
103. Ⓐ Ⓑ Ⓒ Ⓓ
104. Ⓐ Ⓑ Ⓒ Ⓓ
105. Ⓐ Ⓑ Ⓒ Ⓓ
106. Ⓐ Ⓑ Ⓒ Ⓓ
107. Ⓐ Ⓑ Ⓒ Ⓓ
108. Ⓐ Ⓑ Ⓒ Ⓓ
109. Ⓐ Ⓑ Ⓒ Ⓓ
110. Ⓐ Ⓑ Ⓒ Ⓓ
111. Ⓐ Ⓑ Ⓒ Ⓓ
112. Ⓐ Ⓑ Ⓒ Ⓓ
113. Ⓐ Ⓑ Ⓒ Ⓓ
114. Ⓐ Ⓑ Ⓒ Ⓓ
115. Ⓐ Ⓑ Ⓒ Ⓓ
116. Ⓐ Ⓑ Ⓒ Ⓓ
117. Ⓐ Ⓑ Ⓒ Ⓓ
118. Ⓐ Ⓑ Ⓒ Ⓓ
119. Ⓐ Ⓑ Ⓒ Ⓓ
120. Ⓐ Ⓑ Ⓒ Ⓓ
121. Ⓐ Ⓑ Ⓒ Ⓓ
122. Ⓐ Ⓑ Ⓒ Ⓓ
123. Ⓐ Ⓑ Ⓒ Ⓓ
124. Ⓐ Ⓑ Ⓒ Ⓓ
125. Ⓐ Ⓑ Ⓒ Ⓓ

126. Ⓐ Ⓑ Ⓒ Ⓓ
127. Ⓐ Ⓑ Ⓒ Ⓓ
128. Ⓐ Ⓑ Ⓒ Ⓓ
129. Ⓐ Ⓑ Ⓒ Ⓓ
130. Ⓐ Ⓑ Ⓒ Ⓓ
131. Ⓐ Ⓑ Ⓒ Ⓓ
132. Ⓐ Ⓑ Ⓒ Ⓓ
133. Ⓐ Ⓑ Ⓒ Ⓓ
134. Ⓐ Ⓑ Ⓒ Ⓓ
135. Ⓐ Ⓑ Ⓒ Ⓓ
136. Ⓐ Ⓑ Ⓒ Ⓓ
137. Ⓐ Ⓑ Ⓒ Ⓓ
138. Ⓐ Ⓑ Ⓒ Ⓓ
139. Ⓐ Ⓑ Ⓒ Ⓓ
140. Ⓐ Ⓑ Ⓒ Ⓓ
141. Ⓐ Ⓑ Ⓒ Ⓓ
142. Ⓐ Ⓑ Ⓒ Ⓓ
143. Ⓐ Ⓑ Ⓒ Ⓓ
144. Ⓐ Ⓑ Ⓒ Ⓓ
145. Ⓐ Ⓑ Ⓒ Ⓓ
146. Ⓐ Ⓑ Ⓒ Ⓓ
147. Ⓐ Ⓑ Ⓒ Ⓓ
148. Ⓐ Ⓑ Ⓒ Ⓓ
149. Ⓐ Ⓑ Ⓒ Ⓓ
150. Ⓐ Ⓑ Ⓒ Ⓓ

151. Ⓐ Ⓑ Ⓒ Ⓓ
152. Ⓐ Ⓑ Ⓒ Ⓓ
153. Ⓐ Ⓑ Ⓒ Ⓓ
154. Ⓐ Ⓑ Ⓒ Ⓓ
155. Ⓐ Ⓑ Ⓒ Ⓓ
156. Ⓐ Ⓑ Ⓒ Ⓓ
157. Ⓐ Ⓑ Ⓒ Ⓓ
158. Ⓐ Ⓑ Ⓒ Ⓓ
159. Ⓐ Ⓑ Ⓒ Ⓓ
160. Ⓐ Ⓑ Ⓒ Ⓓ
161. Ⓐ Ⓑ Ⓒ Ⓓ
162. Ⓐ Ⓑ Ⓒ Ⓓ
163. Ⓐ Ⓑ Ⓒ Ⓓ
164. Ⓐ Ⓑ Ⓒ Ⓓ
165. Ⓐ Ⓑ Ⓒ Ⓓ
166. Ⓐ Ⓑ Ⓒ Ⓓ
167. Ⓐ Ⓑ Ⓒ Ⓓ
168. Ⓐ Ⓑ Ⓒ Ⓓ
169. Ⓐ Ⓑ Ⓒ Ⓓ
170. Ⓐ Ⓑ Ⓒ Ⓓ
171. Ⓐ Ⓑ Ⓒ Ⓓ
172. Ⓐ Ⓑ Ⓒ Ⓓ
173. Ⓐ Ⓑ Ⓒ Ⓓ
174. Ⓐ Ⓑ Ⓒ Ⓓ
175. Ⓐ Ⓑ Ⓒ Ⓓ

176. Ⓐ Ⓑ Ⓒ Ⓓ
177. Ⓐ Ⓑ Ⓒ Ⓓ
178. Ⓐ Ⓑ Ⓒ Ⓓ
179. Ⓐ Ⓑ Ⓒ Ⓓ
180. Ⓐ Ⓑ Ⓒ Ⓓ
181. Ⓐ Ⓑ Ⓒ Ⓓ
182. Ⓐ Ⓑ Ⓒ Ⓓ
183. Ⓐ Ⓑ Ⓒ Ⓓ
184. Ⓐ Ⓑ Ⓒ Ⓓ
185. Ⓐ Ⓑ Ⓒ Ⓓ
186. Ⓐ Ⓑ Ⓒ Ⓓ
187. Ⓐ Ⓑ Ⓒ Ⓓ
188. Ⓐ Ⓑ Ⓒ Ⓓ
189. Ⓐ Ⓑ Ⓒ Ⓓ
190. Ⓐ Ⓑ Ⓒ Ⓓ
191. Ⓐ Ⓑ Ⓒ Ⓓ
192. Ⓐ Ⓑ Ⓒ Ⓓ
193. Ⓐ Ⓑ Ⓒ Ⓓ
194. Ⓐ Ⓑ Ⓒ Ⓓ
195. Ⓐ Ⓑ Ⓒ Ⓓ
196. Ⓐ Ⓑ Ⓒ Ⓓ
197. Ⓐ Ⓑ Ⓒ Ⓓ
198. Ⓐ Ⓑ Ⓒ Ⓓ
199. Ⓐ Ⓑ Ⓒ Ⓓ
200. Ⓐ Ⓑ Ⓒ Ⓓ

TCS		
3R	3CS
2R	2CS
1R	1CS

Target Score Review Tests Answer Sheet

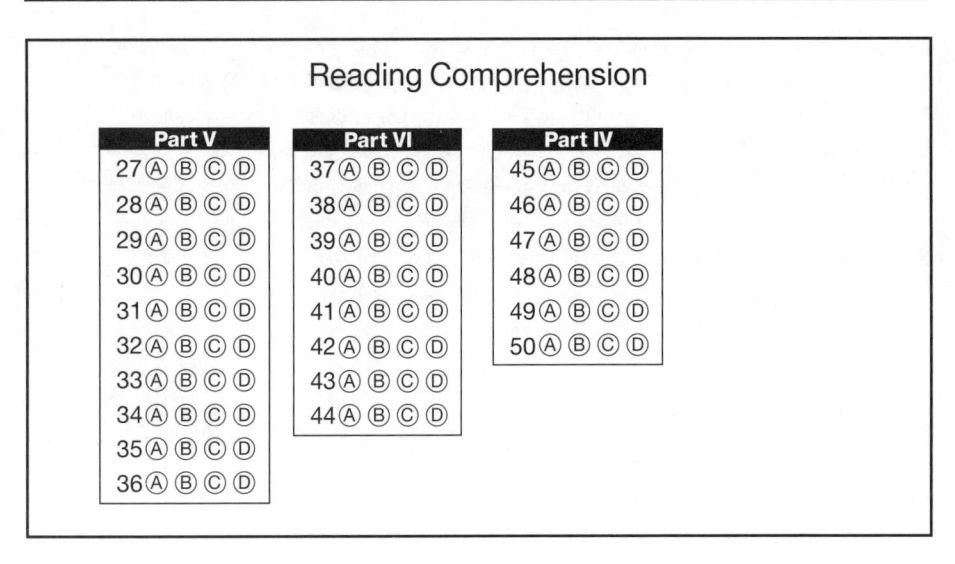

Listening Comprehension

Part I
1. Ⓐ Ⓑ Ⓒ Ⓓ
2. Ⓐ Ⓑ Ⓒ Ⓓ
3. Ⓐ Ⓑ Ⓒ Ⓓ
4. Ⓐ Ⓑ Ⓒ Ⓓ
5. Ⓐ Ⓑ Ⓒ Ⓓ
6. Ⓐ Ⓑ Ⓒ Ⓓ

Part II
7. Ⓐ Ⓑ Ⓒ Ⓓ
8. Ⓐ Ⓑ Ⓒ Ⓓ
9. Ⓐ Ⓑ Ⓒ Ⓓ
10. Ⓐ Ⓑ Ⓒ Ⓓ
11. Ⓐ Ⓑ Ⓒ Ⓓ
12. Ⓐ Ⓑ Ⓒ Ⓓ
13. Ⓐ Ⓑ Ⓒ Ⓓ
14. Ⓐ Ⓑ Ⓒ Ⓓ

Part III
15. Ⓐ Ⓑ Ⓒ Ⓓ
16. Ⓐ Ⓑ Ⓒ Ⓓ
17. Ⓐ Ⓑ Ⓒ Ⓓ
18. Ⓐ Ⓑ Ⓒ Ⓓ
19. Ⓐ Ⓑ Ⓒ Ⓓ
20. Ⓐ Ⓑ Ⓒ Ⓓ
21. Ⓐ Ⓑ Ⓒ Ⓓ

Part IV
22. Ⓐ Ⓑ Ⓒ Ⓓ
23. Ⓐ Ⓑ Ⓒ Ⓓ
24. Ⓐ Ⓑ Ⓒ Ⓓ
25. Ⓐ Ⓑ Ⓒ Ⓓ
26. Ⓐ Ⓑ Ⓒ Ⓓ

Reading Comprehension

Part V
27. Ⓐ Ⓑ Ⓒ Ⓓ
28. Ⓐ Ⓑ Ⓒ Ⓓ
29. Ⓐ Ⓑ Ⓒ Ⓓ
30. Ⓐ Ⓑ Ⓒ Ⓓ
31. Ⓐ Ⓑ Ⓒ Ⓓ
32. Ⓐ Ⓑ Ⓒ Ⓓ
33. Ⓐ Ⓑ Ⓒ Ⓓ
34. Ⓐ Ⓑ Ⓒ Ⓓ
35. Ⓐ Ⓑ Ⓒ Ⓓ
36. Ⓐ Ⓑ Ⓒ Ⓓ

Part VI
37. Ⓐ Ⓑ Ⓒ Ⓓ
38. Ⓐ Ⓑ Ⓒ Ⓓ
39. Ⓐ Ⓑ Ⓒ Ⓓ
40. Ⓐ Ⓑ Ⓒ Ⓓ
41. Ⓐ Ⓑ Ⓒ Ⓓ
42. Ⓐ Ⓑ Ⓒ Ⓓ
43. Ⓐ Ⓑ Ⓒ Ⓓ
44. Ⓐ Ⓑ Ⓒ Ⓓ

Part IV
45. Ⓐ Ⓑ Ⓒ Ⓓ
46. Ⓐ Ⓑ Ⓒ Ⓓ
47. Ⓐ Ⓑ Ⓒ Ⓓ
48. Ⓐ Ⓑ Ⓒ Ⓓ
49. Ⓐ Ⓑ Ⓒ Ⓓ
50. Ⓐ Ⓑ Ⓒ Ⓓ

Target Score Second Edition
Final Practice TOEIC® Test

The TOEIC® test directions and Answer sheet are reprinted by permission of Educational Testing Service, the copyright owner. However, the test questions and any other testing information are provided in their entirety by Cambridge University Press. No endorsement of this publication by Educational Testing Service should be inferred.

TOEIC® is a registered trademark of Educational Testing Service (ETS). This publication is not endorsed or approved by ETS.

Be sure to completely fill in the circle that corresponds to your answer choice. Completely erase errors or stray marks.

	CORRECT	WRONG	WRONG	WRONG	WRONG
EXAMPLE:	Ⓐ Ⓑ ● Ⓓ	Ⓐ Ⓑ ⊘ Ⓓ	Ⓐ Ⓑ ⊗ Ⓓ	Ⓐ Ⓑ ◉ Ⓓ	Ⓐ Ⓑ Ⓒ Ⓓ

LISTENING SECTION

1 Ⓐ Ⓑ Ⓒ Ⓓ	26 Ⓐ Ⓑ Ⓒ	51 Ⓐ Ⓑ Ⓒ Ⓓ	76 Ⓐ Ⓑ Ⓒ Ⓓ
2 Ⓐ Ⓑ Ⓒ Ⓓ	27 Ⓐ Ⓑ Ⓒ	52 Ⓐ Ⓑ Ⓒ Ⓓ	77 Ⓐ Ⓑ Ⓒ Ⓓ
3 Ⓐ Ⓑ Ⓒ Ⓓ	28 Ⓐ Ⓑ Ⓒ	53 Ⓐ Ⓑ Ⓒ Ⓓ	78 Ⓐ Ⓑ Ⓒ Ⓓ
4 Ⓐ Ⓑ Ⓒ Ⓓ	29 Ⓐ Ⓑ Ⓒ	54 Ⓐ Ⓑ Ⓒ Ⓓ	79 Ⓐ Ⓑ Ⓒ Ⓓ
5 Ⓐ Ⓑ Ⓒ Ⓓ	30 Ⓐ Ⓑ Ⓒ	55 Ⓐ Ⓑ Ⓒ Ⓓ	80 Ⓐ Ⓑ Ⓒ Ⓓ
6 Ⓐ Ⓑ Ⓒ Ⓓ	31 Ⓐ Ⓑ Ⓒ	56 Ⓐ Ⓑ Ⓒ Ⓓ	81 Ⓐ Ⓑ Ⓒ Ⓓ
7 Ⓐ Ⓑ Ⓒ Ⓓ	32 Ⓐ Ⓑ Ⓒ	57 Ⓐ Ⓑ Ⓒ Ⓓ	82 Ⓐ Ⓑ Ⓒ Ⓓ
8 Ⓐ Ⓑ Ⓒ Ⓓ	33 Ⓐ Ⓑ Ⓒ	58 Ⓐ Ⓑ Ⓒ Ⓓ	83 Ⓐ Ⓑ Ⓒ Ⓓ
9 Ⓐ Ⓑ Ⓒ Ⓓ	34 Ⓐ Ⓑ Ⓒ	59 Ⓐ Ⓑ Ⓒ Ⓓ	84 Ⓐ Ⓑ Ⓒ Ⓓ
10 Ⓐ Ⓑ Ⓒ Ⓓ	35 Ⓐ Ⓑ Ⓒ	60 Ⓐ Ⓑ Ⓒ Ⓓ	85 Ⓐ Ⓑ Ⓒ Ⓓ
11 Ⓐ Ⓑ Ⓒ	36 Ⓐ Ⓑ Ⓒ	61 Ⓐ Ⓑ Ⓒ Ⓓ	86 Ⓐ Ⓑ Ⓒ Ⓓ
12 Ⓐ Ⓑ Ⓒ	37 Ⓐ Ⓑ Ⓒ	62 Ⓐ Ⓑ Ⓒ Ⓓ	87 Ⓐ Ⓑ Ⓒ Ⓓ
13 Ⓐ Ⓑ Ⓒ	38 Ⓐ Ⓑ Ⓒ	63 Ⓐ Ⓑ Ⓒ Ⓓ	88 Ⓐ Ⓑ Ⓒ Ⓓ
14 Ⓐ Ⓑ Ⓒ	39 Ⓐ Ⓑ Ⓒ	64 Ⓐ Ⓑ Ⓒ Ⓓ	89 Ⓐ Ⓑ Ⓒ Ⓓ
15 Ⓐ Ⓑ Ⓒ	40 Ⓐ Ⓑ Ⓒ	65 Ⓐ Ⓑ Ⓒ Ⓓ	90 Ⓐ Ⓑ Ⓒ Ⓓ
16 Ⓐ Ⓑ Ⓒ	41 Ⓐ Ⓑ Ⓒ Ⓓ	66 Ⓐ Ⓑ Ⓒ Ⓓ	91 Ⓐ Ⓑ Ⓒ Ⓓ
17 Ⓐ Ⓑ Ⓒ	42 Ⓐ Ⓑ Ⓒ Ⓓ	67 Ⓐ Ⓑ Ⓒ Ⓓ	92 Ⓐ Ⓑ Ⓒ Ⓓ
18 Ⓐ Ⓑ Ⓒ	43 Ⓐ Ⓑ Ⓒ Ⓓ	68 Ⓐ Ⓑ Ⓒ Ⓓ	93 Ⓐ Ⓑ Ⓒ Ⓓ
19 Ⓐ Ⓑ Ⓒ	44 Ⓐ Ⓑ Ⓒ Ⓓ	69 Ⓐ Ⓑ Ⓒ Ⓓ	94 Ⓐ Ⓑ Ⓒ Ⓓ
20 Ⓐ Ⓑ Ⓒ	45 Ⓐ Ⓑ Ⓒ Ⓓ	70 Ⓐ Ⓑ Ⓒ Ⓓ	95 Ⓐ Ⓑ Ⓒ Ⓓ
21 Ⓐ Ⓑ Ⓒ	46 Ⓐ Ⓑ Ⓒ Ⓓ	71 Ⓐ Ⓑ Ⓒ Ⓓ	96 Ⓐ Ⓑ Ⓒ Ⓓ
22 Ⓐ Ⓑ Ⓒ	47 Ⓐ Ⓑ Ⓒ Ⓓ	72 Ⓐ Ⓑ Ⓒ Ⓓ	97 Ⓐ Ⓑ Ⓒ Ⓓ
23 Ⓐ Ⓑ Ⓒ	48 Ⓐ Ⓑ Ⓒ Ⓓ	73 Ⓐ Ⓑ Ⓒ Ⓓ	98 Ⓐ Ⓑ Ⓒ Ⓓ
24 Ⓐ Ⓑ Ⓒ	49 Ⓐ Ⓑ Ⓒ Ⓓ	74 Ⓐ Ⓑ Ⓒ Ⓓ	99 Ⓐ Ⓑ Ⓒ Ⓓ
25 Ⓐ Ⓑ Ⓒ	50 Ⓐ Ⓑ Ⓒ Ⓓ	75 Ⓐ Ⓑ Ⓒ Ⓓ	100 Ⓐ Ⓑ Ⓒ Ⓓ

READING SECTION

101 Ⓐ Ⓑ Ⓒ Ⓓ	126 Ⓐ Ⓑ Ⓒ Ⓓ	151 Ⓐ Ⓑ Ⓒ Ⓓ	176 Ⓐ Ⓑ Ⓒ Ⓓ
102 Ⓐ Ⓑ Ⓒ Ⓓ	127 Ⓐ Ⓑ Ⓒ Ⓓ	152 Ⓐ Ⓑ Ⓒ Ⓓ	177 Ⓐ Ⓑ Ⓒ Ⓓ
103 Ⓐ Ⓑ Ⓒ Ⓓ	128 Ⓐ Ⓑ Ⓒ Ⓓ	153 Ⓐ Ⓑ Ⓒ Ⓓ	178 Ⓐ Ⓑ Ⓒ Ⓓ
104 Ⓐ Ⓑ Ⓒ Ⓓ	129 Ⓐ Ⓑ Ⓒ Ⓓ	154 Ⓐ Ⓑ Ⓒ Ⓓ	179 Ⓐ Ⓑ Ⓒ Ⓓ
105 Ⓐ Ⓑ Ⓒ Ⓓ	130 Ⓐ Ⓑ Ⓒ Ⓓ	155 Ⓐ Ⓑ Ⓒ Ⓓ	180 Ⓐ Ⓑ Ⓒ Ⓓ
106 Ⓐ Ⓑ Ⓒ Ⓓ	131 Ⓐ Ⓑ Ⓒ Ⓓ	156 Ⓐ Ⓑ Ⓒ Ⓓ	181 Ⓐ Ⓑ Ⓒ Ⓓ
107 Ⓐ Ⓑ Ⓒ Ⓓ	132 Ⓐ Ⓑ Ⓒ Ⓓ	157 Ⓐ Ⓑ Ⓒ Ⓓ	182 Ⓐ Ⓑ Ⓒ Ⓓ
108 Ⓐ Ⓑ Ⓒ Ⓓ	133 Ⓐ Ⓑ Ⓒ Ⓓ	158 Ⓐ Ⓑ Ⓒ Ⓓ	183 Ⓐ Ⓑ Ⓒ Ⓓ
109 Ⓐ Ⓑ Ⓒ Ⓓ	134 Ⓐ Ⓑ Ⓒ Ⓓ	159 Ⓐ Ⓑ Ⓒ Ⓓ	184 Ⓐ Ⓑ Ⓒ Ⓓ
110 Ⓐ Ⓑ Ⓒ Ⓓ	135 Ⓐ Ⓑ Ⓒ Ⓓ	160 Ⓐ Ⓑ Ⓒ Ⓓ	185 Ⓐ Ⓑ Ⓒ Ⓓ
111 Ⓐ Ⓑ Ⓒ Ⓓ	136 Ⓐ Ⓑ Ⓒ Ⓓ	161 Ⓐ Ⓑ Ⓒ Ⓓ	186 Ⓐ Ⓑ Ⓒ Ⓓ
112 Ⓐ Ⓑ Ⓒ Ⓓ	137 Ⓐ Ⓑ Ⓒ Ⓓ	162 Ⓐ Ⓑ Ⓒ Ⓓ	187 Ⓐ Ⓑ Ⓒ Ⓓ
113 Ⓐ Ⓑ Ⓒ Ⓓ	138 Ⓐ Ⓑ Ⓒ Ⓓ	163 Ⓐ Ⓑ Ⓒ Ⓓ	188 Ⓐ Ⓑ Ⓒ Ⓓ
114 Ⓐ Ⓑ Ⓒ Ⓓ	139 Ⓐ Ⓑ Ⓒ Ⓓ	164 Ⓐ Ⓑ Ⓒ Ⓓ	189 Ⓐ Ⓑ Ⓒ Ⓓ
115 Ⓐ Ⓑ Ⓒ Ⓓ	140 Ⓐ Ⓑ Ⓒ Ⓓ	165 Ⓐ Ⓑ Ⓒ Ⓓ	190 Ⓐ Ⓑ Ⓒ Ⓓ
116 Ⓐ Ⓑ Ⓒ Ⓓ	141 Ⓐ Ⓑ Ⓒ Ⓓ	166 Ⓐ Ⓑ Ⓒ Ⓓ	191 Ⓐ Ⓑ Ⓒ Ⓓ
117 Ⓐ Ⓑ Ⓒ Ⓓ	142 Ⓐ Ⓑ Ⓒ Ⓓ	167 Ⓐ Ⓑ Ⓒ Ⓓ	192 Ⓐ Ⓑ Ⓒ Ⓓ
118 Ⓐ Ⓑ Ⓒ Ⓓ	143 Ⓐ Ⓑ Ⓒ Ⓓ	168 Ⓐ Ⓑ Ⓒ Ⓓ	193 Ⓐ Ⓑ Ⓒ Ⓓ
119 Ⓐ Ⓑ Ⓒ Ⓓ	144 Ⓐ Ⓑ Ⓒ Ⓓ	169 Ⓐ Ⓑ Ⓒ Ⓓ	194 Ⓐ Ⓑ Ⓒ Ⓓ
120 Ⓐ Ⓑ Ⓒ Ⓓ	145 Ⓐ Ⓑ Ⓒ Ⓓ	170 Ⓐ Ⓑ Ⓒ Ⓓ	195 Ⓐ Ⓑ Ⓒ Ⓓ
121 Ⓐ Ⓑ Ⓒ Ⓓ	146 Ⓐ Ⓑ Ⓒ Ⓓ	171 Ⓐ Ⓑ Ⓒ Ⓓ	196 Ⓐ Ⓑ Ⓒ Ⓓ
122 Ⓐ Ⓑ Ⓒ Ⓓ	147 Ⓐ Ⓑ Ⓒ Ⓓ	172 Ⓐ Ⓑ Ⓒ Ⓓ	197 Ⓐ Ⓑ Ⓒ Ⓓ
123 Ⓐ Ⓑ Ⓒ Ⓓ	148 Ⓐ Ⓑ Ⓒ Ⓓ	173 Ⓐ Ⓑ Ⓒ Ⓓ	198 Ⓐ Ⓑ Ⓒ Ⓓ
124 Ⓐ Ⓑ Ⓒ Ⓓ	149 Ⓐ Ⓑ Ⓒ Ⓓ	174 Ⓐ Ⓑ Ⓒ Ⓓ	199 Ⓐ Ⓑ Ⓒ Ⓓ
125 Ⓐ Ⓑ Ⓒ Ⓓ	150 Ⓐ Ⓑ Ⓒ Ⓓ	175 Ⓐ Ⓑ Ⓒ Ⓓ	200 Ⓐ Ⓑ Ⓒ Ⓓ

1R	1CS
2R	2CS
3R	3CS
TCS	

LISTENING TEST

In the Listening test, you will be asked to demonstrate how well you understand spoken English. The entire Listening test will last approximately 45 minutes. There are four parts, and directions are given for each part. You must mark your answers on the separate answer sheet. Do not write your answers in your test book.

PART 1

Directions: For each question in this part, you will hear four statements about a picture in your test book. When you hear the statements, you must select the one statement that best describes what you see in the picture. Then find the number of the question on your answer sheet and mark your answer. The statements will not be printed in your test book and will be spoken only one time.

Sample Answer
Ⓐ Ⓑ ● Ⓓ

Example

Statement (C), "They're standing near the table," is the best description of the picture, so you should select answer (C) and mark it on your answer sheet.

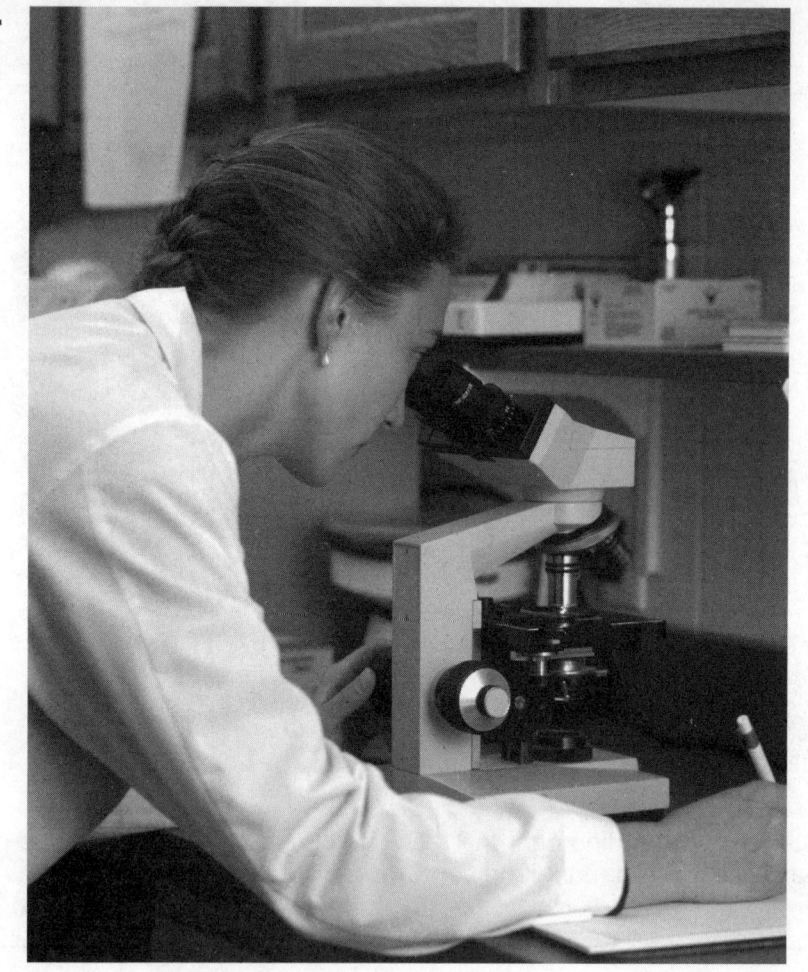

1.

2.

3.

4.

GO ON TO THE NEXT PAGE

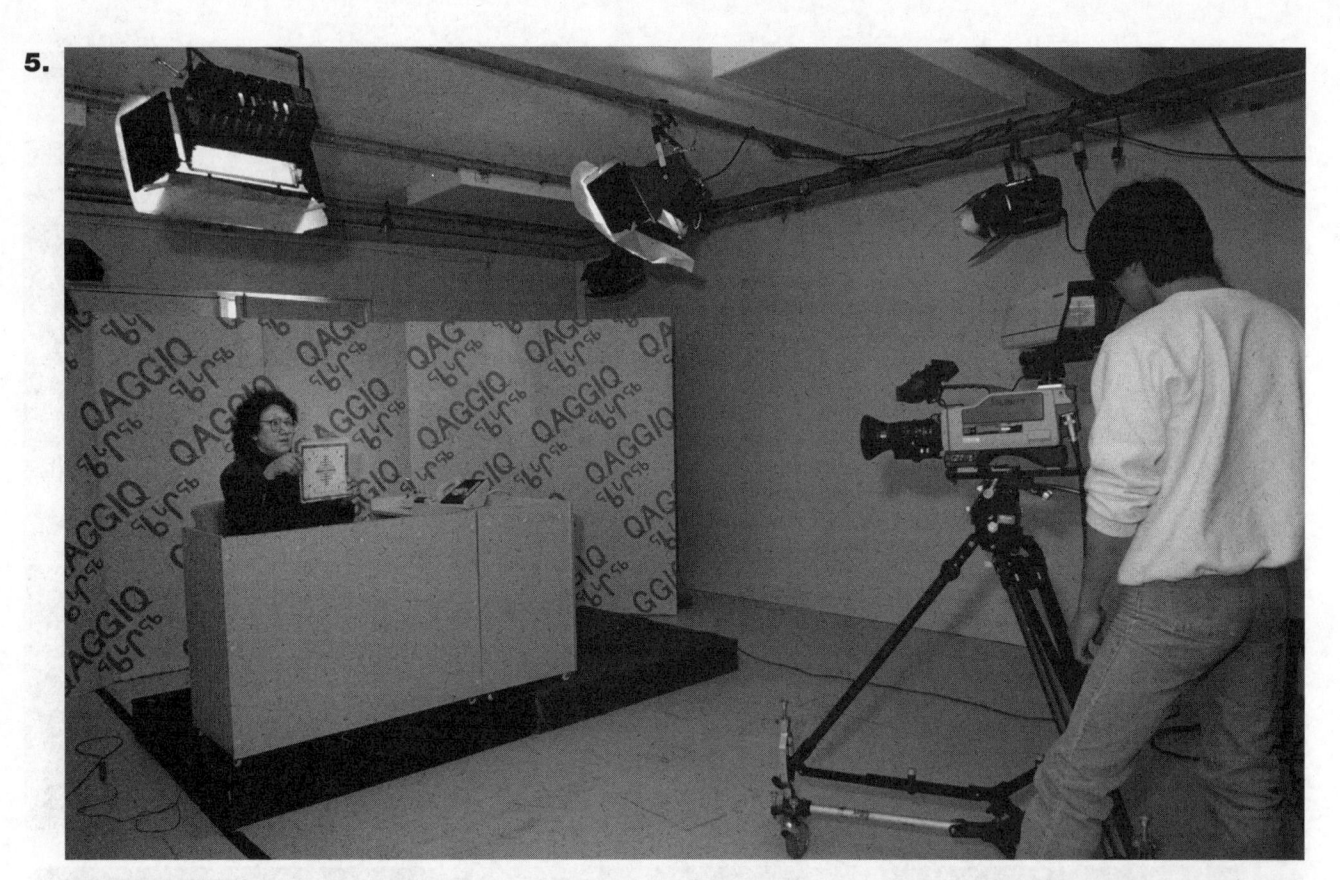

5.

6.

7.

8.

GO ON TO THE NEXT PAGE

9.

10.

PART 2

Directions: You will hear a question or statement and three responses spoken in English. They will not be printed in your test book and will be spoken only one time. Select the best response to the question or statement and mark the letter (A), (B), or (C) on your answer sheet.

Sample Answer
Ⓐ ● Ⓒ

You will hear: Where is the meeting room?

You will also hear: (A) To meet the new director.
(B) It's the first room on the right.
(C) Yes, at two o'clock.

The best response to the question "Where is the meeting room?" is choice (B), "It's the first room on the right," so (B) is the correct answer. You should mark answer (B) on your answer sheet.

11. Mark your answer on your answer sheet.
12. Mark your answer on your answer sheet.
13. Mark your answer on your answer sheet.
14. Mark your answer on your answer sheet.
15. Mark your answer on your answer sheet.
16. Mark your answer on your answer sheet.
17. Mark your answer on your answer sheet.
18. Mark your answer on your answer sheet.
19. Mark your answer on your answer sheet.
20. Mark your answer on your answer sheet.
21. Mark your answer on your answer sheet.
22. Mark your answer on your answer sheet.
23. Mark your answer on your answer sheet.
24. Mark your answer on your answer sheet.
25. Mark your answer on your answer sheet.
26. Mark your answer on your answer sheet.
27. Mark your answer on your answer sheet.
28. Mark your answer on your answer sheet.
29. Mark your answer on your answer sheet.
30. Mark your answer on your answer sheet.
31. Mark your answer on your answer sheet.
32. Mark your answer on your answer sheet.
33. Mark your answer on your answer sheet.
34. Mark your answer on your answer sheet.
35. Mark your answer on your answer sheet.
36. Mark your answer on your answer sheet.
37. Mark your answer on your answer sheet.
38. Mark your answer on your answer sheet.
39. Mark your answer on your answer sheet.
40. Mark your answer on your answer sheet.

GO ON TO THE NEXT PAGE

PART 3

Directions: You will hear some conversations between two people. You will be asked to answer three questions about what the speakers say in each conversation. Select the best response to each question and mark the letter (A), (B), (C), or (D) on your answer sheet. The conversations will not be printed in your test book and will be spoken only one time.

41. What are the speakers doing?
    (A) Asking for directions
    (B) Making a delivery
    (C) Attending a meeting
    (D) Purchasing new office furniture

42. Why is the office being moved?
    (A) It is too small.
    (B) It is too big.
    (C) It is too expensive.
    (D) It is too far from the center of town.

43. Where will the new office probably be located?
    (A) In another town
    (B) In the same part of town
    (C) Overseas
    (D) In another state

44. Where does this conversation take place?
    (A) In a classroom
    (B) In a restaurant
    (C) In a store
    (D) In a waiting room

45. What has the man decided to do?
    (A) Order now
    (B) Change an order
    (C) Pay the bill
    (D) Order later

46. What sort of meal will the clients be having?
    (A) A three-course meal
    (B) An appetizer and a main course
    (C) A main course and a dessert
    (D) A main course only

47. What is the man's profession?
    (A) A dentist
    (B) A guide
    (C) A mechanic
    (D) A musician

48. Why has Mrs. Webster taken her car in?
    (A) To have the engine repaired
    (B) To have the windshield replaced
    (C) To have the lights checked
    (D) To have the car serviced

49. Who will pick up the vehicle?
    (A) Mrs. Webster
    (B) Mr. Webster
    (C) The workshop manager
    (D) A driving instructor

50. How much luggage will the man be checking?
    (A) Three bags
    (B) Two bags
    (C) One bag
    (D) None

51. At what time does boarding begin?
    (A) At three
    (B) At five
    (C) At seven
    (D) At eight

52. Which of the following is NOT true about the man's flight?
    (A) It leaves in the evening.
    (B) It leaves from gate E-3.
    (C) It has business class seating.
    (D) It has been delayed.

53. Why is Margaret moving to New York?
    (A) She is leaving the company.
    (B) She has received a promotion.
    (C) She has been laid off.
    (D) She is retiring.

54. What is Margaret's position?
    (A) Junior manager
    (B) Foreman
    (C) President
    (D) Vice President

55. How long has Margaret been with the group?
 (A) Two years
 (B) Three years
 (C) Four years
 (D) Five years

56. What are they discussing?
 (A) Purchasing a home
 (B) Improving the neighborhood
 (C) Investing in the stock market
 (D) Negotiating a new order

57. How many children does Nancy have?
 (A) 1
 (B) 2
 (C) 3
 (D) 4

58. Which of the following advantages does the Greenwood area offer?
 (A) High quality education
 (B) Low taxes
 (C) Cheap housing
 (D) Easy access to public transport

59. When will Steve take his vacation?
 (A) In a month
 (B) In two weeks
 (C) At the end of this week
 (D) Today

60. What does Steve intend to do during his break?
 (A) Finish some work
 (B) Play golf
 (C) Repair his home
 (D) Take a cruise

61. Where will the woman spend her vacation?
 (A) At a beach resort
 (B) On a ship
 (C) In the mountains
 (D) At a camp site

62. Who will be in Mr. Honda's office on Monday?
 (A) Clients
 (B) Supervisors
 (C) Secretaries
 (D) Workmen

63. What has been installed in the conference room?
 (A) A video projector
 (B) A coffee machine
 (C) Computer equipment
 (D) Electrical cables

64. What will Mr. Honda have to do?
 (A) Change the date of a meeting
 (B) Cancel a conference call
 (C) Move his office furniture
 (D) Meet someone at the station

65. How is the woman feeling?
 (A) Dissatisfied
 (B) Satisfied
 (C) Enthusiastic
 (D) Relieved

66. What has the woman received?
 (A) A bill
 (B) An estimate
 (C) Some brochures
 (D) An invitation

67. Why is the woman calling Mr. Hanser?
 (A) To negotiate a discount
 (B) To request documentation
 (C) To complain about a delivery
 (D) To confirm an appointment

68. What did Anita forget to do?
 (A) Write a report
 (B) Pass on information
 (C) Call Mr. Lee
 (D) Prepare the sales presentation

69. Who will be attending Mr. Lee's presentation?
 (A) The sales staff
 (B) Anita
 (C) Mr. Jensen
 (D) The editor of the newsletter

70. When will Mr. Lee return the item?
 (A) This morning
 (B) This afternoon
 (C) Tomorrow
 (D) At the end of the week

GO ON TO THE NEXT PAGE

PART 4

Directions: You will hear some talks given by a single speaker. You will be asked to answer three questions about what the speaker says in each talk. Select the best response to each question and mark the letter (A), (B), (C), or (D) on your answer sheet. The talks will not be printed in your test book and will be spoken only one time.

71. Where would this talk most likely be heard?
- (A) On a construction site
- (B) In a warehouse
- (C) On a city tour
- (D) In a store

72. When was the building constructed?
- (A) After 1900
- (B) Between 1850 and 1900
- (C) Before 1800
- (D) Between 1800 and 1850

73. What is the unique feature of the building?
- (A) The magnificent view
- (B) The woodwork on its doors
- (C) Its outdoor pool
- (D) Its seven floors

74. Who is the speaker?
- (A) A scientist
- (B) A stockbroker
- (C) A financial consultant
- (D) A trustee

75. How will they use the money?
- (A) To build a new facility
- (B) To reward board members
- (C) To hire new staff
- (D) To give personnel advances

76. What is the purpose of this talk?
- (A) To recruit new researchers
- (B) To celebrate an achievement
- (C) To announce quarterly earnings
- (D) To award bonuses

77. How many companies will merge?
- (A) 2
- (B) 3
- (C) 4
- (D) 6

78. When will the merger likely occur?
- (A) In five years
- (B) In six months
- (C) Next week
- (D) On Tuesday

79. What would the merger allow the new company to do?
- (A) To expand its human resources department
- (B) To specialize in automobile insurance
- (C) To focus on expanding its business insurance sector
- (D) To reduce home insurance costs by 30%

80. What does this organization provide?
- (A) Business loans
- (B) Cash flow
- (C) Advice
- (D) Managers

81. Who would be interested in this announcement?
- (A) Professional counselors
- (B) Financial advisors
- (C) Business mentors
- (D) Small business owners

82. How much does this service cost?
- (A) Thousands of dollars
- (B) A small fee
- (C) Eight hundred dollars
- (D) Nothing

83. Where is the workshop being held?
- (A) At company headquarters
- (B) At the front desk of a hotel
- (C) On a train
- (D) In a mall

84. Who would attend this workshop?
- (A) Dissatisfied customers
- (B) Front desk clerks
- (C) Hospital directors
- (D) Hotel managers

85. What is the purpose of this talk?
    (A) To develop online training tools
    (B) To present a staff training plan
    (C) To review performance
    (D) To announce results

86. To whom is this announcement being made?
    (A) Emergency workers
    (B) Local residents
    (C) Gas salesmen
    (D) Public health officials

87. What are people advised to do?
    (A) Heat their homes safely
    (B) Leave their homes
    (C) Use ovens for heating
    (D) Burn charcoal indoors

88. What is the cause of the problem?
    (A) Electrical storms
    (B) Snowstorms
    (C) High winds
    (D) Heavy rain

89. Who is this message intended for?
    (A) Bank security officers
    (B) Bank customers
    (C) Service representatives
    (D) Customer assistants

90. What happens to all incoming calls?
    (A) They are transferred to a local branch.
    (B) They are recorded.
    (C) They are put on hold.
    (D) They are used for advertising.

91. Which of the following services is NOT offered?
    (A) Information about borrowing money
    (B) Stock transactions
    (C) Information about accounts
    (D) Money transfers

92. Why was the flight cancelled?
    (A) Scheduling conflicts
    (B) Bad weather
    (C) Mechanical failure
    (D) Baggage loading problems

93. Where is the checked baggage?
    (A) In Chicago
    (B) At a hotel
    (C) On the airplane
    (D) At Gate 5

94. What is the airline offering the passengers?
    (A) A coupon for a free flight
    (B) A refund check
    (C) A free night in a hotel
    (D) Complimentary luggage

95. When is the conference dinner?
    (A) Today
    (B) Tomorrow
    (C) On Friday
    (D) On Saturday

96. What does the speaker have to do?
    (A) Pay the caterer in advance
    (B) Tell the caterer how many people will attend
    (C) Reserve the Pine Ridge Ballroom
    (D) Get more seats

97. What is the man announcing?
    (A) The menu has changed.
    (B) It is too late to register.
    (C) It is still possible to sign up.
    (D) The dinner has been postponed.

98. Who is organizing today's event?
    (A) The East Coast Chronicle
    (B) The Chamber of Commerce
    (C) Business Ventures
    (D) LV Associates

99. What sort of business did Benjamin Levitt start?
    (A) An insurance company
    (B) A venture capital firm
    (C) A consultancy
    (D) A business magazine

100. How long will the "Business Start-up" event last?
    (A) Half a day
    (B) One day
    (C) Two days
    (D) One week

GO ON TO THE NEXT PAGE

READING TEST

In the Reading test, you will read a variety of texts and answer several different types of reading comprehension questions. The entire Reading test will last 75 minutes. There are three parts, and directions are given for each part. You are encouraged to answer as many questions as possible within the time allowed.

You must mark your answers on the separate answer sheet. Do not write your answers in your test book.

PART 5

Directions: A word or phrase is missing in each of the sentences below. Four answer choices are given below each sentence. Select the best answer to complete the sentence. Then mark the letter (A), (B), (C), or (D) on your answer sheet.

101. As a result _____ the air traffic controllers' strike all flights have been diverted to alternative destinations.
    (A) with
    (B) from
    (C) of
    (D) for

102. Financial _____ are predicting that a slowdown in consumer spending will affect profit margins.
    (A) analysis
    (B) analysts
    (C) analyze
    (D) analytical

103. In her new position as dean of the university, Dr. Morganti will _____ full responsibility for academic affairs and curricular development.
    (A) resume
    (B) presume
    (C) consume
    (D) assume

104. Transferring our _____ facilities to areas with lower labor costs will lead to greater profitability in the long term.
    (A) manufactured
    (B) manufactures
    (C) manufacturing
    (D) manufacturer

105. Product managers _____ performance is considered exceptional will be awarded an annual bonus.
    (A) whose
    (B) who
    (C) which
    (D) whom

106. With energy prices _____ than ever, many petroleum companies are investing in deep water exploration.
    (A) high
    (B) higher
    (C) highly
    (D) highest

107. Brisbane Associates has revealed that several customers of _____ have recently moved to rival brokerage firms.
    (A) them
    (B) their
    (C) theirs
    (D) themselves

108. Mr. Walton's physical therapist recommended that he _____ the treatment until the swelling has gone down.
    (A) continue
    (B) continued
    (C) has continued
    (D) is continuing

109. Many economists believe that the latest figures show that the risk of inflation has _____ slightly over the past six months.
(A) limited
(B) reduced
(C) cut
(D) lessened

110. Hardly _____ of the parts that we ordered are in stock.
(A) any
(B) few
(C) none
(D) some

111. The warehouse manager has been unable to account _____ the missing supplies.
(A) by
(B) for
(C) to
(D) with

112. Ms. Sato admitted that the sales of her division have been _____ but said she expected better results next month.
(A) disappointed
(B) disappointing
(C) disappointingly
(D) disappointment

113. The hotel complex is located five miles _____ the international airport.
(A) away from
(B) far from
(C) next to
(D) along with

114. _____ Mr. Meyers pointed out at the meeting, centralizing the order processing system will mean standardizing procedures across all business units.
(A) As
(B) Such as
(C) Since
(D) So

115. The human resources manager has warned labor unions that prolonged strikes could _____ the company's plans to invest in a new plant and lead to layoffs.
(A) economize
(B) jeopardize
(C) monopolize
(D) penalize

116. Goods that are returned _____ warranty should be accompanied by proof of purchase.
(A) with
(B) under
(C) over
(D) on

117. Health care workers should always explain the _____ effects of physical exercise to their patients.
(A) benefiting
(B) benefits
(C) beneficiary
(D) beneficial

118. Professor Singh argues that the major aid institutions could make better use of the funds that they have at their _____.
(A) disapproval
(B) dismissal
(C) dispersal
(D) disposal

119. Local residents are launching a new _____ to promote greater involvement in community affairs.
(A) initial
(B) initiation
(C) initiate
(D) initiative

120. Under _____ circumstances are visitors allowed to enter the Research and Development center.
(A) none
(B) no
(C) any
(D) all

121. The report form must be completed and _____ to the workshop supervisor within 24 hours of an accident.
(A) substituted
(B) subscribed
(C) submitted
(D) subjected

122. All personnel are required to report for work, _____ of prevailing weather conditions.
(A) although
(B) despite
(C) even
(D) regardless

123. The increase in profits during the third quarter was _____ due to a national advertising campaign.
(A) almost
(B) most
(C) mostly
(D) much

124. Please note that neither Dr. Johnson _____ Dr. Lang is available for consultation on Monday and Friday mornings.
(A) or
(B) nor
(C) but
(D) and

125. The hospital director _____ following allegations of financial mismanagement.
(A) dismissed
(B) has been dismissed
(C) has dismissed
(D) will dismiss

126. _____ flexible work time was introduced, productivity levels have improved by almost five percent.
(A) As
(B) Before
(C) Since
(D) While

127. The Caribbean islands are still one of the most popular tourist _____ during the winter season.
(A) situations
(B) positions
(C) directions
(D) destinations

128. _____ having an advanced degree in molecular biology, Ms. Dempsey has led several research projects in biotechnology.
(A) Beneath
(B) Beside
(C) Besides
(D) Between

129. All things _____, the board's decision to pay a dividend may not have been the right one.
(A) consider
(B) considerable
(C) considerate
(D) considered

130. It is _____ that permission to build will be refused as the site is zoned for residential use only.
(A) likely
(B) possibly
(C) probably
(D) surely

131. There is _____ chance of the mayor being re-elected unless he can restore confidence in the business community.
(A) few
(B) least
(C) low
(D) little

132. Food and beverage suppliers will once again be _____ the main sponsors of this year's Bellevue city marathon.
(A) along
(B) amid
(C) among
(D) around

133. The proposed alliance between the two companies fell _____ after they failed to reach an agreement about the transfer of technology.
(A) through
(B) down
(C) out
(D) over

134. The most successful investors are _____ who can evaluate the effects that strategic challenges will have on a company's stock price.
(A) those
(B) their
(C) these
(D) them

135. Many domestic appliances are left to run continuously and _____ consume large amounts of electricity.
(A) although
(B) even though
(C) whereas
(D) thus

136. Alternative energies will never become economical unless governments _____ incentives to homeowners and corporations.
(A) is providing
(B) provide
(C) provided
(D) will provide

137. We _____ to the joint venture, if we'd known more about our partner's real intentions.
(A) will not agree
(B) will not have agreed
(C) would not agree
(D) would not have agreed

138. ABC Associates has always _____ to provide its clients with innovative and cost-effective solutions for information management.
(A) sought
(B) searched
(C) prepared
(D) demanded

139. With more than 200,000 domestic accidents every year, household safety is not something that should be taken for _____.
(A) granted
(B) accepted
(C) agreed
(D) given

140. Due to the unusually cool weather last month, the number of visitors to the state's major theme parks was _____ lower than forecast.
(A) extremely
(B) highly
(C) significantly
(D) well

GO ON TO THE NEXT PAGE

PART 6

Directions: Read the texts that follow. A word or phrase is missing in some of the sentences. Four answer choices are given below each of the sentences. Select the best answer to complete the text. Then mark the letter (A), (B), (C), or (D) on your answer sheet.

Questions 141–144 refer to the following letter.

ALBERTA BANK
3895 EDMONDTON

Dear Steve Martin

In response to your request, we are switching your current Express® account to our most popular _____ account FullAccess®.

141. (A) check
(B) checked
(C) checking
(D) checker

As a valued customer, we want to make this operation as simple _____ possible for you.

142. (A) than
(B) more
(C) also
(D) as

As of March 1st, we will automatically transfer your funds to your new account. Please note that your existing account number and bank card number will remain the same.

For more information on the benefits of your new FullAccess® account, please visit our website at www.alberta-bank.ca or visit your neighborhood branch.

We would like to remind you that Alberta Bank also offers a wide range of savings accounts that are ideal for customers who wish to earn _____ from their savings.

143. (A) interest
(B) expenditure
(C) investment
(D) insurance

_____ have any additional questions, please contact me at 373-5764.

144. (A) Would you
(B) Should you
(C) Could you
(D) Do you

Sincerely,

Roxanna Babridge

Roxanna Babridge

GO ON TO THE NEXT PAGE

Questions 145–148 refer to the following advertisement.

Do you know that, last year alone, over 20 million cell phone users in this country _____ to switch to newer models?

145. (A) are deciding
(B) have decided
(C) decide
(D) decided

And what did they do with their old ones, you may ask? Well nothing – and that means that _____ phones have now been added to the growing mountain

146. (A) even more
(B) more than
(C) much more
(D) as many as

of disused telephones which is currently estimated at something like 66 million. So, if you are planning on changing yours sometime soon, then _____ of simply discarding it, make a gesture for the environment.

147. (A) as a result
(B) because
(C) in spite
(D) instead

Enclosed with this issue of your monthly magazine, you will find a postage-paid envelope that you can use to send your old phone to us. For each phone that our readers send in, we will receive a donation of £2.50 from RecyclePhone, _____ is currently the world's leading mobile phone recycling company.

148. (A) that
(B) what
(C) whose
(D) which

This money will be used to help us to finance our 'Be Green Aware' campaign, which we will be launching nationwide in July.

Don't miss this opportunity to make your contribution to intelligent recycling.

Questions 149–152 refer to the following email.

From:	Patricia Marchmont <pmarchmont@cityparkvillage.com>
To:	rtsilva@gmail.com
Date:	24 April
Subject:	Reservation

Dear Mr. Silva,

Thank you for your letter enquiring about the availability of rental accommodation at our City Park Village. I am sorry to have to inform you that the village is currently fully booked during the month of August, which is always the _____ time of year for us.

149. (A) busy
(B) busier
(C) busily
(D) busiest

We do, _____, have two apartments at our Highland Gates residence,

150. (A) however
(B) while
(C) although
(D) yet

which are both vacant during the first two weeks of the month. These are both prestige apartments and feature the same standard of high quality furnishings.
The Highland Gates residence is located on the outskirts of the city and is _____ easy reach of the city center and of all the major festival venues.

151. (A) inside
(B) within
(C) into
(D) along

The price is 200 dollars per day and in order to make a reservation we require a 25% deposit at the time of booking with the _____ to be paid in full one month prior to arrival.

152. (A) balance
(B) discount
(C) deduction
(D) addition

Please find attached a brochure with additional information about the Highland Gates residence.
I look forward to welcoming you and your family at Highland Gates in the near future.

Yours sincerely,
Patricia Marchmont

GO ON TO THE NEXT PAGE

PART 7

Directions: In this part you will read a selection of texts, such as magazine and newspaper articles, letters, and advertisements. Each text is followed by several questions. Select the best answer for each question and mark the letter (A), (B), (C), or (D) on your answer sheet.

Questions 153–154 refer to the following notice.

Required Documents for a Visa

1. A passport valid at least six months after departure date.
2. Two ID photographs.
3. A photocopy of your return ticket.
   For a business visa, please attach a letter from your company indicating the reason for travel and an invitation letter from your host.
   If you are applying by mail, please send a self-addressed stamped registered envelope for return.
   Please allow five business days for processing.

FEE
$50 US
Payment is by cash or money order.
Same-day visa processing is available for an extra $50 US.

VACCINATIONS REQUIRED
none

OPENING HOURS
The Visa Department is open Monday through Friday from 10:00 a.m. to 2:00 p.m.

153. What do business travelers have to provide?
(A) A receipt from their travel agent
(B) A vaccination certificate
(C) An additional photo
(D) A letter from their employer

154. How can you obtain a visa in one day?
(A) By applying in person
(B) By paying an additional fee
(C) By sending an express mail envelope
(D) By submitting an invitation letter

GO ON TO THE NEXT PAGE

Questions 155–157 refer to the following notice.

Water shortage warning

State officials have announced that water restrictions will be introduced starting next Monday. As a result of below average rainfall, lake reserves are now at their lowest levels in fifty years. The regional water management authority has issued the following water conservation measures:

- All water users are required to restrict their water use.

- Public and privately-owned water utilities shall restrict the monthly use of water by their customers. They may do this by interrupting supply or by advising their clients on procedures to reduce their consumption.

- Use of water for domestic gardens and yards is permitted on Wednesdays and Saturdays for residents with even house numbers, and on Mondays and Thursdays for residents with odd house numbers.

- For agricultural businesses, irrigation is now limited to the hours between 7 p.m. and midnight.

---

155. What is the purpose of this notice?

(A) To inform residents of water conservation measures
(B) To warn residents of weather conditions
(C) To announce water pollution levels
(D) To promote mineral water sales

156. What actions are water utility companies authorized to take?

(A) Raise their charges
(B) Cut water supply
(C) Supply more water
(D) Develop new lake reserves

157. When can farmers water their crops?

(A) Anytime
(B) Mornings
(C) Afternoons
(D) Evenings

Questions 158–159 refer to the following advertisement.

Job title: Cabin crew member

Company: Sunbeam Airlines
Posted: January 10th

Sunbeam Airlines currently have an opening for a bilingual Cabin crew member. We are looking for talented individuals to join our onboard customer service staff. Crew members deliver first-class service for our passengers throughout the Americas. You will be trained in airline hospitality and catering services, and in safety procedures. If you are over 21 years of age, a high school graduate, fluent in English and Spanish and have the requisite interpersonal skills, this could be a perfect career opportunity for you.

Send résumé and cover letter to:

Ms. Bettina Jarnik
Human Resources Director
Sunbeam Airlines
3742 West Chesterfield Drive
Atlanta, GA 00725

All applications must be received by March 15th.
Applicants will be contacted by Sunbeam Airlines.
Please do not visit our offices or call us directly.
Sunbeam Airlines is an equal opportunity employer.

---

158. Which qualifications should an applicant have?

(A) A college degree
(B) A pilot's license
(C) A first aid certificate
(D) Fluency in English and Spanish

159. How should an applicant apply for the position?

(A) By calling the personnel director
(B) By visiting the company
(C) By filling out an application form
(D) By mailing a résumé and a cover letter

GO ON TO THE NEXT PAGE

Questions 160–162 refer to the following notice.

EMERGENCY PROCEDURES for Minor Chemical Spills

ATTENTION:

Certain experiments require the handling of hazardous chemicals and materials. Please be familiar with the following emergency procedures.

1. GET AWAY. Extinguish any ignition sources (burners, appliances, etc.) and move to a safe distance.

2. DETERMINE the substance spilled, extent of the spill and degree of hazard. Block off the area.

3. GET HELP. If the spill cannot be handled safely using the equipment and personnel present, activate fire alarm and call 911 for emergency assistance and Security at 777.

4. ASSESS INJURIES. If anyone is injured, call 911.

5. CLEAN UP SPILL WITH PROPER EQUIPMENT AND MATERIALS. Select proper personal protective equipment and clean-up materials for the spill. Place contaminated materials in a container designated for hazardous waste.

6. DISPOSAL. Contact Environmental Health and Safety personnel. Absorbed materials remain hazardous. Treat them with care.

---

160. Where would this notice be posted?
(A) In a restaurant kitchen
(B) In a health food store
(C) In a laboratory
(D) In a garage

161. In case of a spill, what should be done first?
(A) Put on protective gear
(B) Contact the janitor
(C) Turn off open flames and electrical sources
(D) Call the fire department

162. How should contaminated materials be disposed of?
(A) They should be burned.
(B) They should be rinsed thoroughly with water.
(C) They should be placed outside.
(D) They should be placed in special containers.

Questions 163–165 refer to the following letter.

The Nature Conservation Society

Dear Member,

Following the Annual General Meeting, we are proceeding with the election of two new members of the board. Board members are elected for a three-year term and may not serve more than two consecutive periods. As an active member of the society, you are entitled to vote for the candidate of your choice by secret ballot.

The profiles of the four candidates standing for election are enclosed on a separate sheet. You will also find a postal ballot form and a stamped addressed envelope. Photocopies of ballot forms will not be accepted.

Please return your vote to us by October 8th. The results of the ballot will be published on our website and announced in the November newsletter.

Sincerely,

Stan Riley

Stan Riley
Chairman

163. How can members vote in the election?
(A) By attending the yearly meeting
(B) By submitting a postal vote
(C) By connecting to the society's website
(D) By calling Stan Riley

164. How long can a member serve on the board?
(A) Two years
(B) Four years
(C) Six years
(D) Eight years

165. What is NOT included with this letter?
(A) A newsletter
(B) A postal ballot form
(C) A profile of the candidates
(D) A stamped addressed return envelope

Questions 166–168 refer to the following invitation.

The Medical Auxiliary cordially invites you to the

Tenth Annual Community Hospital Charity Auction and Gala Dinner.

Saturday, May 9th at 7 p.m.
at the Rockridge Country Club.

Help the hospital build the new out-patient treatment center with your participation and donations.
All proceeds will be given to the hospital's development fund.

Tickets are $100 per person.
RSVP to Wanda Babbington before April 30th.

Make a bid on a Jaguar XJS, trips to Hawaii and Paris, paintings and artwork,
a canoe, bicycles, sports equipment, and children's toys!
See the full catalog on-line a week in advance at:
www.comm.hospital/charity.auction.html

---

166. Why is this event being held?

(A) To raise money
(B) To welcome patients
(C) To inaugurate the new hospital
(D) To honor the founder

167. How often does this event take place?

(A) Every year
(B) Every other year
(C) Every three years
(D) Every ten years

168. What can you find on the website?

(A) Plans for the new treatment center
(B) Registration forms
(C) Tickets for the event
(D) Auction items

Questions 169–172 refer to the following article.

A recent study of drivers using cell phones has reported that accidents are four times as likely, even if a driver is using a hands-free telephone. This study, the first of its kind to compare extensive data about accidents and cell phone records, draws a direct link between the risk of traffic accidents and general phone use while driving.

The findings show that the use of earpieces and other hands-free telephone devices while driving does not reduce the risk of an accident. The research concludes that the primary cause of phone-related accidents is not the handling of the phone, but rather the act of talking on a phone.

"The brain cannot adequately process the complex information required for driving and talking on the phone at the same time," according to Guiseppe Fontini, a leading researcher in cognitive sciences. "This information overload distracts the driver and makes him less alert, thus leading to a serious compromise." And possibly a serious accident.

The challenge now is for lawmakers. Although many governments have banned the use of normal cellular phones behind the wheel, they have, under pressure from cell phone lobbies, allowed the use of hands-free equipment. But with this new and seemingly conclusive study, lawmakers may decide to prohibit drivers from ever using cell phones while on the road.

169. What is the topic of this article?
 (A) Driver's license requirements
 (B) The latest cell phone technology
 (C) Internet telephone services
 (D) Cell phone use while driving

170. How does talking on the phone affect drivers?
 (A) They lose concentration.
 (B) They drive faster.
 (C) They slow down.
 (D) They're more alert.

171. Who is Guiseppe Fontini?
 (A) A professional driver
 (B) A lawmaker
 (C) A government official
 (D) A scientist

172. According to the article, which statement is true?
 (A) Using a telephone headset while driving reduces accident risk.
 (B) Three out of four drivers use their mobile phones in their cars.
 (C) Cell phones have been prohibited in hotel lobbies.
 (D) Phoning while driving is dangerous.

Questions 173–176 refer to the following instructions.

To replace an ink cartridge on your printer:

Step 1. Turn ON the printer. Open the top cover. The printer's ink cartridge holder will move to the center. The Power ON light will begin blinking.

Step 2. Release the blue lever over the ink cartridge holder by lifting it up.

Step 3. Hold the top of the empty ink cartridge and gently lift it upward until it comes loose. Discard the cartridge, being careful not to spill any remaining ink.

Step 4. Remove the cellophane wrapping from a new ink cartridge. Peel away the yellow protective strip from the head of the cartridge.
Caution: Once you have removed the yellow protective strip, do not touch the ink nozzles or the metal strips. This can damage the head and result in poor print quality or print failure.

Step 5. Set the new ink cartridge into the open slot in the holder. Align it and gently press downward until the ink cartridge clicks into place.

Step 6. Lower the blue lever until it snaps over the ink cartridges.

Step 7. Close the cover of the printer. When the Power ON light stops blinking, the printer can begin printing. If you'd like to run an optional print test, hold the Power ON button down for 3 seconds. If you encounter any printing problems, please consult the Troubleshooting section in your instruction manual.

---

173. When would someone most likely consult this notice?
(A) When there is a paper jam in the printer
(B) When the printer is out of ink
(C) When preparing the printer for storage
(D) When connecting the printer to a computer

174. Which action is NOT necessary to change a cartridge?
(A) Lifting the blue lever
(B) Removing the yellow protective strip
(C) Running a print test
(D) Opening the top cover

175. When is the printer ready for use?
(A) Once the ink cartridge holder moves to the center
(B) As soon as the yellow strip is removed
(C) When the ink cartridge clicks into place
(D) After the Power On light stops flashing

176. According to the notice, what should you do if the printer does not work?
(A) Call the after-sales service
(B) Clean the cartridge head
(C) Refer to the user's guide
(D) Unplug it

Questions 177–180 refer to the following article.

TENSING INC. STOCK SPLIT

Tensing Incorporated, the hi-tech California company specializing in data storage systems, has announced that it will be proceeding with a two for one stock split this Monday. On October 1st, Tensing shareholders will receive one additional share for every share that they already hold in the company.

CEO Julius Barnaby said that the split was decided after the spectacular rise in the Tensing stock price over the last six months. "We've had a great year so far and I'm very confident that the demand for our software solutions will remain strong."

The dramatic rise is due to Tensing's expansion into overseas markets. The company's systems have now been adopted by over 135 major international corporations and further growth is on the horizon.

At the close of the stock market on Friday, Tensing stock was trading at 70 dollars, a 50% increase over last year.

Splitting the stock will make more shares available to investors at half the current price, but it will not increase the overall value of a shareholder's investment. As finance specialist J.J. Holmes of Broker Securities points out, "a stock split does little more than offer shareholders two share certificates instead of one. Tensing has doubled its stock volume and halved the share value. But at 35 dollars, it's a more tempting buy." What would you rather have: a twenty dollar bill or two tens?

177. What type of business is Tensing Inc?
- (A) An investment bank
- (B) A software supplier
- (C) A brokerage firm
- (D) A livestock trading company

178. What is the company going to do?
- (A) Pay a cash dividend
- (B) Buy back its own stocks
- (C) Increase the number of shares
- (D) Invest in storage facilities

179. How much will each share be worth after the split?
- (A) 70 dollars
- (B) 35 dollars
- (C) 20 dollars
- (D) 10 dollars

180. Why has Tensing stock risen 50% since last year?
- (A) The company transferred its headquarters.
- (B) Financial specialists promoted the stock.
- (C) The company has had increased sales abroad.
- (D) The company has cut its costs in half.

GO ON TO THE NEXT PAGE

Questions 181–185 refer to the following advertisement and form.

TeamWise

Choosing the right event for your staff to develop their team-working skills is the starting point for a successful collective experience. And that's where our own very special team here at **TeamWise** can be of assistance. With over ten years' experience of arranging team events for a wide variety of corporate and government clients, **TeamWise** can provide you with tailor-made programs and training solutions to match your exact needs and requirements. Whether your priority is integrating new team members, motivating existing teams or simply rewarding your staff by giving them a chance to share an unforgettable experience – why not let **TeamWise** look after your next team activity?

Contact Us!

Please complete and submit the request form below. Or, if you prefer to discuss your activity or team building event with one of our event managers, please call us at 01539 730890.

Postal Address: The Manor House, Castleford, West Leighton, N48 7JR, United Kingdom

Contact name and title	Jenna Jonman Managing Director
Organization	MasterClass plc
Telephone No	03 4558 6565
Address	10 West Point Boulevard, Auckland Ny8 9JW
Email	JJonman@masterclass.uk

Please indicate which activities you are interested in. (You may check more than one.)
Outdoor ✓   Sports ✓   Problem-solving ☐   Team building ☐
Adventure excursions ☐   Competitive team challenge ☐

Please specify the objectives of your activity and the approximate date
We would like to organize a two day motivation event. This event would take place before the start of the school year, during the last week of August. All transport arrangements will be made by us.

Please indicate the number and type of participants
There would be 25 participants who are all directors of regional schools.

Please indicate whether overnight accommodation will be required and for how many participants.
We would need to arrange accommodation and meals for two days for the whole group.

181. What type of organization is TeamWise?

(A) An employment agency
(B) A travel agency
(C) A sports club
(D) A training company

182. Who would be most likely to hire the services of TeamWise?

(A) Private individuals
(B) Students
(C) Personal assistants
(D) Managers

183. Who is Jenna Jonman?

(A) The director of TeamWise
(B) An event manager
(C) The director of MasterClass
(D) A sports instructor

184. Which of the following would be a suitable event for MasterClass?

(A) An indoor football tournament
(B) An interactive computer game
(C) A cooking class
(D) A golf outing

185. What will TeamWise have to provide?

(A) Room and board
(B) Simultaneous translation
(C) Individual coaching
(D) Transport for all participants

GO ON TO THE NEXT PAGE

Questions 186–190 refer to the following press release and email.

Solar Trophy: Call to Competitors

The Solar Trophy, inaugurated one year ago with only three boats completing an ocean crossing from Cape Town to Hobart, has established itself as a truly unique event in the calendar of ocean racing. Each of the 20 meter boats was powered only by the energy provided by solar panels. The race was won by a four-man team captained by Hans Larssen from Stockholm aboard Icarus 2.

Following the success of the first race, the race committee has decided to hold the event every three years. Teams wishing to participate in the next edition of the race are hereby invited to submit their applications. The full application package and race regulations can be downloaded from the Solar Trophy website (www://solartrophy.org).

The organizers would like to remind applicants that only solar-powered yachts are authorized to compete and that all vessels must correspond to the specifications in the race regulations.
If you have additional questions regarding the application process, please contact Carmen Johannsen by e-mail at C.Johannsen@solartrophy.org or by telephone on 04 95 35 47.

To: Hank Martin <hmartin@solarwattage.com>
From: Anna Sabiani <asabiani@solarwattage.com>
Date: August 23 11:47
Subject: Promotional opportunity

Hi Hank,

I am forwarding the press release about the Solar Trophy that I mentioned to you this morning. I met Bill Bradley, the race coordinator, at the solar energy conference in Manila where he was giving a presentation about the event. I understand from him that the first race was a huge success and generated enormous media coverage both in traditional media and on the Internet. For the next edition of the race he is expecting applications from as many as twenty yachts from seven different countries, including Japan. He suggested that we might like to sponsor one of the crews especially as we are already supplying marine versions of our solar panels to a number of boatyards in Europe and Asia. He particularly recommended that we contact Sven Hadrada of SailYard boats as they are apparently considering entering the race.

We've both worked with SailYard on several occasions. Do you think you could contact them as soon as possible and set up a meeting to explore ways of working together on this? You could arrange to supply our solar panels free of charge in exchange for appropriate publicity space onboard and in the press.

Best regards
Anna

186. What is the Solar Trophy?
 (A) A competition for road vehicles
 (B) A solar energy research award
 (C) A boat race
 (D) A shipping company

187. Which type of craft can enter the Solar Trophy?
 (A) Ocean liners
 (B) Inflatable boats
 (C) Sailboats
 (D) Solar-powered yachts

188. How many times has the Solar Trophy been held?
 (A) Once
 (B) Twice
 (C) Three times
 (D) Ten times

189. Who is Hank Martin?
 (A) The race coordinator
 (B) The previous race winner
 (C) A boat builder
 (D) An employee of a solar panel manufacturer

190. Why is Anna contacting Hank?
 (A) To invite him to finance a venture
 (B) To explore sponsorship possibilities
 (C) To ask him to attend an energy conference
 (D) To nominate him for a prize

GO ON TO THE NEXT PAGE

Questions 191–195 refer to the following conference program and email message.

Sports Medicine Conference Program
Freiburg-im-Breisgau, Germany

FRIDAY, 5TH SEPTEMBER

9:30 – 12:00	Registration
10:00 – 12:00	**Welcome and <u>Plenary Lecture I</u>:** Professor Clive Baker *Growing pains: adolescents and interscholastic sports*
12:00 – 13:30	**Workshop** with Toshiro Takata, MD *Diagnosing and treating contact sport injuries*
13:30 – 14:30	LUNCH
14:30 – 16:00	**Panel presentations (1):** *New trends in sports medicine*
16:00 – 16:30	Refreshments
16:30 – 18:00	**Panel Discussion:** *Breaks and fractures*
18:00 – 19:00	RECEPTION

SATURDAY, 6TH SEPTEMBER

8:30 – 9:30	Breakfast buffet
9:30 – 11:00	**Workshop** with Kim Hyung, MD: *The aging athlete: on and off the field*
11:00 – 11:30	Coffee break
11:30 – 13:00	**Panel presentations (2):** *Wilderness sports medicine*
13:00 – 14:00	LUNCH
14:00 – 16:00	**Plenary Lecture II:** Professor Hamida de Oliviera *Breakthroughs in women's sports medicine*
16:00 – 16:30	Refreshments
16:30 – 18:00	**Video conference:** *Advances in sports medicine technology* with Professor Beatrice Oaksmith, live from Stansland University, CA, USA.
19:00 – late	CONFERENCE DINNER

From: Chris Rogers chris.rogers@pacific.clinic.com
Sent: Saturday, August 10, 11:39 AM
To: Phil Hurvitz hurvitz@uni.2.de
Subject: Scheduling

Hello Phil,

We'll have to make some changes to the conference program. Professor de Oliviera has been scheduled to speak on Saturday even though she said she would only be available on Friday. She is working at the European Women's League Basketball Tournament all day on the sixth in Turino. Could you call Clive Baker to see if he'd be able to switch his plenary talk to Saturday? If he can, we would then move de Oliviera to Friday; otherwise, we'll have to cancel the second plenary. Let me know what Clive says asap.

Best,
Chris

191. Who would be most likely to attend the conference?

(A) A physical therapist
(B) A marine biologist
(C) A nuclear physicist
(D) A financial analyst

192. Whose talk will focus on young athletes?

(A) Professor Baker's lecture
(B) Doctor Takata's workshop
(C) Doctor Hyung's workshop
(D) Professor Oaksmith's video conference

193. What is the problem?

(A) One of the lecturers is injured.
(B) One of the lecturers cannot speak on the scheduled day.
(C) One of the lecturers cannot attend the conference.
(D) The video conference has been postponed.

194. According to the email, where will Hamida de Oliviera be on Saturday, 6th September?

(A) At a conference
(B) At a sporting competition
(C) At the hospital
(D) On vacation

195. What do the organizers propose to do?

(A) Add a panel discussion
(B) Cancel the workshops
(C) Exchange the two plenary lectures
(D) Invite a new lecturer

GO ON TO THE NEXT PAGE

Questions 196–200 refer to the following expense form and letter.

EXPENSE REPORT FORM
(please use one form for each currency)

TRANSNATIONAL TECHNOLOGIES TNT

Full Name:	Conte, Pierre	Department:	Bur. #78	Currency used:	Euros
Event:	Next Generation Trade Show – Milan, Italy			Euro/Currency	1

EXPENSES

Date	Hotel	Meals	Transport.	Misc. (explain below)	Total in currency	Total	Explanation
04/25			airfare		895.00	895.00	Roundtrip: Detroit – Milan 04/25 – 04/28
04/25	1 night				125.00	125.00	Airport Express Hotel
04/26–27	2 nights				2 x 150.00	300.00	Milan Guest Inn
04/26			taxi		42.00	42.00	Taxi fare to trade show
04/28			taxi		35.00	35.00	Taxi fare to airport
04/26		meals			51.40	55.00	Breakfasts and lunches
04/26		dinner			185.00	185.00	Dinner with TNT client (Top Textiles 3 people)
04/26				fee	50.00	50.00	Trade Show Registration Fee
Total spent						1,687.00	
Advance Received						800.00	
Remaining	if "+" TNT owes you, if (–) you owe Transnational					887.00	

I hereby certify that all information contained on this report is accurate and correct, and that this claim represents expenses incurred for Transnational Technologies business.

Employee Signature: *Pierre Conte*

Dear Pierre,

We received your completed expense report form for your recent trip to Milan and most of the corresponding receipts. However, the taxi receipt of 28/04 is missing. Could you please send us this receipt for our records? Thank you.

We noticed that you listed an Advance Received of 800.00 euros, but our records show that you only received 500.00. In addition, the receipt that you submitted for the Trade Show Registration indicates that you actually paid 250 euros and not the 50 euros that you are claiming. These adjustments increase the amount TNT owes you to 1387.00 in euros, which comes to 1870.51 USD.

Please find enclosed a reimbursement check for the said amount.

Best regards,

Carrie Wilson
Accounting Department
TransNational Technologies

196. Who most likely filled out the expense form?

(A) Carrie Wilson
(B) A Next Generation employee
(C) Pierre Conte
(D) A Milan Guest Inn clerk

197. Why did Pierre Conte go to Milan?

(A) To tour the city
(B) To review two hotels
(C) To attend a professional trade fair
(D) To receive new equipment for the company

198. What does Carrie Wilson ask Pierre Conte to do?

(A) Reimburse the company
(B) Submit his airline tickets
(C) Pay his taxi fare himself
(D) Send in a receipt

199. What is included in the letter?

(A) A bank statement
(B) A check
(C) A new expense form
(D) A bill

200. How much did it cost Mr. Conte to register for the Trade Show?

(A) 50 euros
(B) 100 euros
(C) 200 euros
(D) 250 euros

Photo acknowledgements

© Bryan & Cherry Alexander/Alamy: p.6t; © J Moscrop/Axiom: p.6b; © Vince Streano/Corbis: p.7t; © Tom Craig@directphoto.org 2006, photographersdirect.com: p.8b; Anthony Galván III, photographersdirect.com: p.5t; Phototake/Robert Harding: p.4b; Michael Klinec, photographersdirect.com: p.8t; Charles Talcott: pp.4t; Topfoto/Image Works: pp 5b, 7b; Copyright © by Educational Testing Service. All rights reserved.

Picture research by Sandie Huskinson-Rolfe of PHOTOSEEKERS.

Target Score Second Edition
Final Practice TOEIC® Test
Annotated Answer Key and Audioscript

Part 1

1. **D** There are no motor vehicles in the parking area (*parking lot*) and so (B) no cars *are parked in the shade*. The space is neither (A) a *park* nor (C) a *square*.

2. **A** The lab technician is working with a *microscope* and not (B) a *magnifying glass*. (C) She is *looking through* the instrument, not *some files*. (D) She is *examining* something, not having her eyes examined.

3. **C** The people are looking at the paintings on display in a museum and not (A) in a private home. (B) The works of art are not for sale. (D) A woman is taking a photograph and not *painting a picture*.

4. **B** The couple is sitting next to each other and the waiter is taking their order not (A) *serving* a *meal.* (C) The other tables are empty. (D) The waiter is working on a train but is not *training staff*.

5. **D** The news presenter is sitting in front of the camera. (A) She is seated at her desk and is not *moving* it. (B) They are recording a television broadcast, not *watching a TV show*. (C) The *cameraman* is filming the woman and she is not *developing a film*.

6. **B** The cyclists are going through an *open gate*. (A) They are cycling not *resting*. (C) They are biking and not *hiking*. (D) They cannot be *loading the bikes* since they are riding them.

7. **A** The men are wearing protective headgear (*hard hats*). (C) They are *installing* heavy equipment not *software* and (B) neither man is *smoking a pipe*. (D) They are working in an oil field and are not *at the gas station*.

8. **D** The man is working on his *laptop* which is open in front of him. (A) He is sitting alone and not *studying with a friend*. (B) He is not sitting in a *computer lab* classroom. (C) There is a book on the table but he is not *checking it out* from the *library*.

9. **A** They are on *the platform*. (B) The train is stopped. (C) The people are carrying *their bags* and not *packing* them. (D) They are in a train station so they cannot be *boarding a plane*.

10. **B** The man is talking to members of the audience who (A) are standing next to the stage and not *in front of* it. (C) He is *delivering* a speech, not *equipment*. (D) He is *addressing* the audience, not *exchanging addresses*.

Part 2

11. **A** The speaker asks about a *train fare*, which varies according to travel time. (B) is about a *refund*. (C) is the answer to a question with *where*.

12. **C** The speaker wants to know if she can pay by *credit card* and this answer gives information about the minimum purchase required. (A) is about receiving a cash payment. (B) is expressing agreement but does not refer to payment.

13. **B** The speaker asks if the *seats* are available and is told that they are *reserved*. Answer (A) refers to the cost of a *buffet*. (C) talks about the surroundings (*setting*) and not the seating.

14. **C** The question expresses concern about the man's plan to quit his job. (A) is about a brief absence. (B) is about *signing* and not *resigning*.

15. **B** The question asks who will present the *award* and a *manager* is the correct answer. (A) answers the question *when* and (C) is about *being present* and not about *presenting something*.

16. **C** *Why don't you* makes a suggestion and this is the only appropriate answer. (A) answers the question *why* about the cause of a past event. (B) refers to an amount of money that was spent.

17. **A** The speaker wants to know about the bus schedule. The bus only operates during the week . (B) is about the *weather* and (C) is about physical activity and not about transportation.

18. **B** The question asks when a vacant position will be filled and *pretty soon* answers this question. (A) answers the question *how far* and (C) answers the question *how long* about the duration of a visit.

19. **A** This question makes a suggestion about organizing a visit and (A) is the appropriate answer. (B) is about *products*. (C) answers a question about *duration*.

20. **C** The question *How did it go?* means *What happened?* and this is explained in answer (C). (A) is about a future event. (B) is about means of travel.

21. **C** The invitation to the *concert* is politely refused. (A) is about duration and (B) refers to a past performance.

22. **A** *In January* is the correct answer to the question *when*. (B) answers the question *how long* and (C) is about a physical ailment (*her back*) and not about when Ms. Davies will return.

23. **B** The speaker asks *where to meet* so *at your place* is the correct answer. (A) is a suggestion about arranging the furniture and (C) a *snack* refers to eating and not to meeting.

24. **B** The speaker asks when the man last had a *medical* examination which was *three years* ago. (A) is about duration and (C) is advice to see a doctor.

1

25.	A	The question asks whether the man has read an author's books and the answer reveals that he is a regular reader or *fan*. (B) is a response to an offer and (C) is about a reservation (*booking*) and not a book (*novel*).
26.	C	The question asks if a diner is ready to order from the menu. *I'll have today's special* is the appropriate response. (A) *out of order* refers to something that is not working and (B) is an order or command being given.
27.	C	The speaker asks for the name of the caller so *Leo Jensen* is the right answer. (A) answers the question *where* and (B) answers the question *when*.
28.	B	The question asks *when* the model will go on sale so the right answer is *in the fall*. (A) is about having lunch and not a product *launch* and (C) is about a flight departure time.
29.	A	The speaker suggests inviting the training manager, which has already been done. (B) is about a manager's performance and (C) refers to an event that has already taken place.
30.	B	The speaker politely asks the man to record what will be said in a meeting (*take the minutes*) and *not at all* indicates his agreement. (A) is the answer to the question *What time is it?* and (C) is an offer to lend something.
31.	B	This speaker asks if the woman has a *copy of* a *contract* and is told that the original is *at the office*. (A) answers the question *What happened?* and not *Do you happen to know?*. (C) is a response to a suggestion about taking a coffee break.
32.	C	The speaker proposes to meet *at nine* which the man agrees to. (A) is the answer to the question *How is* and not *How about*. (B) refers to the *afternoon* and not to the morning.
33.	A	This statement explains why the elevator isn't working. (B) answers a question about which *floor* to get off on. (C) gives the reason why a person is not at work.
34.	A	This answer explains that *safety procedures* call for the building to be evacuated. (B) The distracter *bill* refers to invoicing and (C) the distracter *vacation* refers to a holiday and not to leaving a building.
35.	B	The question asks if the reservations have been cancelled and this is an appropriate response. (A) *Doubts* refers to misgivings and not to a booking (*reservation*). (C) The distracter *can* refers to ability and not cancelling.
36.	A	The question asks who made a decision so *our consultants* is the correct answer. (B) answers a question about ownership. (C) answers a question about *favorite colors*.
37.	A	This question asks how Roberto can be reached, which is by email. (B) refers to the location of something. (C) The distracter *board* refers to a professional group and not to traveling to another country.
38.	B	The question asks about physical fitness so *regular exercise* and *healthy food* is the correct answer. (A) refers to size. (C) The distracter *run* refers to managing and not physical fitness.
39.	C	The speaker asks to borrow a pen and the woman offers one. (A) The distracter *ten* refers to a time. (B) is about the price of shares on the stock market.
40.	C	The speaker asks if information has been sent, so the right answer is that it was sent by *fax*. (A) refers to a location. (B) is about general progress and not a specifc action.

Part 3

41.	C	The keywords and phrases *move on to, item, agenda, turn to the issue of* indicate a meeting. The distracters *move on*, *turn to* and *relocate* do not refer to (A) *directions* or (B) *delivery*. (D) There is no mention of *purchasing furniture*.
42.	A	The man says they are looking for a *bigger place* and therefore not (B) a smaller one. Neither (C) cost nor (D) distance are mentioned as reasons for the move.
43.	B	They are looking for an office in the same area or *neighborhood* and not in (A), (C), (D) another location.
44.	B	The keywords *appetizer, main course, to order* indicate a restaurant. *Main course* refers to a dish and not (A) *a class*. This conversation would not occur in (C) or (D).
45.	A	*We'd like to order* indicates that the man has decided to place an order and not (B) modify an existing one or (D) request more time before ordering. (C) He does not ask to pay for the meal.
46.	D	The word *just* is a synonym for *only* so answers (A), (B) and (C) are incorrect.
47.	C	A *tune-up, oil and filter change, vehicle* and *10,000 miles* indicate that they are talking about car maintenance, which is done by a *mechanic*, not by the professions (A), (B) or (D).
48.	D	The garage is conducting routine maintenance or *servicing* on the car and not (A) *repairing* or (B) *replacing* damaged parts. (C) Although the *lights* may be checked, this is not the reason why the car has been *taken in*.
49.	B	Mrs. Webster's *husband* (Mr. Webster) will be collecting the car as she *won't be able* to do this herself. (A), (C) and (D) are therefore incorrect.
50.	D	The man says that he *just* has *carry-on luggage* and *a laptop* computer, which are not *checked*. Therefore, (A), (B) and (C) are incorrect.
51.	C	Boarding begins at *seven*. (A) *three* refers to the number of the gate. (B) *Five* and (D) *eight* are distracters.
52.	D	Answer (D) is the only untrue statement as there is no reference to the flight being late or *delayed*. (A), (B) and (C) are true because the flight is *overnight*, it leaves from *gate E-3* and it has *business class* passengers.
53.	B	Margaret has been *promoted* to a new position and has been *transferred* to another job location. She is therefore not (A) *leaving the company*, she has not (C) been *laid off* and she has not (D) *retired*.

2

54.	D	She has been appointed as a *Vice President*. She is a senior manager and not (A) *a junior* one. She will be working under (C) the *President*. (B) *Foreman* is a distracter for *four*.
55.	C	In the dialogue the man mentions that Margaret *joined the group* four years ago so she has been there for *four* years and not for (A) *two*, (B) *three*, or (D) *five*.
56.	A	They are discussing the woman's plan to *buy* (purchase) a home in a particular *neighborhood* which does not need (B) *improving*. The woman will be investing in real estate and not in the (C) *stock market*. (D) She is *negotiating the price* but not *an order*.
57.	B	The woman says she has *two kids* that she would like *to enroll*. (A), (C) and (D) are incorrect.
58.	A	Greenwood has *great schools*. There are no references to (B) *taxes* (C) *cheap housing* or to (D) *public transport*.
59.	C	The woman says that Steve will be on vacation *as of Friday*, meaning *at the end of this week*. (A) The woman will take her vacation *next month*. (B) Steve's vacation will *last two weeks*. (D) *Today* is not discussed.
60.	B	Steve hopes to *play some golf*. (A) He says that he will not be *taking any work* with him. (C) He will not be at *home* but on *a trip*. (D) The woman will be going on a *cruise*.
61.	B	The woman is taking a *cruise* and will therefore be on board a *ship*. Answers (A), (C) and (D) are incorrect as they refer to locations on land.
62.	D	The woman tells Mr. Honda that he must *vacate (his) office* because *electricians* (workmen) *will be installing new cables next Monday*. (A), (B) and (C) would not do this type of work.
63.	C	*Workstations,* which include professional computer equipment, have been *set up* or installed and not (A) *a video projector* or (B) *a coffee machine*. (D) *Electrical cables* will be installed but not in the conference room.
64.	A	He will have to *reschedule* a meeting that was to take place in the (B) *conference room*. (C) He will have to *move* out of his office but not *move* the furniture. (D) He will have to *meet* someone but not at the station.
65.	A	The woman is unhappy because there is a printing error on the documents that she ordered and not (B), (C) or (D) which all refer to positive emotional reactions.
66.	C	She has received a delivery of *brochures* and not (A) a *bill*. (B) *An estimate* is received before work is ordered and not after. She has not received (D) *an invitation*. She is inviting her supplier to reprint the brochures.
67.	C	The reason for her call is to express dissatisfaction or *to complain*. (A) She may be *negotiating* but not *negotiating a discount*. (B) She *requests* new *brochures* and not *documentation* which is information in document form. (D) She does not refer to an *appointment*.
68.	B	Anita forgot to *tell Mr. Jensen* something. There is no mention of her having to (A) *write a report* or (D) *prepare a sales presentation*. She offers to (C) *call Mr. Lee*.
69.	A	Mr. Lee is giving his presentation to members of *staff* from the *sales department* and not to (B), (C) or (D).
70.	B	Mr. Lee promised to return the report *after lunch* and not (A), (C) or (D).

Part 4

71.	C	The speaker describes the façade of a *historical* building on *a city tour*. Since the talk takes place outside, it isn't (B) *in a warehouse* or (D) *in a store*. Although she mentions the building's construction, they are not on (A) *a construction site*.
72.	D	The *early 1800s* refers to the first years or decades of the 19th century and not (A) to a date in the 20th century or (B) to a date in the second half of the 19th century or (C) to a date in the 18th century.
73.	B	The speaker highlights the *carved wooden doors*. (A) The speaker says that the building is *coming into view* but does not mention the view from the building. (C) There is no mention of an *outdoor pool*. (D) The building has seven *doors*, not seven *floors*.
74.	A	The keywords *researchers*, *laboratory*, the name *ScienTech*, *advances and discoveries* designate the speaker as a research *scientist*. (B) and (C) would not use such vocabulary. The speaker thanks the (D) *trustees* for the award.
75.	A	The speaker says that the *grant … will finance the construction of a new laboratory* or facility. (B) The word *award* is used in the talk, but not *reward*, which is a distracter. (D) The word *advances* refers to progress, not money for *personnel*. There is no mention of (C) *hiring new staff*.
76.	B	The speaker is accepting an award for work that has been *accomplished*. He is not addressing an audience of (A) new recruits. (C) He is talking about *results* but not in financial terms. (D) He does not mention any financial reward or *bonus* for employees.
77.	B	The news broadcast refers to *three insurance providers*. (A), (C) and (D) are not correct.
78.	B	The report says that it *will take six months to reach an agreement*. (A) *Five years* refers to future business projections. (C) *Next week* is not mentioned. (D) *Tuesday* the day that the news report was issued.
79.	C	The merger will enable the new company *to concentrate its resources on insuring businesses*. There is no mention of (A) expanding human resources, (B) specializing in car insurance or (D) *reducing home insurance costs*.
80.	C	This public service announcement informs listeners that SMART offers *business advice*. The organization provides advice on *how to get a small business loan* and how to improve *cash flow management* but does not provide (A) *loans*, (B) *cash flow* or (D) *managers*.
81.	D	The announcement targets *small businees owners*. (A), (B) and (C) would most likely work *for* SMART, providing counsel, advice and mentoring to small businesses.

3

82.	D	The service is *free*, which means *at no charge*. (A) *Thousands* refers to the number of *people* who *get advice*. (B) *A small fee* sounds similar to *free*. (C) *Eight hundred* is part of the telephone number.
83.	A	The speaker thanks the audience for coming to *today's workshop here at our home office* or at company headquarters. The workshop focuses on *training front desk personnel* for the company's hotels. So, (B) and (C) are incorrect. There is no mention of (D) *a mall*.
84.	D	The speaker uses the words *your front desk personnel* and *your hotels*. The audience is told that *at the end of today's session you will ... return to your hotels with the full training package*. (A) *Customers*, (B) *clerks* and (C) *hospital directors* would not be in charge of training in a hotel.
85.	B	The purpose of the talk is to introduce *front desk personnel training tools*. (A) *online training tools* are mentioned, but they are not being developed in this session. (C) There is no mention of *performance reviews* and (D) no *results are announced*.
86.	B	The announcement is addressed to people living in *homes and apartments* and it aims to prevent casualties. It is not targeted at either (A) *emergency workers* or (C) *employees of a gas company*. (D) The announcement is being made *by* public health officials and not *to* them.
87.	A	The announcer advises people *to stay warm* by heating their homes safely. (B), (C) and (D) are all actions that people are warned not to do.
88.	B	The power failure has been caused by *snowstorms* and not by (A), (C) or (D), which are other types of storms.
89.	B	The telephone message is intended for *bank customers*, who can find out about their *accounts*, *money transfers*, and *loans*. (A), (C) and (D) are not the target audience of this message.
90.	B	All calls to the center are *recorded* but not (A) rerouted. Recorded calls may be used for training but not for (D). (C) Only some calls – those from non-touchtone phones – are *put on hold*.
91.	B	Only *stock transactions* are not referred to. (A) *Loans*, (C) *account balance information* and (D) *money transfers* are all mentioned.
92.	B	The flight *has been cancelled* because of *heavy snowfall and high winds*. There is no mention of (A) *scheduling conflicts*, (C) *mechanical failure* or (D) *baggage loading problems*.
93.	C	*Checked baggage ... has already been loaded onto the aircraft*. The airplane is in *Houston* not (A) *in Chicago*. (B) *Passengers* have the option of staying at a *hotel*, but without their checked luggage. (D) A *service representative* is *at Gate 5*, not the baggage.
94.	C	The *airline is providing complimentary hotel and meal vouchers*, which are *coupons* for a free hotel room and a free meal. The airline is not offering (A) flight vouchers or *coupons for a free flight*, (B) *refund checks* or (D) *complimentary luggage*.
95.	D	The speaker talks about *the formal conference dinner this Saturday*. He must be making this announcement on Thursday because he mentions *Friday noon, that is, tomorrow*. So (A), (B) and (C) are not possible.
96.	B	The *caterer* wants the speaker to confirm *a day in advance* how many guests will attend the dinner. (A) is about *payment*. (C) The *Pine Ridge Ballroom* is already reserved. (D) There are *seats available*, so he does not need to get more.
97.	C	The speaker says that *places are still available* so answers (B) and (D) are incorrect. (A) The menu is mentioned but has not been *changed*.
98.	B	This is a *Chamber of Commerce event* and is not organized by either (A), (C) or (D) which are the organizations that the speakers belong to.
99.	C	He is co-founder of a *business consultancy* and not of (A), (B) or (D) which are other types of business ventures.
100.	B	The program for the event has two parts, one in the morning and one in the afternoon. (A), (C) and (D) are incorrect.

Part 5

101.	C	*As a result* is followed by the preposition *of*. (A), (B), and (D) are incorrect.
102.	B	(B) is a noun that refers to a profession. (A) is a noun that describes an act. (C) is a verb and (D) is an adjective.
103.	D	Someone *assumes responsibility*. (A) *To resume* means to take something up again, not to start something *new*. (B) and (C) do not follow common and correct usage.
104.	C	(C) is an adjective that describes the *facilities*. (A) is the past participle. (B) is the third person singular of the verb. (D) is a noun.
105.	A	(A) is the possessive form of the relative pronoun and refers to *managers*. (B), (C) and (D) are also relative pronouns, but do not express possession.
106.	B	The comparative form of the adjective is used with *than*. (A) is the simple adjective form. (C) is an adverb. (D) is the superlative form.
107.	C	(C) is the possessive pronoun for *Brisbane Associates*. (A) is an object pronoun. (B) is a possessive adjective. (D) is a reflexive pronoun.
108.	A	(A) is the subjunctive form. Verbs in *that* clauses that are introduced with *recommend* take the infinitive without *to*. (B) is the simple past or a past participle. (C) is the present perfect. (D) is the present continuous.
109.	D	(D) is an intransitive verb in the past participle form, describing the action of the noun *inflation*. (A), (B) and (C) are the past participle forms of transitive verbs, which require a direct object.
110.	A	The adverb *hardly* is used with *any*. (B), (C) and (D) are incorrect.
111.	B	Someone *accounts for* something. The other prepositions (A), (C) and (D) are incorrect.
112.	B	(B) is an adjective describing *the sales*. (A) is the past participle. (C) is an adverb. (D) is a noun.

113. A Only (A) is appropriate when used with units of measurement. (B), (C) and (D) refer to positions and not to specific distances.

114. A (A) is a conjunction that expresses agreement. The main clause restates what Mr. Meyers said *in the same way*. (B) is used to present examples. (C) expresses cause. (D) is a conjunction meaning *therefore*.

115. B (B) means to endanger. The words *warned, prolonged strikes, layoffs* indicate risk. (A), (C) and (D) cannot be used to describe the effect on the *company's plans*.

116. B Goods are *under warranty*. (A), (C) and (D) do not follow correct and common usage.

117. D (D) is an adjective, which describes *effects*. (A) is the present continuous. (B) is a plural noun or the third person singular form of the verb. (C) is a noun for the person who receives the benefits of something.

118. D An institution has *funds at its disposal*. (A), (B) and (C) do not follow common and correct usage.

119. D (D) is a noun describing a new action. (A) is an adjective indicating *at the beginning*. (B) is a noun that refers to the process of introducting someone to a group and (C) is the verb form.

120. B *Under no circumstances* is a common adverbial phrase. (A), (C) and (D) do not follow correct and common usage.

121. C Someone *submits a report*. (A), (B) and (D) do not follow correct and common usage.

122. D The adverb *regardless* is followed by the preposition *of*. (A) is a conjunction. (B) is followed by a noun and not the preposition *of*. (C) is an adverb used to add emphasis.

123. C (C) is an adverb, indicating the primary cause. (A) does not make sense. Note: *almost* would be correct if the phrase read *almost entirely due to*. (B) is a superlative form. (D) is a determiner, pronoun or adverb. (A), (B) and (D) do not follow correct and common usage.

124. B The conjunction *neither* is followed by *nor*. (A), (C) and (D) do not follow correct and common usage.

125. B (B) is the passive form that the sentence requires. (A) is the past. (C) is the present perfect. (D) is the future.

126. C *Since* expresses the starting point of a period of time and is used with the present perfect. (A), (B) and (D) are incorrect.

127. D A *tourist destination* is a common collocation. (A), (B), and (C) are incorrect as they are not used in this way.

128. C The adverb *besides* means *in addition to*. (A), (B) and (D) are prepositions refering to the position of objects.

129. D The common expression *all things considered* uses the past participle form of the verb *to consider*. (A) is the present simple or the infinitive without *to*. (B) and (C) are adjectives.

130. A (A) is an adjective that expresses probability. (B), (C) and (D) are adverbs, and are not correct in this context.

131. D (D) is a determiner that expresses *not much* for the non-count noun *chance*. (A) is used with count nouns. (B) is a superlative that requires *the*. (C) is an adjective that is not used with *chance*.

132. C (C) is a preposition that expresses inclusion in a group. Although the other answers are also prepositions, their meanings emphasize position: (A) *next to*, (B) *in the middle of* or *surrounded by*, and (D) *in the area*.

133. A To *fall through* is the common phrasal verb used when a plan (*the alliance*) fails to happen. (B), (C) and (D) are not used in this context.

134. A (A) is a demonstrative pronoun used to add information. (B) is the possessive adjective. (C) does not follow common and correct usage. (D) is an object pronoun.

135. D (D) is an adverb that expresses consequence or result. (A), (B) and (C) are conjunctions that express contrast.

136. B The first conditional is formed with the simple present in the *if* clause, which in this case begins with *unless*. (A) is the present continuous. (C) is the past simple. (D) is the future.

137. D In the third conditional, the *then* clause is formed with *would* + the present perfect. (A) is the future. (B) is the future perfect. (C) is the second conditional.

138. A (A) is the simple past of the verb *to seek*. (B), (C) and (D) do not follow common and correct usage.

139. A The idiomatic expression is *to take for granted*. (B), (C) and (D) do not follow common and correct usage.

140. C The adverb *significantly* expresses how much *lower*. (A), (B) and (D) cannot be used with a comparative adjective.

Part 6

141. C The adjective *checking* correctly completes the collocation *checking account*. (A), (B) and (D) do not follow common and correct usage.

142. D The adverbial clause *as ... as* is a common idiom. (A), (B) and (C) cannot be used after *as* followed by an adjective or an adverb.

143. A (A) is the only direct object possible after the transitive verb *earn*. (B), (C) and (D) do not form a logical or correct pair with the verb.

144. B The sentence is a conditional statement that opens with a dependent clause and ends with the imperative *please contact me*. (A), (C) and (D) are used to introduce questions.

145. D After an adverb of time indicating a period that is finished, the correct verb form is the past simple. The present continuous (A), the present perfect (B) and the present simple (C) form of the verb are incorrect.

146. A (A) is the correct adjective form. (B), (C) and (D) are inappropriate comparative forms.

147. D The adverbial phrase *instead of* correctly introduces an alternative. (A) and (B) express effect and cause. (C) indicates that something is done without any effect.

148.	D	The relative pronoun *which* correctly introduces the clause giving further information. (A) and (B) do not introduce non-defining relative clauses and (C) is a relative pronoun that indicates possession.
149.	D	The superlative is correct. (A) is a simple adjective form. (B) is the comparative form. (C) is the adverbial form.
150.	A	(A) is an adverb that indicates contrast and can be separated from the rest of the sentence by commas. The conjunctions (B) and (C) must introduce phrases and clauses. (D) indicates contrast but cannot be separated from the rest of the sentence by commas.
151.	B	The preposition *within* forms an idiom with *reach* expressing distance. (A), (C) and (D) do not correctly form an idiom with *reach*.
152.	A	A *balance* refers to the difference between an amount due and an amount paid. (B), (C) and (D) do not express this.

Part 7

153.	D	The notice implies that *business travelers* would need a *visa* and are thus asked to *attach a letter from* (their) *company* or *employer*. There is no mention of (A) a *receipt from the travel agent* or (C) an *additional photo*. (B) *Vaccinations* are *not required*.
154.	B	The notice states that *same-day visa processing is available for an extra $50 US*, that is, you must *pay an additional fee* to *obtain the visa in one day*. (A), (C), or (D) do not enable you to obtain your visa in one day.
155.	A	This *Water shortage warning* announces *water restrictions*, and specifically addresses *residents*. (B) Although *weather conditions* such as *below average rainfall* may have produced the need for *water conservation measures*, the purpose of the notice is not to *warn residents of such conditions*. There is no mention of (C) *water pollution* or (D) *mineral water sales*.
156.	B	*Interrupting* is a synonym of *cutting*. There is no reference to either (A), (C) or (D).
157.	D	*Farmers* would be among those who run *agricultural businesses* and who *irrigate*. The notice states that they may water their crops (*irrigate*) *between 7 p.m. and midnight*, in other words, *evenings*. (A), (B), and (C) are incorrect.
158.	D	The job advertisement lists being *fluent in English and Spanish* as necessary qualifications. (A) An applicant must be *a high school graduate*, not a *college* graduate. There is no mention of (B) or (C) as qualifications.
159.	D	The applicant is asked to *send a résumé* and a *cover letter* to a mailing address. (A) No telephone numbers are listed and the advertisement asks applicants not to *call directly* and (B) not to *visit the offices*. (C) No *application form* is mentioned.
160.	C	The notice mentions *experiments* that *require the handling of chemicals*. This would only occur in a scientific *laboratory* and not in (A), (B) or (D).
161.	C	The first item on the procedures notice says to *get away* after *extinguishing any ignition sources*. (A) *protective gear* and (D) *call the fire department* are mentioned later and (B) *janitors* are not mentioned at all.
162.	D	Item 5 states that contaminated materials should be placed in *a container designated for hazardous waste*. There is no mention of (A) *burning* (B) *rinsing* or (C) *placing outside* the material.
163.	B	The letter to Society members includes a *postal ballot form and a stamped addressed envelope*, which indicates that the election will be conducted by mail and not (A) at an Annual General Meeting. (C) The *results* of the election *will be published on the website*. (D) There is no mention of *calling Stan Riley*.
164.	C	*Board members are elected for a three-year term* and *may not serve more than two consecutive periods* or terms. Two three-year terms add up to *six years*. (A), (B) and (D) are incorrect.
165.	A	The letter states that (B) a *postal ballot form*, (C) a *profile of the four candidates*, and (D) a *stamped addressed envelope* to *return your vote* are *enclosed with this letter*. Mention of the *November newsletter* is a distracter.
166.	A	The event is a *Charity Auction*. The guests are invited to *help build the new treatment center* by *participating and* (giving) *donations*. The money collected from the ticket sales and the auction (*the proceeds*) will be given to the *development fund*. This is a *fund-raising event*. (B), (C) and (D) are not mentioned.
167.	A	The event is *annual*, which means that it is held *every year*. (B), (C) and (D) are not correct. (D) draws on the distracter *tenth*, which indicates that this will be the *tenth time* the event has been held.
168.	D	The invitation states that *the full* (auction) *catalog* will be *on-line a week in advance*. The catalog would present all the *auction items*. There is no mention that the website would present (A) *plans*, (B) *registration forms*, or (C) *tickets for the event*.
169.	D	The article is based on a *study of drivers using cell phones*. There is no mention of (A) *driver's license requirements* or (C) *internet telephone services*. Although *earpieces and other hands-free telephone devices* are discussed, the (B) *latest cell phone technology* is not the primary topic.
170.	A	Cell phone use while driving is said to produce an *information overload* that *distracts the driver and makes him less alert*. The driver thus *loses concentration*. (D) states the opposite of the article and (B) and (C) are not mentioned.
171.	D	Guiseppe Fontini is presented as a *researcher in cognitive sciences*, which best corresponds to (D) *A scientist*. (A) is not mentioned, and (B) and (C) do not correspond to his profile.
172.	D	The only true statement is (D) *Phoning while driving is dangerous*. (A) is false because *using a telephone headset while driving increases accident risk*. (B) is not mentioned. (C) is incorrect. The word *lobbies* in the text

6

refers to advocacy groups that promote their interests, not hotel reception areas.

173. B The notice describes how to *replace an ink cartridge*. Step 3 mentions that the cartridge is *empty*. (A), (C), and (D) are not mentioned.

174. C Step 7 states that you can *run an optional print test*. As *optional* it is not necessary. You must do (A), (B), and (D) to change a cartridge.

175. D Step 7 specifies that *the printer can begin printing when the Power ON light stops blinking* or flashing. (A), (B) and (C) are all preliminary steps that must be completed before Step 7.

176. C The instructions state that *if you encounter any printing problems*, you should *consult the instruction manual* or *the user's guide*. There is no mention of (A), (B) or (D).

177. B The article describes Tensing Inc. as a *hi-tech company specializing in data storage systems* and *software solutions*. Although Tensing Inc. stock is being sold and traded by investors and brokers, the company is neither (A) an investment bank, nor (C) a brokerage firm. (D) is a distracter referring to the sale of animals.

178. C Key expressions are *2 for 1 stock split* and *shareholders will receive one additional share for every share*. The stock split is defined as *making more shares available* and as *doubling the stock volume*. There is no mention of (A), (B), or (D).

179. B On *Friday, Tensing stock was trading at 70 dollars*. The stock split will occur on Monday with *shares available to investors at half the current price*. The *finance specialist* says that Tensing will *halve the share value* and he mentions the figure *35 dollars*. (A), (C), and (D) are incorrect.

180. C The article attributes Tensing's success to *expansion into overseas markets*. (A), (B) and (D) are not mentioned.

181. D TeamWise *provides ... programs and training solutions* to help *develop ... team-working skills*. Employment (A) and travel (B) are not mentioned. Although *sports* events are available, TeamWise is not a (C) *club*.

182. D The ad mentions *your staff* and *corporate and government clients* indicating a service for managers and professionals, not for (A) and (B). (C) normally would not manage staff and would not *hire* such services.

183. C Her *title* is *Managing Director*. Her *Organization* is *MasterClass plc*. (A), (B) and (D) are not indicated.

184. D The client is interested in *Outdoor* activities and *Sports*. (D) is the only sport that is listed as being played outside. (A) is played *indoors*. (B) and (C) are not sports.

185. A The last box in the form indicates that the group will require *accommodation and meals*, which is a synonym of *room and board*. (B) and (C) are not mentioned. *Transport arrangements* (D) are being made by *MasterClass*.

186. C The SolarTrophy is described as an *ocean racing event*, involving *boats* and *yachts*. (A) *Road vehicles* and (B) *research awards* are not mentioned. No (D) *shipping companies*, that is, companies involved in transporting goods, are mentioned.

187. D The boats or yachts in the race are *powered only by the energy provided by solar panels* and *only solar-powered yachts are authorized to compete*. (A) and (B) are not mentioned. (C) All sailboats are not solar-powered.

188. A The race was *inaugurated one year ago* and after this first and only race the race committee *has decided to hold the event every three years*. (B), (C) and (D) are not possible.

189. D The letter to Hank refers to *our solar panels* and implies that he and the sender *work together*. Bill Bradley is (A) the race coordinator. Hans Larssen won the race (B) the year before. The only boat builder (C) mentioned is Sven Hadrada.

190. B Anna mentions Bill Bradley's suggestion *to sponsor one of the crews* and later suggests *supplying our solar panels free of charge in exchange for publicity space*, which indicates a sponsorship agreement. (A), (C) and (D) are not discussed.

191. A A *Sports Medicine* conference that addresses topics such as *diagnosing and treating contact sports injuries*, dealing with *breaks and fractures*, treating the *ageing athlete*, etc. would most likely interest a *physical therapist*. (B), (C) and (D) would be less likely to have any direct professional interest in such topics.

192. A Professor Baker's lecture deals with *adolescents* and *interscholastic sports*, which are the sports that *schools and their students organize in order to compete against each other*. His talk would most likely focus on *young athletes*. Although (B), (C) and (D) could mention young athletes, they would not be the focus of the talks.

193. B Professor de Oliviera was scheduled to speak on Saturday, but *she said she would only be available on Friday*. (A) and (D) are not mentioned. (C) All of the lecturers can attend the conference, but not necessarily on both days.

194. B She will be working at a *Basketball Tournament*, which is a sporting competition between basketball teams. The email does not say she will be at (A) or (C). (D) is incorrect because the email says that she *is working* at the tournament.

195. C The email suggests *switching* or exchanging Clive Baker's plenary talk with Professor de Oliviera's plenary talk. The organizers would *move* de Oliviera's talk to Friday. (A) and (D) are not mentioned. (B) The organizers will only *cancel* the *second plenary* if they cannot exchange the plenary speakers. They do not discuss canceling any workshops.

196. C The form lists *Pierre Conte* as the person who has filled in the expense report. In her letter, Carrie Wilson refers to Pierre Conte as the person who *listed* the expense information and *submitted* the form. (A) Carrie Wilson is processing the report in the accounting department. (B) *Next Generation* is the name of the *Trade Show*. (D) Pierre is reporting expenses incurred at the *Milan Guest Inn*.

197.	**C**	The form and the letter refer to a *Trade Show* or trade fair that he attended for the company he works for, *TransNational Technologies*. The purpose of his trip is primarily professional, not to (A) *tour the city*. There is no mention of (B) or (D).
198.	**D**	Carrie Wilson asks Pierre Conte to *send us* the *taxi receipt*. (A) is not correct because Pierre is requesting that the company reimburse him. The letter also refers to a *reimbursement check enclosed* for Pierre. There is no mention of (B). The Accounting Department is reimbursing Pierre for his travel expenses, so (C) is not logical.
199.	**B**	The letter refers to a *reimbursement check enclosed* for Pierre. It does not refer to (A), (C) or (D).
200.	**D**	Although Pierre lists the *Trade Show Registration Fee* as only 50 euros, Carrie Wilson corrects this in her letter. According to the registration fee receipt, Pierre *paid 250 euros* and not the *50 euros* he *claimed*. (A) is the incorrect amount Pierre first listed. (B) and (C) are also incorrect.

Audioscript

PART 1: PHOTOGRAPHS

1. (A) The picnic area is outside the park.
   (B) The cars are parked in the shade.
   (C) There is a statue in the middle of the square.
   (D) There aren't any cars in the parking lot.

2. (A) She's examining a sample under a microscope.
   (B) The magnifying glass is kept in the drawer.
   (C) She's looking through some files.
   (D) She's having her eyesight checked.

3. (A) The painting's on the living room wall.
   (B) The artwork's being sold at auction.
   (C) The visitors are admiring the collections.
   (D) She's painting a picture.

4. (A) He's serving their meal.
   (B) The couple is sitting side by side.
   (C) The dining car is full.
   (D) The waiter's training the new staff.

5. (A) They're moving the desk.
   (B) They're watching a television show.
   (C) She's developing the film.
   (D) The woman is facing the camera.

6. (A) They're resting at the top of the hill.
   (B) The gate has been left open.
   (C) They're hiking through the countryside.
   (D) They're loading the bikes onto a rack.

7. (A) The workers are wearing hard hats.
   (B) One of the men is smoking a pipe.
   (C) The men are installing new software.
   (D) They're filling up at the gas station.

8. (A) He's studying with a friend.
   (B) Class is being held in the computer lab.
   (C) He's checking out a book at the library.
   (D) The laptop is set up on the table.

9. (A) The passengers are on the platform.
   (B) The train is pulling away from the station.
   (C) They're packing their bags.
   (D) They're boarding the plane.

10. (A) The audience is seated in front of the stage.
    (B) They're listening to his speech.
    (C) He's delivering some equipment.
    (D) They're exchanging addresses.

PART 2: QUESTION-RESPONSE

11. What's the cheapest round-trip train fare?
    (A) That depends on when you travel.
    (B) You can return them for a full refund.
    (C) It's fairly close to the station.

12. Do you accept all major credit cards?
    (A) I didn't expect to be paid in cash.
    (B) Yes. I agree with you about that.
    (C) As long as your bill is over 15 dollars.

13. Excuse me. Are these seats free?
    (A) There's no charge for the buffet.
    (B) I'm sorry. They're all reserved.
    (C) Yes, the setting is beautiful.

14. You're not going to resign, are you?
    (A) Yes, I'll be away until midweek.
    (B) Yes, both parties must sign.
    (C) I am considering it.

15. Who's going to present the award to Mrs. Sato at the ceremony?
    (A) After the president's speech.
    (B) Her manager will say a few words.
    (C) No, I won't be able to attend.

16. Why don't you get someone to help you with the budget?
    (A) Because they couldn't help it.
    (B) No, I didn't spend much at all.
    (C) I could certainly use some assistance.

17. Do you know whether the number 40 bus runs on Sundays?
    (A) No, it doesn't. Only on weekdays.
    (B) It'll be sunny and hot.
    (C) Yes, he goes jogging every weekend.

18. How long will it be before they appoint a new director?
    (A) About thirty miles in this direction.
    (B) I think we should know pretty soon.
    (C) Each appointment lasts twenty minutes.

19. Do you think we should take Mr. Lee on a tour of our production plant?
    (A) I'm sure he'd be delighted to see it.
    (B) Cereals and flour are the main products.
    (C) No. It shouldn't take more than two hours.

20. How did the meeting with the safety inspectors go?
    (A) We have to be ready at the site by ten.
    (B) They all came by car.
    (C) It was very interesting to hear their opinions.

21. I have an extra ticket for the concert tonight. Would you like to come along?
    (A) Yes. It's much too short.
    (B) I thought they gave a great performance.
    (C) No, thank you. I have a prior engagement.

22. When will Ms. Davies be back from her sabbatical?
    (A) She's returning in January.
    (B) For one month, starting next week.
    (C) Her back is much better now.

23. Where shall we arrange to meet?
    (A) Let's move the table over by the window.
    (B) At your place around nine.
    (C) Just a snack will be enough.

24. When was the last time you had a complete medical exam?
    (A) It will only take two hours.
    (B) It must be three years now.
    (C) You should see a specialist about that.

25. Have you read any of her novels?
    (A) Yes. I'm one of her biggest fans.
    (B) No. I don't need anything, thanks.
    (C) Yes. I've changed our booking.

26. May I take your order, sir?
    (A) I'm sorry, it's out of order.
    (B) Yes. Tell them to call me immediately.
    (C) I'll have today's special, please.

27. Who shall I say is calling?
    (A) I'm calling from Spain.
    (B) Later today would be fine.
    (C) This is Leo Jensen from ATO.

28. When is the marketing team planning to launch the new model?
    (A) They're meeting for lunch tomorrow.
    (B) It will be available in the fall.
    (C) Their flight leaves at five.

29. Shouldn't we invite the training manager to attend our presentation?
    (A) I already did.
    (B) She manages the department very well.
    (C) Yes, he probably should have.

30. Would you mind taking the minutes?
    (A) Sure, it's quarter to three.
    (B) Not at all.
    (C) No. But I can lend you mine.

31. Do you happen to have a copy of the Lonsdale contract?
    (A) No. I don't know how that happened.
    (B) No. But the original is back at my office.
    (C) Yes. I think it's time we had a break.

32. 7:30 is too early to meet. How about nine?
    (A) She's very well, thank you.
    (B) I'm busy this afternoon.
    (C) That's fine with me.

33. Why isn't the elevator working today?
    (A) They're doing routine maintenance.
    (B) Get off on floor eight.
    (C) No. She's not on duty today.

34. Will we have to vacate the building during the fire drill?
    (A) That's the standard safety procedure.
    (B) We'll bill them directly.
    (C) During summer vacation.

35. Have you cancelled the reservations?
    (A) I have some doubts about it myself.
    (B) No, I completely forgot.
    (C) Yes, I can.

36. Whose decision was it to change the colors of the company logo?
    (A) Our consultants suggested we do it.
    (B) No. It doesn't belong to me.
    (C) Red and green are my favorite colors.

37. Is there any way to contact Roberto while he's abroad?
    (A) You can email him at his usual address.
    (B) He's left them on his desk.
    (C) Yes. He's now on the board.

38. How do you manage to stay in such good shape?
    (A) It's a perfect fit.
    (B) Regular exercise and healthy food.
    (C) I run the after-sales service.

39. I don't suppose you'd have a spare pen, would you?
    (A) It's open until ten. Sure.
    (B) Stocks are up again.
    (C) Take this one.

40. Have you forwarded the latest figures to Mr. Summers?
    (A) I'll put it back where it was.
    (B) Yes, we've made a lot of progress.
    (C) I faxed them to him earlier today.

PART 3: SHORT CONVERSATIONS

Questions 41–43
(M) Are there any further comments before we move on to the next item on the agenda?
(W) No, I think we've covered everything.
(M) Good. Let's now turn to the issue of relocating the branch office.
(W) OK. Our lease expires in May. Why don't we just extend it for another six months? That would leave us more time to look for a bigger place in the same neighborhood.

Questions 44–46
- (W) Would you like to begin with an appetizer this evening?
- (M) No thank you. I think we'll just be having a main course.
- (W) Are you ready to order now or would you like me to come back in a few minutes?
- (M) I think we're ready. We'd like to order two seafood platters, please. One with prawns and one with crab.

Questions 47–49
- (M) Would you like a full tune-up with the oil and filter change today, Mrs. Webster?
- (W) Yes. It's been about 10,000 miles since the last one.
- (M) OK. Just sign here and we'll have your vehicle ready by four this afternoon.
- (W) In fact I won't be able to pick up the car myself. But my husband will drop by before you close.

Questions 50–52
- (W) And will you be checking any bags this evening, sir?
- (M) I just have carry-on luggage and my laptop.
- (W) Allright. Here is your boarding pass with your seat assignment. The flight will begin boarding at 7:00 from gate E-3. Enjoy your trip.
- (M) I'm sure I will. Traveling business class is always a pleasure, especially on an overnight flight like this.

Questions 53–55
- (W) Don, is Margaret really leaving the company?
- (M) No, she's been transferred to New York. They made her a Vice President.
- (W) Really? That's great news. I had no idea she'd been promoted.
- (M) She's managed to do really well, considering she only joined the group four years ago.

Questions 56–58
- (M) Hi Nancy. Tom said you're looking to buy a place in the Greenwood area.
- (W) As a matter of fact, we've found something but we're still negotiating the price.
- (M) Well I sure hope you get it. Greenwood's a nice neighborhood.
- (W) It certainly is and it has some great schools, too. I would really like to enroll our two kids there next year.

Questions 59–61
- (W) Hey Steve. I hear you're on vacation as of Friday.
- (M) Yeah. I'm taking two weeks for a trip with the family and hopefully to play some golf. And you?
- (W) I'm taking one week off next month. We're going on a Mediterranean cruise. Listen, enjoy the break, you sure deserve it.
- (M) Yup and for once I won't be taking any work along with me.

Questions 62–64
- (W) Mr. Honda, the electricians will be installing new cables next Monday. I'm afraid you'll have to vacate your office all day.
- (M) All right. But is there another office I can use?
- (W) We've set up several workstations in the conference room upstairs. You can use one of them if you'd like.
- (M) Wait a minute. We'd reserved that room for a client meeting in the afternoon. We'll have to reschedule that immediately.

Questions 65–67
- (M) Print Express. Edward Hanser speaking. How can I help you?
- (W) This is Edwina Lewis from Assist Communication. It's about the new brochures that you delivered to us yesterday. I'm afraid there's a serious error in the text.
- (M) Really? I'm very surprised to hear that. What exactly is wrong?
- (W) Well I'm afraid you've misspelled our company's name on the front cover of the brochure. It should be 'Assist Communication' with a double 's' after the A in the first word – and, as printed, there's only one 's'. I'm very sorry but we are going to have to ask you to reprint another batch as soon as possible.

Questions 68–70
- (M) I'm looking for my copy of the Harris report. I thought I left it here on my desk last night. You haven't seen it, have you Anita?
- (W) Oh I'm terribly sorry Mr. Jensen. I completely forgot to tell you – Mr. Lee asked me if he could borrow it – he wants to include some of the figures in the presentation he's giving to the sales department.
- (M) Well I wish you'd told me earlier. I've been looking everywhere for it. I have to write up a summary for the next edition of our newsletter. Did he say when he'd bring it back?
- (W) He said he needed it for a couple of hours and promised to bring it back after lunch. Do you want me to call him?

PART 4: SHORT TALKS

Questions 71–73 refer to the following announcement.

Coming into view is one of the most prominent buildings in the old town, the House of the Seven Doors. Built in the early 1800s, the house earns its name from seven magnificently carved wooden doors. Doors were often the first part of the house to be constructed because the door stood as a symbol of the prosperity and status of the household. The elaborate carvings on each of the seven doors represent trade products, such as sugar, spices, coffee and tea.

Questions 74–76 refer to the following talk.

On behalf of all the senior and junior researchers in the special applications laboratory and the rest of the staff here at SienTech, I would like to thank the trustees, the board and the selection committee for this exceptional research award. We are very honored and very happy to receive the generous 20 million dollar grant, which will finance the construction of a new laboratory. The advances and discoveries we've made over the last five years are the result of extraordinary teamwork. We could not have accomplished any of this without the generous support of wise patrons, great colleagues, kind friends and, of course, our families. Thank you.

Questions 77–79 refer to the following news broadcast.

According to Tuesday's Newsline report, three European insurance providers are involved in negotiations for a strategic merger.

Although the talks for the proposed merger are in the inital stages company spokesmen say they expect to reach an agreement in six months. The merger would create the largest insurance provider on the continent, allowing the companies to consolidate their home and car insurance sectors. But more significantly, the newly formed company, with its large capital base, would be able to concentrate its resources on insuring businesses. With the demand for specialized business insurance up 30%, the merger could make the company the leading business insurance provider within the next five years.

Questions 80–82 refer to the following announcement.

For free confidential business advice call SMART at 1-800/522-0245 or log on to www.smart.org. Every year, thousands of people get advice from SMART when starting or expanding their companies and you can be one of them.

Your SMART counselor can teach you how to create a business plan so that you can get a small business loan.

SMART's business mentors can help with cash flow management and market analysis.

If you're a small business owner or thinking about starting a company, call SMART today at 1-800/522-0245 or visit smart dot org for confidential advice at no charge.

SMART is a nonprofit association.

Questions 83–85 refer to the following talk.

Thank you for coming to today's workshop here at our home office. This morning we are going to focus on improving the performance of your front desk personnel. To begin, I'd like to draw your attention to three key numbers: 9, 3 and 30. The first refers to the number of people that a dissatisfied hotel guest will talk to about their experience. The second number refers to the cost of finding a new customer compared to keeping an existing one, that is, it costs three times as much. The last is 30, which is the percentage increase in direct revenue that can be achieved by implementing our simple hospitality and customer service training program. At the end of today's session you will all be able to return to your hotels with the full training package that we have developed here at the home office. These training tools, including an interactive DVD, will significantly enhance the performance of your front desk personnel to ensure customer loyalty and satisfaction.

Questions 86–88 refer to the following announcement.

This is a public service announcement.

Many homes and apartments are without electricity after the severe snowstorm that hit the region last night. If you are without electricity DO NOT burn charcoal or use gasoline generators indoors to heat your home. Never use gas ovens to heat your home and do not use kerosene and gas heaters in closed rooms. These devices can produce dangerous carbon monoxide gas. For more information about how to stay warm and safe during the winter power outage, please stay tuned for an interview with Public Health official, Janet Sharpe at 10:00. Thank you for your attention.

Questions 89–91 refer to the following announcement.

Thank you for calling Security Bank. All incoming calls to our telephone banking center are recorded and may be used for security monitoring and for training our customer service staff.

For checking and savings account balances, press 1.

To transfer funds, press 2.

To find out about a home or car loan, press 3.

If you are not calling from a touchtone phone, please hold and the next available customer service assistant will answer your call.

Questions 92–94 refer to the following talk.

All passengers on Flight 520 to Chicago, may I have your attention for a special announcement. This evening's flight has been cancelled due to heavy snowfall and high winds in the Chicago area. The flight has been re-scheduled for 8 a.m. tomorrow morning, weather permitting. For security reasons, you will not be able to collect checked baggage as it has already been loaded onto the aircraft. For those passengers needing overnight accommodation in Houston, the airline is providing complimentary hotel and meal vouchers. Please see our service representative at Gate 5 check-in. We apologize for the inconvenience.

Questions 95–97 refer to the following talk.

Yesterday, many of you asked me about the formal conference dinner this Saturday evening. And yes, there are places still available. The caterer has asked me to confirm the number of participants a day in advance, so if you'd like to attend, please sign up at the registration desk in the lobby by Friday noon, that is, tomorrow at the latest. The cost – 40 dollars per person – includes pre-dinner drinks, a delicious five-course meal, followed by dancing to the Dixie Jazz Ensemble. Dinner will be served starting at eight o'clock in the Pine Ridge Ballroom.

Questions 98–100 refer to the following talk.

I'd like to welcome you all to this special Chamber of Commerce event. This is the first time we've organized a "Business Start-Up" seminar and workshop. Today, you will hear presentations from two distinguished speakers.

Our first presenter, Benjamin Levitt, is co-founder of the well-known business consultancy, LV associates. Benjamin will be giving a few pointers for starting your own business venture.

Our second presenter is Emily Jego, the best-selling author of *Starting a Business – The Easy Way* and she'll be sharing her insights into how to make your business start-up a real success story.

After the presentations, there will be a panel discussion with Dave Garrett, business correspondent with the Coast Chronicle and Lucinda Bellcroft, CEO of Business Ventures. They will be discussing the current climate for business development and answering questions.

So that's the program for this morning.

During the lunch break you can sign up for one of the five workshops that the Chamber of Commerce will be offering this afternoon.

So let's get started … allow me to present our first speaker … Benjamin Levitt.

Answer Key for Target Score Second Edition Final Practice TOEIC® test

1.	D	41.	C	81.	D	121.	C	161.	C
2.	A	42.	A	82.	D	122.	D	162.	D
3.	C	43.	B	83.	A	123.	C	163.	B
4.	B	44.	B	84.	D	124.	B	164.	C
5.	D	45.	A	85.	B	125.	B	165.	A
6.	B	46.	D	86.	B	126.	C	166.	A
7.	A	47.	C	87.	A	127.	D	167.	A
8.	D	48.	B	88.	B	128.	C	168.	D
9.	A	49.	B	89.	B	129.	D	169.	D
10.	B	50.	D	90.	B	130.	A	170.	A
11.	A	51.	C	91.	B	131.	D	171.	B
12.	C	52.	D	92.	B	132.	C	172.	D
13.	B	53.	B	93.	C	133.	A	173.	B
14.	C	54.	D	94.	C	134.	A	174.	C
15.	B	55.	C	95.	D	135.	D	175.	D
16.	C	56.	A	96.	B	136.	B	176.	C
17.	A	57.	B	97.	C	137.	D	177.	B
18.	B	58.	A	98.	B	138.	A	178.	C
19.	A	59.	C	99.	C	139.	A	179.	B
20.	C	60.	B	100.	B	140.	C	180.	C
21.	C	61.	B	101.	C	141.	C	181.	D
22.	A	62.	D	102.	B	142.	D	182.	D
23.	B	63.	C	103.	D	143.	A	183.	C
24.	B	64.	A	104.	C	144.	B	184.	D
25.	A	65.	A	105.	A	145.	D	185.	A
26.	C	66.	C	106.	B	146.	A	186.	C
27.	C	67.	C	107.	C	147.	D	187.	D
28.	B	68.	B	108.	A	148.	D	188.	A
29.	A	69.	A	109.	D	149.	D	189.	D
30.	B	70.	B	110.	A	150.	A	190.	B
31.	B	71.	C	111.	B	151.	B	191.	A
32.	C	72.	D	112.	B	152.	A	192.	A
33.	A	73.	B	113.	A	153.	D	193.	B
34.	A	74.	A	114.	A	154.	B	194.	B
35.	B	75.	A	115.	B	155.	A	195.	C
36.	A	76.	B	116.	B	156.	B	196.	C
37.	A	77.	B	117.	D	157.	D	197.	C
38.	B	78.	B	118.	D	158.	D	198.	D
39.	C	79.	C	119.	D	159.	D	199.	B
40.	C	80.	C	120.	B	160.	C	200.	D

Target Score Sample Test Scoring Conversion Table

No. of Correct answers	Listening Score	Reading Score
0	5	5
1	5	5
2	5	5
3	5	5
4	5	5
5	5	5
6	5	5
7	10	5
8	15	5
9	20	5
10	25	5
11	30	5
12	35	5
13	40	5
14	45	5
15	50	5
16	55	10
17	60	15
18	65	20
19	70	25
20	75	30
21	80	35
22	85	40
23	90	45
24	95	50
25	100	60
26	110	65
27	115	70
28	120	80
29	125	85
30	130	90
31	135	95
32	140	100
33	145	110
34	150	115
35	160	120
36	165	125
37	170	130
38	175	140
39	180	145
40	185	150
41	190	160
42	195	165
43	200	170
44	210	175
45	215	180
46	220	190
47	230	195
48	240	200
49	245	210
50	250	215
51	255	220

No. of Correct answers	Listening Score	Reading Score
52	260	225
53	270	230
54	275	235
55	280	240
56	290	250
57	295	255
58	300	260
59	310	265
60	315	270
61	320	280
62	325	285
63	330	290
64	340	300
65	345	305
66	350	310
67	360	320
68	365	325
69	370	330
70	380	335
71	385	340
72	390	350
73	395	355
74	400	360
75	405	365
76	410	370
77	420	380
78	425	385
79	430	390
80	440	395
81	445	400
82	450	405
83	460	410
84	465	415
85	470	420
86	475	425
87	480	430
88	485	435
89	490	445
90	495	450
91	495	455
92	495	465
93	495	470
94	495	480
95	495	485
96	495	490
97	495	495
98	495	495
99	495	495
100	495	495

Number of Correct Listening Responses = Listening Score

Number of Correct Listening Responses = Listening Score +

Total Estimated Test Score =